Christianity and Power Politics Today

Christianity and Power Politics Today

Christian Realism and Contemporary Political Dilemmas

Edited by Eric Patterson

First published in 2008 by
PALGRAVE MACMILLAN™
175 Fifth Avenue, New York, N.Y. 10010 and
Houndmills, Basingstoke, Hampshire, England RG21 6XS.
Companies and representatives throughout the world.

PALGRAVE MACMILLAN is the global academic imprint of the Palgrave Macmillan division of St. Martin's Press, LLC and of Palgrave Macmillan Ltd. Macmillan® is a registered trademark in the United States, United Kingdom and other countries. Palgrave is a registered trademark in the European Union and other countries.

ISBN-13: 978-0-230-60264-9
ISBN-10: 0-230-60264-9

Library of Congress Cataloging-in-Publication Data

Christianity and power politics today : Christian realism and contemporary political dilemmas / edited by Eric Patterson.
    p. cm.
Includes bibliographical references and index.
ISBN 0-230-60264-9
    1. Christianity and politics—United States. 2. United States—Church history. I. Patterson, Eric, 1971-

BR516.C47 2008
261.70973—dc22   2007030425

A catalogue record of the book is available from the British Library.

Design by Scribe Inc.

First edition: March 2008

10 9 8 7 6 5 4 3 2 1

Printed in the United States of America.

For my father,
William Louis Patterson, Jr.

Contents

CHAPTER 1

Christianity and Power Politics
Themes and Issues

Eric Patterson

While the Nazis advanced across Europe in 1940, Reinhold Niebuhr released a volume of his previously published essays under the title *Christianity and Power Politics*. The intellectual and political context was grave: European governments were falling to Hitler, whose army was temporarily in league with the Soviets, and in the Far East Japan continued its brutal Asian campaign. Totalitarian and authoritarian philosophies were on the ascendant, yet the United States was sitting out the conflict. Meanwhile, many Christians in the West deplored the use of violence and retreated into political pacifism.

A major theme of Niebuhr's *Christianity and Power Politics* was that such retreat was immoral, and that Christian realism provided the intellectual resources for coming to grip with the "isms" of the day (i.e., fascism and Communism) while serving as a starting point for thoughtful, real-world policies.

This volume takes its inspiration from the troubled context and questions of its namesake. As in the 1930s and1940s, our world has become a confusing place where various models claim to explain the international order (e.g., globalization, neoliberal economics, institutionalism) and point us to peace and brotherhood via understanding, consensus, democracy, human rights, and the United Nations. Nonetheless, there is widespread unease about the legitimacy and durability of such conventions. We live in a world where at least two great political worldviews are in conflict: one is Western individualistic, capitalist democracy, and the other being all forms of collectivist, hierarchical, quasi- (or pseudo-) organic culture, the most obvious being Islamic fundamentalism. Moreover, we see bloody ethnoreligious fault lines in Eastern Europe, Africa, and Asia that pit representatives of the great civilizations against one another in places like Kosovo, Palestine, and Kashmir. The Christian realists of the 1930s and 1940s—Reinhold Niebuhr, Herbert Butterfield, John C. Bennett, John Foster Dulles, Martin Wight, and others—would have found it all familiar: the poverty of the masses in the Third World, Western military intervention in poor countries, the castigation of "power politics" by religious elites, coupled with the corresponding call for nonviolent solutions, and so forth.

The Christian realists would also recognize, and cautiously welcome, the reemergence of religious discourse in public affairs and scholarly endeavor, after decades of banishment. At the writing of this book, the American president and British prime minister openly practice their obviously devout faith. Their speeches have been often couched in religious language, and both Bush and Blair have drawn fire from critics at home and abroad for using "evil" as a noun rather than an adjective in international affairs. Similarly, in an ironic twist, the use of force has gained a new notoriety as academic and elite religious voices seem to have finally achieved a consensus that there is a case to be made for military intervention, as long as it is a case of gross human rights violations or genocide (e.g., Darfur). Moreover, the West is exerting modest but real pressure, for the first time since the presidency of Ronald Reagan, on regimes that persecute their citizens on religious grounds.

Although the Christian realists of the past would have welcomed a religious lens providing a perspective on politics, they would have advised caution. They were ever concerned that matters of the spirit would be shortchanged when appropriated for use in the political. It is tempting for a politician to use religious images to evoke patriotic or nationalistic impulses. It is even more tempting to believe in the perfect congruence of eternal and temporal ideals. Therefore, Christian realism is a religious and moral voice, but it retains a critical edge and is willing to scrutinize not only the political, but also the shortcomings of the religious and spiritual.

Hence, this book. The questions motivating this book include the following: What contemporary resources does Christian realism have to illuminate our understanding of present political dilemmas? Can Christian realism provide an intellectual framework for approaching political theories as well as real-world policy alternatives? Furthermore, can Christian realism suggest concrete proposals for the vexing issues of contemporary life, such as the war on terrorism, violent ideologies, genocide, and nurturing stable political institutions?

In short, the answer is "yes." Christian realism is a vibrant intellectual approach for evaluating political phenomena that starts with considerations of *power, order, security,* and *responsibility.* Christian realist analysis is useful in revealing the power dynamics of all political scenarios, the primacy of political order in domestic and international life, and the opportunities and limitations of individual human agency in the political context. Following an introduction to the themes of classical Christian realism, the rest of this chapter explicates some applications of those themes found in three of Reinhold Niebuhr's books, and then concludes with an overview of the subsequent chapters.

What Is Christian Realism?

According to Roger L. Shinn, "both words in that phrase are important." Shinn writes:

> The ethic was Christian in its serious appropriation of biblical motifs and classical doctrines: the uniqueness of biblical revelation, the sinfulness of man and society, the judging and redeeming activity of God, the faith in justification by a divine grace that produces works worthy of repentance, the distinctive quality of Christian love. It was realistic in its criticism of naïve idealism or utopianism and its confrontation with the brute facts and power struggles of the contemporary world. This Christian realism, at least at its best, was not an artificial combination of two unrelated motifs. It was realistic in its appropriation of Christian faith, and it was Christian—often recovering orthodox traditions neglected in the modern church—in its realism. It was alert both to the Word of God and to the latest news from European and Asiatic battlefronts, and it constantly sought the relation between the good news of the gospel and the daily news of the world.[1]

In short, Christian realism was a perspective committed to understanding and involvement in politics based on a realistic standpoint. What made the Christian realists feel that their perspective on human nature and political phenomena was "realistic" was not pessimism, but faith in the biblical doctrines of sin and the Fall.

The Augustinian Theology of Christian Realism

Roger Epp has called the rise of mid-twentieth century Christian realism the "Augustinian Moment" in international politics.[2] By "Augustinian," Epp is specifically referring to the doctrinal foundation of Christian realism that emanates from Augustine's political treatise *The City of God*. Certainly, many

Christian realists expressed their intellectual debt to Augustine. For instance, Niebuhr wrote, "[Augustine] . . . proves himself a more reliable guide than any known thinker. A generation which finds its communities imperiled and in decay . . . might well take counsel of Augustine in solving its perplexities."[3] Likewise, Cambridge historian Herbert Butterfield, reflecting on the deepening Cold War and the atomic age, stated that "we in this part of the world find ourselves . . . in the midst of the very kind of catastrophic history that Augustine viewed when writing his seminal *The City of God* in the fifth century."[4] Even secular Niebuhrians agreed that Augustine was valuable. As Arthur Schlesinger, Jr., quipped, "Whatever you say about Augustine, at least he would not have been much surprised by the outcome of the Russian Revolution."[5] More recently, Jean Bethke Elshtain, writes that "classic Augustinian thinking" can help us come to grips with the terrorism associated with September 11 and Al Qaeda terrorism training videos captured in Afghanistan: "Augustinians are painfully aware of the temptation to smash, destroy, damage, and humiliate. Such temptations may be struggled against, capitulated to, or even extolled as a form of strength and the path to victory. Violence unleashed when what Augustine called the *libido dominandi*, or lust to dominate, is unchecked, is violence that knows no limits."[6]

Epp argues that Niebuhr and other Christian realists "reclaimed" Augustine's understanding of political life in four ways. First, the Christian realists parallel Augustine's view of human nature. Augustine saw humankind as God's penultimate creation—made in God's very image with tremendous creative potential, but marred by Adam's sin. Because Christian realists tended to emphasize sin and evil in stark contrast to the religious and secular liberals of their day, they were often wrongly stereotyped as cynics or pessimists. Second, like Augustine, Christian realists saw history as meaningful, linear, and moving toward an ultimate fulfillment. As Cambridge historian Herbert Butterfield wrote, "[T]he ultimate faith is the belief that all things will have a final reconciliation—a final share in the redemptive purpose of Christ."[7] A third Augustinian theme is the Christian realist emphasis on order in political life. Augustine's conception of "concord" and his application of it to Rome, in the context of barbarian attacks on the empire, provided the essential justification for law and government. Rome provided the benefits of commerce, education, and communication despite also being responsible for evil such as slavery and war. Augustine did not apologize for Rome's wrongs, but made it clear that they were lesser evils when the alternative was social disorder and political chaos. Finally, Christian realists appropriate from Augustine the notion of *caritas*, "the love of God and Neighbors as the proper motivation of the will transformed by grace."[8] This "law of love" is the ultimate standard for individual conduct.

Applying the City of God to the Earthly City

Christian realism begins by rejecting the modernist idea that biblical revelation and judgment is inappropriate for contemporary society. Instead, the Christian realists realized in the New Testament a call for action in dealing with contemporary social and political situations. Most Christian realists were political liberals and sympathetic to the Social Gospel's call for social justice. Nevertheless, Christian realists tended to be critical of idealism that was unwilling to deal with the realities of political power and face the judgmental portions of Christ's message.

Christian realism emphasized the universality of sin: No individual and no collective is free from guilt of pride and sin. Unlike idealists, who could not differentiate between temporary political projects because they all fell short of the law of love, Christian realists argued that distinctions can be made between lesser and greater evils. This was the position of various Christian realists toward Nazi aggression in the 1940s. Germany was no evil incarnate, nor was America perfect, but the tyranny of National Socialism was certainly more evil than the foibles of the Western powers and therefore demanded a forceful response.[9]

Thus, one finds in the writings of the Christian realists frequent allusions to the tension between individual responsibility and the law of love. In fact, perhaps an ethic of responsibility should be the fifth pillar for understanding the Augustinian roots of Christian realism. On the one hand, Christians are citizens of the world and therefore must use the tools of the world (e.g., politics, force) to act, participate, and fight against injustice. On the other hand, Christians must humbly recognize that every behavior falls short of the ideal of the law of love and is therefore censured by the ideal. Individual Christians should act while not neglecting repentance for their own pride and evil.

In general, Christian realism relied heavily on Augustine's distinction between the City of God and the City of Earth and was unsparing in its attacks on those, such as pacifists and Social Gospel liberals, who confused the realities of the temporal political order and its justice with the eternal city and its ideals. The City of God is founded on the law of love, and it is an ideal that cannot be realized in this world. In contrast, we live in the earthly city and must work within its limitations to achieve "approximate" conditions of order and justice. In sum, Christian realists enjoined everyone to keep in mind the ideals of Christ's eternal kingdom but to work within the constraints of the present imperfect world.

Christian realists recognized the tension in collective life between the need for order and the law of love. Augustine discussed the tension between the demands of the law of love and the behavior of representatives of the state, who, acting on the state's behalf, might violate the law of love. For example, the soldier serving in Rome's legions would have to kill at times to protect political order. Augustine condoned such behavior on behalf of the state, arguing that there could be no ultimate resolution of the tension between social order and ultimate moral ideals in the earthly city and that the state and its representatives were obligated to act to preserve the political order. Niebuhr agreed that "order precedes justice in the strategy of government."[10]

The Christian realists had another concern about morality and social life: Although individual behavior may be guided at times by ethical concerns, this is generally not the case for collectives. Indeed, groups generally behave based on self-interest, and Niebuhr argued that groups amplify the self-interest of their members. Consequently, one finds in the writings of Niebuhr and Bennett criticism of the moralist rhetoric of foreign policies that claims ethical purposes but actually obfuscates self-interested motives.[11] Moreover, Christian realists such as Butterfield were especially chary of marrying religion or ideology to nationalism, both because it made political concessions impossible and because it bordered on idolatry.[12]

Finally, Christian realists were strident in their calls for political action to resist tyranny aboard and promote justice everywhere. Niebuhr and his contemporaries argued for the value of democracy, proposed an international body resembling the United Nations, warned of complaisance toward the Nazis and later the Communists, advocated containment, argued over nuclear deterrence, and urged the United States to assume a global leadership role. Nevertheless, they did not find in ethical systems, religious tradition, or Scripture concrete policy proposals. Indeed, Christian realists such as Bennett and Butterfield routinely claimed that the insights of the social sciences were both useful and necessary for dealing with the problems of politics and economics.[13] In short, Christian realism had no delimited policy platform or any specific political formula. Instead, Christian realism called for individuals to work from an ethical worldview in a spirit of humility, recognizing that even though one's efforts might be in vain, one has a responsibility to try.

In sum, Christian realism was a practical, flexible, and ethical response to the liberal idealism of the day. Christian realists tended to prioritize a language of "power," "responsibility," and "order" in their discussions of political phenomena. In a time of upheaval and uncertainty characterized by the rise of fascism and Communism, the Second World War, atomic weapons, and the Cold War, the prophetic voice of Christian realism was heeded not only by those in positions of power, but also by many in the mass public. As Michael Howard wrote:

> The Christian eschatology, long disdained by liberal humanists even within the Church itself, once again became terrifyingly relevant to human affairs. . . . And the teachers who best provided an adequate framework for understanding were the philosophers and the theologians Niebuhr, Bonhoeffer, Karl Barth, Tillich, who accepted uncomplainingly the remoteness, the inscrutability of God, who saw the focus of Christianity as the Passion rather than the Sermon on the Mount, men for whom the march of humanitarian, utilitarian liberalism, including its change of gear into Marxian socialism, had simply been a long excursion into the desert in search of a mirage.[14]

Christianity and Power Politics

Reinhold Niebuhr was the preeminent twentieth century Christian realist. He authored dozens of books and thousands of essays and sermons. Among his most famous books are three that are a useful starting point for reconsidering the themes of Christian realism and their application to contemporary world affairs: *Christianity and Power Politics, The Irony of American History*, and *The Children of Light and the Children of Darkness*.

Niebuhr's 1940 collection, *Christianity and Power Politics*, consists of sixteen essays, many of which are famous in their own right, most notably "Optimism, Pessimism, and Religious Faith" and "The Christian Church in the Secular Age." The themes of these two chapters represent the book's larger thesis: Christianity is the most realistic and meaningful perspective for apprehending world affairs at the individual and corporate levels.

Christian realists, especially Niebuhr, have been derided as "dark," "doomsdayers," "pessimists," and "cynics."[15] This is due to their insistence on the fact of human sinfulness, in opposition to the progressivism of liberal Christianity and the Social Gospel of that period. In his chapter "Optimism, Pessimism, and Religious Faith," Niebuhr explores why he and the "Judeo-Christian alternative" are "realistically optimistic," writing that "an adequate religion is always an ultimate optimism which entertains all the facts which lead to pessimism."[16]

Niebuhr began by investigating two competing philosophies: democratic idealism (which he often calls liberalism) and Marxism. He argues that both worldviews tend to be hopelessly idealistic in their belief in human progress, social evolution, the ability of individuals to overcome their interests in the collective, and faith in international peace. Equally damning is that neither worldview presents a holistic view of human beings, history, and God.

Instead, these materialistic and naturalistic theories are "flat" and "horizontal," lacking an appreciation of individuals as spiritual beings and the relational presence ("vertical") of a transcendent God in history.

Niebuhr also calls the reader's attention to the consequences of liberal and Marxian failure: When the heady optimism falls short due to the realities of this world, the believers tend to become pessimistic. Niebuhr cites National Socialism as a case in point, a quasi-religious, pseudoscientific utopian doctrine that preached glory but used increasingly diabolical means in the pursuit of its ends. Niebuhr suggests that Marxist variants are more calculating and in-tune with power realities than liberal idealism, but that after the third or fourth or fifth Five-Year Plan fails, nothing is left but despair for the citizen, who has already been robbed of all spiritual meaning.

Therefore, for Niebuhr, the test of "an adequate" religion, or worldview, was whether it was in touch with the full range of humankind's reality—not just the material, but also the spiritual. For Niebuhr, life and history had meaning because of a transcendent Creator God (source of meaning) who is also judge of the world (the end of all things). This theme runs throughout the chapters of this volume: Human experience and potential run deeper and broader than a mere social science of statistics. Like the classical Christian realists, the contributors to this book assert that we should return the humanistic and normative elements of political life to a privileged place in our scholarship.

Another chapter of *Christianity and Power Politics* is "The Christian Church in a Secular Age." In it, Niebuhr considered the failings of Christendom that led to widespread secularism in the West, which he defines as "the explicit disavowal of the sacred." Niebuhr recognizes that contemporary philosophies such as humanism and socialism have turned their back on Christianity because of failings ("profanization") in the Church's history, such as overintimacy between religious and political authorities during the medieval era and the failure of Protestant "ascetics" to go beyond the spiritual needs of the poor to provide for their physical wants.

In the end, however, he focuses on the sin of self-glorification that is explicit in other philosophies: the intellectual pride of (Enlightenment) liberal rationalists; the egotism of exclusivist, Romantic fascists; and the universalist pretensions of Marxism. Niebuhr says that this self-glorification is "a very old religion, dressed in a new form . . . [and] it is a very old religion because it involves the quintessences of human sin": the deification of self, one's tribe, or an ideology.[17] Today we call such tendencies "fundamentalism" and "nationalism."

Niebuhr asks whether Christianity has something to offer in an increasingly secular world where the transcendent is consistently disavowed in favor of the immediate. He concludes that Christianity does offer at least two things. The first is *repentance*. Not only can and should the Church repent of its historic sins, but it also must assert a prophetic voice regarding the moral content of social and political issues and remind people and governments everywhere that their actions and motives are judged by God. Politics do have moral content.

Christianity also offers *hope*. "Just as the Christian gospel calls the proud to repent, it assures those who despair of a new hope."[18] Niebuhr asserts that Christianity provides answers to the meaning of life and history, and that the contradictions of human experience can find consolation. He writes that "through it [faith] we are able to understand life in all of its beauty and its terror, without being beguiled by its beauty or driven to despair by terror."[19] These themes also permeate the chapters of this book—the relevance of moral questions to inquiry about foreign and domestic policy and the qualified optimism, or better, hope, that the spiritual and intellectual resources of humanity can ameliorate some of the imperfections of our time.

Niebuhr's Irony in American History

In 1952 Reinhold Niebuhr published his famous monograph *The Irony of American History*. Niebuhr defines irony as "apparently fortuitous incongruities, which, upon closer examination, are not merely fortuitous."[20] What makes something ironic is the element of the comedic and the unexpected— that which appears to be strength is often the very mechanism of weakness or downfall. For Niebuhr, the ironic is marked by a certain pretension (e.g., strength, virtue) that obscures unconscious weakness. For example, Niebuhr observed the irony that the United States trumpets its prosperity, believing it to be evidence of its virtues, while critics abroad see American wealth and boasting as evidence of imperialism. He observes that "every effort we make to prove the virtue of our 'way of life' is used by our enemies and detractors as proof of our guilt."[21]

Niebuhr's central thesis in *The Irony of American History* is that the juxtaposition of American naïveté with inordinate American power in the immediate postwar world was ironic. On the one hand, the United States had existed in splendid isolation and eschewed the immoral politics of European colonialism and continental conflict. On the other hand, U.S. capacity, especially its economic power, resulted in it achieving superpower status and responsibilities in a very short period time. Hence, Niebuhr observed an adolescent United States motivated by the rhetoric and reality of its own unique history infused with a youthful idealism. Niebuhr did not dispute that there were elements of the American experience that truly made it a "city on a hill," but he critiqued the "messianic dream" that underscored American exceptionalism. Indeed, it was the pretension that America acted exclusively in terms of a higher morality without regard to self-interestedness that Niebuhr indicted. As Niebuhr observed, "our sense of responsibility to a world community beyond our borders is a virtue, even though it is partly derived from a prudent understanding of our own interests."[22] The irony of American naïveté was its lack of appreciation for how its own moral discourse obfuscated politics based on national interests (e.g., Manifest Destiny, the Spanish-American War).[23]

What made the situation in 1952 considerably more complicated was the dawn of American military, political, and economic superiority. Niebuhr feared that it was possible that such power, especially military power, might be combined with the vanity of American moral exceptionalism and result in aggressive policies for the "higher good." This was especially possible, Niebuhr thought, if restless America became frustrated that its goodwill efforts at diplomacy and sharing democracy did little to result in quick fixes for international dilemmas. Indeed, Niebuhr pointed out, American diplomatic engagement, combined with awesome Yankee power, ironically generated insecurity—the classic security dilemma—rather than trust in some parts of the globe. He wrote, "[T]he paradise of our domestic security is suspended in a hell of global insecurity . . . we are the poorer for the global responsibilities we bear. And the fulfillments of our desires are mixed with frustrations and vexations."[24] Such *a propos* sentiments could have been written in 2007, rather than 1952.

Although Niebuhr criticized U.S. policy on many counts, he did not call for American withdrawal or isolation from world politics. Instead, he returned again and again to the idea of American responsibility in international life due to its wealth, history, worldview, and unique position in world affairs. Nonetheless, Niebuhr simultaneously highlighted the unintended consequences of states (responsibly) seeking their own security, from arms races to inflaming nationalistic pride.

A second point from *Irony* for today relates to American values and American power. It is certainly the case that Americans take their ideals of political liberty and human rights very seriously. However, it is also true that Americans feel uncomfortable being transparent regarding how American interests (e.g., oil) overlap with our ideals. In some ways, America remains naïve because we expect the world to embrace not only our values, but us as well. For better or worse, this expectation is sure to lead to disappointment. The simple fact that America is not universally loved demonstrates not only the fickleness of humanity worldwide, but our own vanity, which makes it difficult for us to distinguish universal values (e.g., human rights) from the unique historical contingencies that put American in the vanguard of rights advocacy.

The chapters of this book deal with such ironies, be it the balance of unilateral responsibility with multilateral engagement, the Bush doctrine, or America's role in the global economy. A common theme is that it is impossible to transcend such ironies, either by ignoring their existence or trying to completely overcome them (such as the myth of "absolute security"). Instead, it behooves us to accept the ironies of the *civitas terrene* and work within those limitations while keeping an eye fixed on the *civitas dei*.

The Children of Light and the Children of Darkness

In 1944, Reinhold Niebuhr gave a series of lectures that ultimately became his volume *The Children of Light and the Children of Darkness*. The book claims to be a "compelling justification" and "a more realistic vindication" of democracy than the idealistic democratic theories of his day. Niebuhr's *Children* has direct relevance for the contemporary observer of domestic and international politics in its critique of the children of light and darkness, as well as its defense of democracy as a mechanism for balancing competing claims and social forces in society.

Who are the children of light? For Niebuhr, the children of light are the moral idealists who optimistically believe that reason, progress, and planning will allow society to overcome the challenges that it faces. The children of light assure themselves that individual self-interest can be overcome as men and women willingly submit their unique self-interest to a higher morality.[25] Niebuhr points to two strands of this idealism in his day. The first is the innocent American bourgeoisie children of light who naïvely believe that the lesson of American history is that the ideals of the Enlightenment combined with the evolution of society and the invisible hand of the market make the realization of a harmony of interests across society possible.[26] Niebuhr identifies a more virulent idealism in the utopianism of prewar Communism, which also envisioned progress toward a halcyonic society based on progress, science, and planning.

Niebuhr calls the children of light "virtuous, but foolish." In contrast, he calls the children of darkness "wise, but evil."[27] The children of darkness are characterized by a moral cynicism that elevates the individual or the tribe by dint of power and prejudice. The children of darkness know no law beyond their own will and interest, and therefore they are willing to use any means at their disposal to advance their interests, regardless of others. Moreover, the children of darkness are wise in not only advancing their own cause, but in exploiting the contradictions in other communities for their own ends. Hence, the Nazis provided Niebuhr with his contemporary exemplar of the children of darkness. The Nazis were motivated by an exclusionist, absolutist ethic that elevated their tribe to prominence at the expense of others. The Nazis were wise in their use of power for the better part of a decade, ruthlessly punishing some foes on the battlefield (or in the concentration camp) while cleverly exploiting the weaknesses of the children of light. For instance, Hitler's annexation of the Sudetenland demonstrated the curious mixture of temerity and good intentions on the part of children of light, like Neville Chamberlain. Similarly, the Nazis realized that the fractures in Western society between the ruling classes and their subordinates based on economic interests (e.g., "Red" labor unions) and race (e.g., blacks, Jews) diminished the effective resistance of the Western powers to German revanchism.[28]

So, in 1944, Niebuhr observed a world in which the children of light were virtuous in their ideals, shortsighted in recognizing how their ideals overlay their interests, and foolish regarding the realities of power politics. In short, the children of darkness had the upper hand because they understood the power of self-interest and had the audacity to act on behalf of their interests without being constrained by intangibles such as international or customary law.

Niebuhr on Democracy

Interestingly, Niebuhr suggests that democracy itself provides a set of solutions to the perennial struggle between the children of light and the children of darkness. Niebuhr begins with the assertion that the Christian doctrine of original sin is the starting point for any theory of politics.[29] He writes, "[The book is] informed by the belief that a Christian view of human nature is more adequate for the development of a democratic society than either the optimism with which democracy has become historically associated or the moral cynicism . . . [associated with] tyrannical political strategies."[30] Niebuhr agrees with classical Christian doctrine that human beings are made in the image of God and therefore have tremendous creative potential. However, human beings are also marred by the Fall and therefore are a complex blend of light and darkness. Democracy is responsive to both elements of human nature: "Man's capacity for justice makes democracy possible; but man's inclination to injustice makes democracy necessary."[31]

Niebuhr's analysis of democracy has no elaboration of constitutions, models of representation, theories of partisan groups, or the like. He completely disregards such, assuming that his reader will generally understand that he is talking about a society governed by the rule of law that protects individual liberties to some degree and adjudicates between the various constituencies that make up the country. Nevertheless, Niebuhr provides a spirited defense that democratic forms of governance are the best formal mechanism to date for realistically dealing with the aspirations and villainies of the children of light and the children of darkness.

Niebuhr's fundamental principle of practical democracy is not one of political equality, suffrage, or individual liberty. Rather, it is the institutionalization of checks on power. Democracy checks the license of the governed with the rule of law and formalizes mechanisms for distribution of authority and resources. Democracy likewise checks the power of factions and communities and similarly limits the power even of government authorities. He argues that "the democratic techniques of a free society place checks upon the power of the ruler and administrator and thus prevent it from becoming vexatious."[32] Niebuhr cites Madison's caution about factions and points to the three great divides in Western public life: ethnicity, religion, and class.[33] Niebuhr recognizes that it is only in democracy that these competing claims can be adjudicated and that the interests of all can be partially served. In fact, it is only in democracy that groups can safely call for change, and at times get it, without resorting to revolutionary upheaval. In sum, these "checks and balances" are pragmatic in their appreciation of the need to balance power with countervailing power and allow for peaceful conflict.

Moreover, Niebuhr suggests that democracy is unique in its flexibility to evolve with "human potencies" and novel situations. These potencies refer to the ongoing creative process in the arts, sciences, economics, philosophy, and elsewhere that create changing conditions for human societies (e.g., the Industrial Revolution). It is the general practice of tyrannies to react violently against such "potencies" in order to restrict change, but the free society provides outlets for the debate of ideas and the adjudication of grievances that such potencies spur. In essence, democracy is a laboratory within which the new can challenge the old and disputes can be resolved. He provides the example of historical England, where democracy became the alternative to war and social convulsion as a means to arbitrating conflicting interests. Moreover, Niebuhr describes how democracy broadened to include new groups identified by differing religious or cultural characteristics.[34]

What makes Niebuhr's analysis different from other political theorists is that he does not expect subgroups to dissolve in the "melting pot" of American society.[35] Hence, he offers a realistic appraisal of their conflicting interests and the need to check the power of the powerful and find room at the table for the less well-off or new groups that develop as part of novel historical contingencies (e.g., organized labor).

Niebuhr's Democratic Theory in the Twenty-First Century

What lessons can be applied from Niebuhr's analysis to our present state of affairs? First and foremost, Niebuhr reminds us of the complexity of human nature and human collectives. We should recognize the vast potential inherent in humankind (light) while also being aware of the propensity for pride and self-promotion of individuals and communities (darkness). Second, in the "third wave" of democratization since the Cold War's end, we should be cautious in building political structures in transitioning countries based on utopian views of capitalism or representative government.[36] Instead, democratic governance should be based on the orderly rule of law that checks the ambitions of the governed as well as those who govern.

Furthermore, Niebuhr cautioned his contemporaries on relying on "fatuous and futile schemes" for resolving conflict.[37] Overreliance by children of light on international goodwill, diplomatic documents, the United Nations General Assembly, and the like to solve the dilemmas of (in)security, poverty, genocide, and war is simply foolish. Perhaps the crimes against humanity in Bosnia, Rwanda, and now in Sudan provides cases in point. Such problems can only be adequately analyzed with a discerning eye toward the human dynamics of the situation, especially the interplay of power politics and chauvinism of any kind. Then, realistic policy alternatives that stress the interplay of power on power can be considered for real action, if appropriate.

Moreover, Niebuhr's warnings about the children of darkness should give us pause in confronting those who subscribe to an apocalyptic fundamentalist Islam. There are children of light today who think that dialogue, overtures, and payoffs can alleviate the threat posed by violent Islamists. Niebuhr would chide such children of light for failing to recognize that the West is confronted with the classic tribal will-to-power, a subculture of death and destruction that utilizes the same language of power as the Nazis: intimidation, confrontation, violence, murder, sectarianism. Niebuhr would recognize the violent prejudices directed at religions, races, and women. The West can only grapple with the threat of suicide bombers, chiliastic Islamists, patriarchal and religious chauvinism, and ethnic hatred (e.g., anti-Semitism) by realizing the self-interest and power-seeking propensities that underlie the religious rhetoric. And, as Niebuhr argued, the children of light must "be armed with the wisdom of the children of darkness but remain free from their malice."[38]

Overview of the Book

Perhaps some of the dilemmas of contemporary international politics are novel, but it seems that most of them are perennial problems of power, competition, the security dilemma, and human frailty. This book reminds us that, in Christian realism, there is a rich foundation from which to reflect on and problem-solve the twenty-first century issues of domestic and international politics.

For instance, Alberto Coll argues for the relevance of Christian realism for today's political dilemmas. He contrasts the moral realism associated with classical Christian realists like Niebuhr to the *realpolitik* of historical realists such as Thucydides. He argues that Christian realism is far more useful in finding solutions to real-world problems than the utopianisms of the past and present. Moreover, he finds in Christian realism the theoretical and ethical resources necessary to combat twenty-first-century dilemmas, such as the dangers of multi-polarity and environmental degradation.

One of the pressing issues of our time is violence, from the genocides of the 1990s to suicide bombings to the global war on terrorism. A question that Christian realists have pondered since the days of Augustine is the moral content of war itself. Keith Pavlischek criticizes Niebuhrian realism for lacking robust limits on the use of force and turns to classical just war theory—a historic "Christian realism"—for guidance. Pavlischek also suggests that Niebuhr shared the presupposition of pacifism that the use of force is always wrong or, at best, "the lesser evil." Instead, he reminds us that for Augustine and others, the use of force was the moral duty of the state to preserve order, punish wrongdoers, and protect the weak.

When Ernest W. Lefever was a young man, he was a contemporary of the classical Christian realists in their waning years. In his chapter on moral realism, first published in 1972 and updated with current events in mind, he articulates the potential and limits of moral reasoning in U.S. foreign policy. On the one hand, he advocates an ethical approach to political problems, but he castigates the soft moralism pretending to be ethical reflection that informs a great deal of political debate. He also warns of demonizing ones opponents, although he suggests it is typical of historical U.S. foreign policy during times of conflict.

Charles Jones returns our focus to the study of war, regretting that most scholarship on war has become mechanistic or utopian. Jones is similarly critical that Thomistic and Augustinian versions of the just war tradition have proved vulnerable to idealism in the form of the legalism that has come to haunt the former and the self-righteousness that periodically overwhelms the latter. He suggests a third kind of realism to help us grapple with the issues of morality and war that consists of close observation of cultural representations of modern warfare, the extrapolation of their ethical implications, and the use made of them by those in authority. Jones provides exemplars from film and literature to illustrate this approach, persuasively arguing that such contemplation renews "moral comprehension of warfare" in the radically changed conditions created by unipolarity, arms proliferation, and mass media.

John Lunn turns our focus to economic matters, in particular international political economy. He begins with traditional Christian realist concerns about power, the egoism of individuals and collectives, and opportunity for the have-nots. Lunn draws an excellent distinction between the economic assumptions of Niebuhr's writings in the 1930s and 1940s with the economic landscape of the twenty-first century. In the end, the chapter argues that the decentralized, competitive process of contemporary market-based economics appears to be consistent with Niebuhr's views concerning the necessity for multiple loci of power competing and balancing one another. Today, we witness several factors that limit the power of any one institution, be it a firm or a nation. They include competition, multilateral negotiations, and a type of balance of power that is gradually shifting away from the West.

Mark Amstutz analyzes the Bush doctrine from the perspective of what he defines as "Niebuhrian realism." Amstutz focuses on the integration of moral ideals with the realistic demands of power politics found in President Bush's speeches and documents, such as the National Security Strategy of the United States of America. The chapter's purpose is not to analyze the doctrine's efficacy, but to assess its moral legitimacy using the Christian realist perspective. Amstutz finds that the Bush doctrine is congruent with Niebuhrian realism by emphasizing freedom and democracy, privileging power in international politics, and affirming the existence of human evil in the world. However, Amstutz points out that the Bush administration may diverge from the cautious, limited perspective of Christian realism by overt triumphalism, excessive confidence in democratization as "the end of history," and in the ability to fundamentally change international affairs.

Peter Lawler uses Christian realism as a paradigm from which to evaluate the philosophical claims of civil and natural theology. Civil theology literally refers to "the gods of the city," and it is the notion that human beings only find their meaning and personal significance in society. This view reifies the political order far beyond the individual. Lawler defines natural theology as a rational deism that depersonifies God the person and simultaneously denies individual human dignity and experience as children of God. In short, both are based on reductionistic misunderstandings of what a human being is. Lawler argues that Christian realism provides a better way to understand human worth and society.

Daniel Young asserts a grand vision of the potential of international institutions. Young locates his argument in the work of British international relations scholar and Christian realist Martin Wight, who is generally considered to also be a founder of the English School of international relations theory. Wight and his contemporaries such as Bennett and Butterfield did believe that positive change was possible in international life, foreshadowing contemporary English School and constructivist scholarship. Young begins from this point, arguing that there are important and logical roles for international institutions to play in evolving international society, and that Christian realism can help us locate and define those roles in the future.

Finally, Eric Patterson takes a critical look at multilateralism in Western political discourse. He argues that the typical case made for multilateral approaches, as opposed to unilateral (or bilateral) policies, is utopian and misleading. Contemporary multilateralism is utopian in its faith that all parties are willing to solve their differences through negotiation and accommodation, without recourse to the realities of individual state interests and calculations of power. Moreover, the promises of utopian multilateralism are misleading in that they measure success in terms of meetings held and agreements signed, rather than concrete actions that actually alter the status quo. Patterson sketches a realistic recourse to multilateralism as one tool, among others, for foreign policy based on an understanding of power and interests.

Notes

1. Roger L. Shinn, "Theological Ethics: Retrospect and Prospect," in *Theology and Church in Times of Change: Essays in Honor of John Coleman Bennett*, ed. Edward LeRoy Long, Jr., and Robert T. Handy (Philadelphia: Westminster, 1982).
2. See Roger Epp, "The 'Augustinian Moment' in International Politics: Niebuhr, Butterfield, Wight, and the Reclaiming of a Tradition" (Research Paper no. 10, Department of International Politics, University of Wales, Aberystwyth, 1991).
3. Reinhold Niebuhr, *Christian Realism and Political Problems* (New York: Scribner, 1953), 143.
4. Herbert Butterfield, *Christianity and History* (London: Bell, 1949), 3.
5. Arthur Schlesinger, "Niebuhr's Vision of Our Time," review of *Discerning the Signs of the Times*, by Reinhold Niebuhr, *New Republic*, June 22, 1946, 754.
6. Jean Bethke Elshtain, *Just War Against Terror* (New York: Basic Books, 2003), 153.
7. Butterfield Papers, box 92, "Christianity," typescript for Christmas number of Methodist Recorder, 3.
8. Epp, "Augustinian Moment," 5.
9. See, for example, Reinhold Niebuhr, *Europe's Catastrophe and the Christian Faith* (London: Nisbet, 1940); "To Prevent the Triumph of Intolerable Tyranny," *Christian Century*, December 18, 1940, pp. 1578–80; and "Our Responsibility in 1942," *Christianity and Crisis* 2, no. 2 (January 12, 1942), 1–2. Also see John C. Bennett, "The Churches and the War," *Christianity and Crisis* 2, no. 15

(November 2, 1942), 29–31; "American Christians and the War," *Student World* 36, no. 1 (1943), 81–89.

10. Quoted in Epp, "Augustinian Moment," 123.

11. For example, see Reinhold Niebuhr, *The Irony of American History* (New York: Scribner, 1952); and John C. Bennett, "The Self-Defeating Attitudes of America's Reactionaries," *Christianity and Crisis* 10, no. 4 (May 15, 1950), 21–23.

12. Concern about ideologically driven foreign policy can be seen in Herbert Butterfield, *International Conflict in the Twentieth Century: A Christian View* (London: Routledge and Kegan Paul, 1960). Also see Reinhold Niebuhr, "The Anatomy of American Nationalism," *New Republic*, February 28, 1955, 16–17.

13. For instance, see Butterfield, *International Conflict*; and John C. Bennett, *Christian Realism* (New York: Scribner, 1952).

14. Michael Howard, "Temperamenta Belli: Can War Be Controlled?" in *Restraints on War*, ed. Michael Howard (Oxford: Oxford University Press, 1979), 14.

15. I record a long list of such charges in the article "Niebuhr and His Critics: Realistic Optimism in World Politics," in *International Relations* 14, no. 5 (August 1999), 51–76.

16. Reinhold Niebuhr, "Optimism, Pessimism, and Religious Faith," in *The Essential Reinhold Niebuhr*, ed. Robert McAfee Brown (New Haven, CT: Yale University Press, 1986), 6.

17. Reinhold Niebuhr, "The Christian Church in a Secular Age," in Brown, *The Essential Reinhold Niebuhr*, 85.

18. Ibid., 84–85.

19. Ibid., 85–86.

20. Ibid.

21. Ibid., 110.

22. Niebuhr, "Optimism," in Brown, *Essential Reinhold Niebuhr*, 7.

23. Ibid., 15, 18–19, 22–23.

24. Ibid., 7.

25. Reinhold Niebuhr, *The Children of Light and the Children of Darkness* (New York: Scribner, 1944), 9.

26. Niebuhr, *Children*, 7.

27. Ibid., 10.

28. Ibid., 11.

29. Ibid., 16.

30. Ibid., xiii.

31. Ibid., xi.

32. Ibid., xii.

33. See ibid., 121–25.

34. Surprisingly, Niebuhr foreshadowed the major work of sociologist Liah Greenfeld, who a half century later made a similar assessment regarding how democracy broadened as rising classes challenged the dominant class in early modern Europe. See Greenfeld's *Nationalism: Five Roads to Modernity* (Cambridge, MA: Harvard University Press, 1992).

35. Greenfeld, *Nationalism*, 21.
36. Samuel P. Huntington coined the phrase in *The Third Wave of Democratization in the Late Twentieth Century* (Oklahoma City: Oklahoma University Press, 1993).
37. Niebuhr, *Children*, 17.
38. Ibid., 41.

CHAPTER 2

The Relevance of Christian Realism to the Twenty-First Century

Alberto R. Coll

The Christian realists who made such a significant contribution to international relations theory in the twentieth century did so in a particular context. Specifically, Reinhold Niebuhr (1892–1971), George Kennan (1904–2005), Martin Wight (1913–72), and Herbert Butterfield (1900–79) wrote in response to several long-term trends and events that shaped decisively their world during their lifetime.[1] These developments included the apogee and demise of an optimistic Victorian liberalism predicated on human perfectibility, the inevitability of progress, and the feasibility of abolishing war through free trade, education, and science; the shattering of this confident worldview by two cataclysmic world wars, Nazism, and the Holocaust; the subsequent division of European civilization into two ideologically hostile camps armed with nuclear weapons; the long cold war under the shadow of mutual assured destruction, the end of which only George Kennan lived to see; and the beginnings of the transformation of a Western-dominated world into a multicultural global civilization. It is legitimate to ask how relevant the insights of these Christian realist thinkers are to the world of the early twenty-first century. My answer is that, in spite of the different outlines of our contemporary world and the fresh nature of some of the problems we face, Christian realism continues to offer compelling insights. In the rest of this essay, I suggest various ways in which Christian realism illuminates the salient features of contemporary international politics and the policy dilemmas those features pose for the United States.

The End of Unipolarity and the Rise of a Multipolar World

In 2007, in spite of earlier triumphant predictions by Charles Krauthammer and others, we no longer live in a unipolar world.[2] Partly as a result of imperialist policies promoted by Krauthammer and other unilateralists, especially the disastrous war in Iraq, the last seven years have seen a dramatic transformation in the shape of international politics. The United States has seen a good deal of its moral, financial, and political standing in the world visibly diminish at the same time that the European Union, China, India, and Russia have gained strength in different categories of power relative to the United States. While the United States remains militarily unchallengeable, it has found that it cannot translate such military superiority into strategic political outcomes. The war in Iraq, far from strengthening American credibility and cowing U.S. adversaries into submission as the war's neoconservative champions had expected, has exposed the limits to U.S. military power. On key issues such as the rise of Iran and North Korea as nuclear powers, the United States has had to abandon unilateral approaches and turn, however belatedly, to what the Christian realists would have recognized as the other "great powers," principally China, Europe, and Russia, to find a satisfactory diplomatic solution.[3] If, in the future, the United States were to use military force to address the Iranian or North Korean nuclear problem it would learn, as it did so painfully in Iraq, that such use of force would not translate into a desirable political outcome and would create new, unpredictable complications.

Economically, while American policymakers have been stuck in the Iraqi quagmire at a cost of half a trillion dollars to the American economy, the global economy has become decidedly multipolar through the rise of China, India, and the so-called "emerging markets."[4] This is a development that was already in motion before the Iraq War and would have continued forward regardless of whether the war had occurred. But the Iraq War certainly has accentuated the irrelevance of unipolar military superiority to other categories of power, such as economic power, which over the long term may wind up shaping and thus, in a sense, indirectly trumping to a large extent the sheer possession of immense military power. Thus far, since the start of the U.S. "global war on terror," for example, the size of China's economy has almost doubled.[5] The economic rise of the "emerging economies" also means that the world economy is moving back to its historical norm. As late as 1820, the share of world GDP produced by China, India, and the other countries in Asia and Latin America was about 80 percent, a figure that these countries are expected to reach again sometime within the next two decades.[6]

In 1990, when Krauthammer and others made their famous prediction about the long-lasting durability of the United States' "unipolar moment," the Christian realists would have been highly skeptical, as indeed George Kennan, the only one among them still living, was. The Christian realists' chief argument would have revolved around one of the key concepts dear to their intellectual framework: the balance of power. The realist argument, whether secular or Christian, from Thucydides down to Hans Morgenthau and Herbert Butterfield, has been that a state's position of hegemony in an international system tends to generate resistance, outright opposition, and eventually the rise of a coalition of other states determined to put the brakes on the hegemon's power.[7] Butterfield was insistent on another point. It did not matter whether the hegemon used its power benevolently or unthreateningly, or whether it was motivated by noble, altruistic intentions. Eventually, because of original sin and the arrogance bred by power—one of Butterfield's most quoted aphorisms was Lord Acton's "power tends to corrupt, and absolute power corrupts absolutely"—the hegemon would start acting in ways that it might not see as threatening to others but which others would perceive as threatening or unsettling to their long-term interests and well-being.[8] It was only a matter of time before other states would attempt to check the hegemon's power and bring it down a notch or two.

Butterfield would not have been surprised that this is precisely what has happened to the United States since the end of the cold war two decades ago left it in a position of unparalleled predominance. Throughout the 1990s, commentators friendly to American power, such as the European writer Josef Joffe, argued that the realist "law" of the balance of power would not apply to the United States because it was a nonthreatening superpower prepared to use its economic and military might cooperatively for the benefit of other states in the international system.[9] The diplomatic style of the George H. W. Bush and first Clinton administrations certainly seemed to support Joffe's arguments. Under the Bush-Baker-Scowcroft team, moderation, international cooperation, and the nurture and care of America's global alliances were the byword of American foreign policy as Washington fought a major war in the Middle East fully financed by allied contributions and with the backing of the United Nations Security Council, watched circumspectly the collapse of Communism in Eastern Europe and the Soviet Union itself with hardly any lapse into triumphalism, and pushed for German reunification and continued European integration. Bill Clinton's first term saw a continuation of this moderate statecraft as Defense Secretary William Perry promoted new models of "cooperative security" in the place of traditional balance of power security policies, and the United States continued reducing its massive military budget in real terms.[10]

But even then, there were complaints already from France, Russia, and China that the United States was too strong, and too free to flex its muscles, for the good of the rest of the world.[11] These fears were further abetted during Clinton's second term by the war in Kosovo, which Secretary of State Madeleine Albright, President Clinton, and British Prime Minister Tony Blair insisted on fighting in spite of the absence of United Nations Security Council authorization and in the face of opposition from two great powers, China and Russia, which the United States believed were not strong enough to stop it. It was during this time also that the United States decided to push vigorously for NATO's expansion up to the very borders of pre-Petrine Old Russia, to include the Baltic states, while fueling expectations that Ukraine and Georgia also might join in the future.

What eventually proved Joffe wrong, and the Christian realists right, however, was the coming to power of the administration of George W. Bush in January 2001. During his campaign Bush had criticized the Clinton team as too interventionist, and he called for a "humbler" American foreign policy.[12] This was, of course, the very opposite of what he did once he assumed the presidency, even though it actually had little to do with Bush himself and a lot to do with the people with whom he surrounded himself. All throughout the Clinton years a group of prominent, intellectually articulate younger leaders, coalescing around the "Project for a New American Century," had begun to call for a more assertive, unilateralist, even imperial American role in the world.[13] Led by such bright minds as William Kristol and Robert Kagan, and working with the support of powerful establishment figures such as Richard Cheney, Paul Wolfowitz, and Donald Rumsfeld, all of whom had felt considerable unease about the moderate statecraft of the George H. W. Bush and Clinton years, they believed the United States should increase its military spending sharply, overthrow the regime of Saddam Hussein in Iraq, and pursue a more muscular global strategy on the basis of America's uncontested military primacy. As they sought to promote a more vigorous American political and military expansion throughout the world, regardless of how Europe, Russia, or China might perceive it, some of them were fond of talking privately about the reality of an existing American empire, and drawing explicitly on Thucydides' *History of the Peloponnesian War*, they echoed the Athenian perspective that "whether it was right or not for us to take up an empire, now that we have one it would be dangerous to lay it down."[14]

It is interesting to note that much of the intellectual impetus for this new imperialism came for the most part from people who had no memories of the cataclysms of World War II or the dangers of the early years of the cold war, as well as no personal experience of the humbling Vietnam debacle. It was a new, younger generation that had grown up under the comfortable shadow of

American primacy, and for whom the old axioms of "the balance of power" seemed as old-fashioned and constricting as traditional economics seemed to the younger Wall Street financiers then immersed in the "dot-com" financial bubble of the late 1990s. In a highly perceptive essay on the role of the generations in history, as well as some of his other writings, Butterfield had warned of similar dangers.[15]

Always preoccupied with the relation of the study of history to the management of international relations, Butterfield argued that one of the problems with foreign policy was that the recurrent concepts at its core, such as the balance of power, usually were learned only through hard experience, with difficulty and as a result of some great historical catastrophe. Unfortunately, the people who learned the "lessons" eventually died and were replaced by newer generations with little awareness or understanding of those same concepts. One of Butterfield's favorite examples was the redoubtable chancellor and founder of the modern German state, Otto von Bismarck (1815–98), who learned about the balance of power during the course of a long lifetime, but was succeeded by the young Kaiser Wilhelm II. Along with his generation, Wilhelm was full of *hubris* about the need for his country to assert its power in a more muscular fashion, and eventually wound up sinking Germany in the hellish quagmire of the First World War. Famously, Butterfield argued that at the end of that war, the victorious Allies should have left Wilhelm on the German throne because, like Frederick the Great at the end of his own life in the aftermath of numerous exhausting wars in the eighteenth century, he probably had learned his lessons about the workings of the balance of power and might have steered his country along a more moderate course in the 1930s (the kaiser lived to a ripe old age until 1940). Whether or not this would have been true of Wilhelm and Germany, it seems clear that the Bush-Baker-Scowcroft team would have epitomized for Butterfield a generation that had learned its lessons about the balance of power the hard way. They had lived through World War II, a harrowing cold war with the Soviet Union, during which they had stared at the prospect of nuclear annihilation several times, and the humiliation of Vietnam. It was no coincidence that they were also fairly skillful and moderate in their use of American power, or that they lacked the *hubris* of their younger counterparts in the George W. Bush administration.

The policies pursued by the Bush administration—its "war on terror," including most famously its blunt advocacy of preemptive war as a key strategic concept at the core of American national security doctrine;[16] its invasion of Iraq in the face of opposition from all the great powers, save for Great Britain, in the name of protecting the world from weapons of mass destruction that turned out to be nonexistent; and its subsequent occupation of that country under circumstances highly reminiscent of the Vietnam War—all have done massive damage to the United States' moral and political standing, and to its credibility and professed right to world leadership, besides reminding American voters of the huge costs of imperial interventionism for the sake of less than vital interests.[17] As international perceptions of the United States have turned more negative, so have American power and influence markedly diminished.[18] As of late 2007, there was no anti-American coalition in view, nor was there likely to be one anytime soon, but something perhaps more significant had occurred. The United States was at the end of its ability to shape the course of world politics, either unilaterally or through the use of sheer military force. The unipolar moment was over. China, India, Russia, and the European Union might not be capable of prevailing over the United States in a military contest, but Washington could not shape any significant strategic outcome anywhere on the globe, whether in the Middle East, the Korean peninsula, or Central Asia, without their consent or active involvement.[19] While far from exhausted, the United States had been brought down a notch or two in less than a decade, much as Great Britain had been at the end of its American intervention in 1776–83. The balance of power had reasserted itself.

The "Global War on Terror"

The Christian realists would have been highly skeptical of, if not downright aghast at, much of the American response to the terrorist attacks of September 11, 2001. They emphasized several themes that policymakers in Washington would have done well to consider relevant. First, all of them warned against self-righteousness and the tendency to turn political or military conflicts into ideological crusades. Second, like that eminent secular realist Carl von Clausewitz, they believed that war was highly unpredictable, full of fog and friction, and had to be thoroughly dominated by a compelling and sober political logic.[20] Third, some of them, especially Martin Wight, had a deep appreciation for the historical complexities and hardiness of ancient non-Western civilizations and cultures, including that of Islam, and their inherent resistance to westernization and modernization. Like Samuel Huntington, the Christian realists would have been prepared to recognize the possibility of a clash of civilizations between fundamentalist, radical Islam and the West, but unlike Huntington's more enthusiastic followers, they would have pointed out the folly of creating, through our own immoderate policies and behavior, such a self-fulfilling prophecy.[21] They would have urged Western political leaders to do everything in their power to avoid turning the struggle against fanatical Islamic terrorists into a broader ideological or cultural war between Islam and the West.

Christian realists such as Butterfield, Wight, and Kennan were keenly aware of the calamities brought about by the sixteenth century wars of religion. They only could have shuddered at President Bush's reference to American policy in the Middle East as "a crusade for freedom," his Manichean assertions that "you are either with us or with the terrorists," his placement of several countries at the core of an "axis of evil," as if all evil were specially concentrated in them, and his obsessive emphasis on the use of military force at the expense of diplomacy and political work. With its goal of remaking the entire political and economic fabric of the Middle East, the war in Iraq would have struck all of them as the height of "hubris," and they would have been hardly surprised at its abysmal failure and unintended catastrophic consequences. With their strong sensitivity to historical continuities and their appreciation for the workings of the balance of power, the Christian realists also would have questioned (as George H. W. Bush and Brent Scowcroft did in their joint memoir in the early 1990s) whether it made sense to upset the historic balance of power in the Middle East by invading and occupying Iraq, thereby leaving Iran as the most powerful state in the region.[22]

The Christian realists would have raised another highly awkward question for the entire West. While uncompromisingly opposed to all acts of terrorism as barbaric and unacceptable, they would have urged the West to think of its own responsibility for the rise of fanatical Islamic terrorism, and to take appropriate steps to acknowledge such responsibility and craft new policies that over the long term could help to address some of the root causes of terrorism. Christian realists such as Butterfield were intensely aware of the position of all individuals and all nations as standing "under God's judgment." At the end of World War II, Butterfield had noted that if Germany had been under God's judgment, so were "all of us."[23] This awareness of the universal character of God's judgment called for a statecraft and a political perspective rooted in the virtues of moderation, humility, and a sense of limits; a recognition of one's own corruptibility and fallibility; and skepticism toward one's own motives and actions in the midst of the pursuit of political and moral objectives.

Christian Realism and the "Just War" Tradition

The Christian realists would have cautioned us about the use of "just war" theory to support the unmeasured militaristic policies of the Bush administration in the Middle East. Among all of them, Niebuhr in particular stood out for his skepticism toward just war theory.[24] Niebuhr, of course, was respectful of the tradition, and he recognized that it embraced such great minds as Augustine, Aquinas, and the Spanish fathers Vitoria and Suarez. What concerned him most was not so much the intellectual framework of the just war tradition, which he recognized as formidable, but its tendency when applied in the sinful world of power politics to supply governments with justifications for whatever they wished to do.[25] This was most obvious in the strong disagreements between Niebuhr and "just war" defenders of the Vietnam War, such as the eminent Princeton ethicist Paul Ramsey (1913–88).[26] While Ramsey's arguments for American military intervention in Vietnam were sound in the abstract, they failed to recognize such power politics realities as the artificiality of the South Vietnamese state created under the tutelage of the Eisenhower administration in violation of the 1954 Geneva Accords; the deceptiveness with which successive American administrations distorted the perception of events on the ground; the hopeless corruption of the South Vietnamese allies; the long-term tensions between Vietnam and China, which U.S. intervention only encouraged them to paper over; and the inordinate moral and material costs of the American intervention to the people of both Vietnam and the United States. For Niebuhr, the September 11 attacks certainly would have justified a response against its perpetrators—the Al Qaeda terrorist network—and that response could have included military attacks designed to destroy the network and prevent it from reconstituting itself. It is dubious that September 11 would have justified a full-scale war against a secular regime that had not been involved in the attacks, and even less, the establishment through military force of democracy throughout the Middle East.

Perhaps it is not surprising that some of the strongest "just war" defenders of the Bush administration policies in the Middle East, such as the well-known Catholic writer George Weigel, are among the harshest critics of Niebuhr, whom Weigel sees as philosophically incoherent.[27] Weigel faults Niebuhr for being too closely wedded to a skeptical realist framework that does not account for the kind of moral differentiation or clarity necessary to face the threats posed to the West by its enemies, be they those of Communism during the cold war years or Islamic fanaticism today. Another just war critic of Niebuhr, Keith Pavlischek, faults him in this book on three general grounds. First, Niebuhr's insistence that the use of violence was "tragic" and a "lesser evil" shows that he never fully left his pacifist sentiments behind about the use of force, in contrast to the Augustinian tradition, which suggests that the use of force by proper authorities can be a noble and virtuous duty, such as when it is wielded to right wrongs and punish evil. Second, Niebuhr supposedly was unable to limit *jus in bello* (how war should be fought), as evidenced by his lukewarm acceptance of firebombings. Because he rejected the just war framework, Niebuhr had an *ad hoc* approach to non-combatant immunity and discrimination. Third, because of Niebuhr's view of the use of force as a "lesser evil" and his skepticism of authority, he tended to raise the *jus ad bellum* (deciding when it is justifiable to start a war) bar unreasonably high, again, in contrast with Augustine and Aquinas.

While these are thoughtful criticisms, they miss the mark in some significant ways. Whether or not Niebuhr ever left behind his pacifist sentiments, he never forgot that the use of force, especially when it involves the taking of human life, is at best a lesser evil because it involves destroying a creature made in God's image and therefore cannot be a good in itself. This is an insight that Augustine himself recognized in some of his earlier writings. The earlier Augustine, indeed, was more insistent on this point than the latter, less measured Augustine who went as far as to advocate war against heretics.[28] It is all well and good to speak of the use of force as a virtuous and noble duty, but in the real world of sin, human ambition, and power politics, such uses are more the exception than the norm. Take a truly just war. Such wars are extremely rare.[29] We might include the efforts by the Poles and the Russians in World War II to resist enslavement by Nazi Germany, as an example.[30] And most Americans would add to the short list the American Civil War, though only as fought from late 1862 on, when it had as one of its objectives the abolition of slavery.[31] But for every just war fought in human history, there have been scores of wars that, though sanctified by the ruling elites and the Church as just conflicts, have turned out to be little more than naked struggles for power, economic interest, or the idol of national glory. In this long list one could include the Crusades, myriad wars of colonization waged by the Western powers in the past five centuries, and countless other conflicts waged in the name of self-defense or bringing the blessings of civilization to inferior peoples.

The same ambiguities about the use of deadly force by legally constituted authorities are present in the taking of human life in a domestic political and legal order. The use by police of deadly force is often necessary to deter and stop serious crimes, even to save human lives. But mistakes are routinely made, and they generally are made not against the rich and well-connected but against minorities and the disadvantaged.[32] Defenders of capital punishment also would argue that the state acts justly when it takes away a life in cases of particularly hideous offenses. Statistics, however, show that in addition to taking the lives of many innocent people, capital punishment works disproportionately against those without the financial resources to mount a skillful legal defense.[33] None of these points suggests that the state is never justified in using deadly force for the ends of maintaining order and justice. But the ambiguities explain why it was proper for Niebuhr to emphasize more the tragic aspects of the use of force than to exalt in its appropriateness. Advocates of just war theory are often surprisingly unrealistic in their inability to take seriously enough the pervasiveness of universal sin and the way it corrupts and warps every political and legal institution.

The criticism that Niebuhr did not have a rigorous approach to the question of *jus in bello* (how war should be fought) is accurate, but it obscures a larger issue that many just war theorists prefer to avoid, and that is whether modern war can be fought at all in full accordance with the principles of noncombatant immunity and discrimination.[34] Perhaps Niebuhr, much to our disappointment and dismay, was representative of an entire generation of public intellectuals that gave up on the effort. In retrospect, neither the American nor the British air bombing campaigns against Germany and Japan met the classic requirements of the *jus in bello*, whether with regard to the conventional bombings of Hamburg, Berlin, Dresden, and Tokyo, or even less the atomic bombings of Hiroshima and Nagasaki.[35] The Allies fought their just wars against Nazi Germany and Imperial Japan using some highly unjust, dirty means, and very few people in Niebuhr's generation questioned this decision.[36]

Could it have been otherwise? In other words, could the Allies have won even while using more restricted means that would have met the classic *jus in bello* requirements of noncombatant immunity and discrimination? While it is easier to say so in hindsight than it would have been in 1943, the answer is probably yes. Yet, not surprisingly, it did not happen that way. The passions aroused by Nazi and Japanese aggression were too intense, and the stakes in what became a conflict for world primacy too high, for reason and moderation to prevail. Secular realists such as Thucydides and Clausewitz have argued that this is the risk implicit in every war, as illustrated by the course of many conflicts, from the Peloponnesian War in the fifth century BCE to the two world wars of the twentieth century.[37] As passions escalate, as the contenders expand their objectives from a limited expansion of their power to crushing the enemy in absolute victory, and as the very survival of entire nations comes into play, the parties cast aside all restraints and what was once unthinkable behavior becomes the accepted norm.

This, in turn, provides an answer to the criticism that Niebuhr raised too high the bar against the decision to use military force or to start a war. In Niebuhr's defense, one can argue that modern warfare is radically different from the kind of warfare that prevailed during the millennium and a half, roughly from 300 CE to 1800, when the classic just war theorists developed their doctrines. Especially since the development of advanced airpower and nuclear weapons during World War II, the tempting possibilities opened up by science and technology to statesmen and military commanders have made it extremely difficult, if not practically impossible, to fight war in accordance with the canons of noncombatant immunity and discrimination.[38] Any casual study of World War II or the Vietnam conflict would bear this out.[39] Faced with this dilemma, Western thinkers have chosen different paths.

One group, including the late William V. O'Brien, James Turner Johnson, George Weigel, Keith Pavlischek, and others, whom we will call "just war conservatives," insist that, in spite of the changes wrought by modern science and technology, it is still possible to fight modern war in accordance with the *jus in bello*.[40] For example, throughout his long and distinguished career, O'Brien argued vigorously that the Vietnam War was not only a war the United States was justified in fighting, but also that the United States fought it justly; that is, in keeping with classic notions of discrimination and non-combatant immunity.[41] This group of thinkers also has argued that the elaborate system of nuclear deterrence maintained by the United States and all other nuclear powers, predicated on the willingness not just to threaten but actually to use nuclear weapons against millions of innocent people, is morally justifiable by classic just war criteria.[42]

A sharply different view is taken by a second group, whom we will call "just war classicists." In 1987, three of them, Joseph Boyle, Joseph Finnis, and Germain Grisez, launched a strong attack on the entire system of nuclear deterrence, arguing that it was fundamentally incompatible with the just war tradition.[43] With regard to conventional war, they argue that while it is theoretically possible to fight modern war in accordance with classic notions of noncombatant immunity and discrimination, in practice this happens rarely and only with great difficulty. Therefore, although the *jus in bello* is still a compelling norm, the bar to the *jus ad bellum* needs to be raised so as to reflect the truly awful and radically immoral nature of modern warfare. In some fundamental respects, the decision to go to war today should be made more difficult precisely because once you are at war, modern military technology makes it so easy to violate norms of discrimination and noncombatant immunity.

Indeed, the classic just war tradition contains within its framework two very useful instruments for raising the bar to the *jus ad bellum*: (1) the requirement of proportionality, meaning that the injury suffered or the evil to be averted must be proportional to the damages and evils that will come about as a result of the war, and (2) the requirement of exhausting all possible nonviolent alternatives before resorting to the use of military force—in other words, the use of force must be a "last resort," absolutely necessary in the sense that there are no viable nonmilitary options to it. In the context of modern warfare, these two traditional *jus ad bellum* requirements raise the bar considerably to the resort to military force. First, modern warfare is so devastating and its weapons so indiscriminate, in spite of the best efforts military planners might make to limit its destructiveness, that only an extremely serious injury or monstrously compelling threat could possibly justify it under the rubric of proportionality. Second, the existence of extensive international legal and diplomatic institutions, and widely available technologies for verifying the existence and urgency of a threat, mean that the scope for defining "last resort" has been widened considerably. One can argue, for example, that the resort to force against Iraq in March 2003 fell far short of meeting the "last resort" requirement. The weapons inspectors could have been given more time to carry out their work, as British Prime Minister Tony Blair unsuccessfully argued to President Bush; larger numbers of inspectors could have been sent to Iraq, as France wanted to do; third parties such as China and Russia could have been brought into the process for active mediation and negotiation; and a number of stricter deterrence and containment measures could have been put in place against the Saddam Hussein regime before resorting to full-scale war.[44]

In other words, the "proportionality" and "last resort" tests have become a stronger firewall against the use of force both because of the much higher destructiveness of modern warfare and because of the availability of numerous nonmilitary options that can be tried before a party reasonably can be said to have exhausted all available alternatives to war. In the past few decades, growing numbers of Catholics, including the late Pope John Paul II and most of the Catholic bishops in the United States and elsewhere, have used these two traditional elements of just war doctrine to raise the bar to the *jus ad bellum*, much to the frustration of the "just war conservatives," who have viewed this development as a worrisome form of creeping pacifism that makes resort to war extremely difficult, if not outright impossible, to justify.[45] While Niebuhr may have shown less philosophical rigor or consistency than the "just war classicists" as he wrestled with the problems posed by the destructiveness of modern war, he wound up raising the bar to the *jus ad bellum*, as many Catholics today have done. It is interesting, too, that as of late 2007, in the midst of the growing moral uncertainties generated by the U.S. war in Iraq, Niebuhr was enjoying an unexpected renaissance, with two presidential candidates, Barack Obama and Hillary Clinton, publicly acknowledging Niebuhr's influence on their thinking about faith and politics.[46]

Niebuhr was unwilling to go as far as the just war classicists and reject nuclear deterrence altogether. In fact, he vigorously attacked those in his own day who advocated unilateral nuclear disarmament. On the other hand, unlike the just war conservatives, he did not delude himself about the moral justness of a system that relies for its functioning on the capacity and willingness to destroy millions of innocent lives. This is why he spoke about the tragedy of using force and the character of force as a lesser evil.[47] The weapons of war, especially nuclear war, were dirty, and they were to be held reticently, with deep humility and an awareness of their intrinsic evil.

Two other Christian realists, Butterfield and Kennan, went almost as far as the just war classicists, at least by questioning publicly whether the West should rely on nuclear deterrence at all. In the late 1950s, Butterfield wondered whether it might not be best for the West to give up its nuclear deterrent unilaterally rather than continue to depend on it.[48] He asked whether submission to Soviet power might not be preferable to the great moral cost involved in relying on nuclear weapons. His doubts were not so much a statement in favor of unilateral nuclear disarmament as a question that he felt needed to be debated with much more vigor and a greater degree of agony than most of his contemporaries were willing to tolerate. Many attacked him at that time for this position, which they rightly argued was as morally troubling as the one he criticized. In the 1980s, Kennan also had increasing misgivings about nuclear weapons, though he did not go as far as Butterfield and simply called instead for radical, deep unilateral reductions that might prompt the Soviet Union to do likewise.[49]

In a sense, the entire debate among "just war conservatives," "just war classicists," and the various strands of Christian and secular realism about nuclear deterrence proves Niebuhr's larger point. There is no single position on this issue that is fully satisfying morally. Any particular stand one might take, whether principled or purely pragmatic, is fraught with difficulties. Hence, Niebuhr argued, it is best not to pretend that there is a morally clear course of action, and to recognize the evil and dirty nature of the weapons, even as one holds them for deterrent purposes. His position, itself not free from substantial difficulties, echoes a much earlier Christian thinker with an existentialist bent who remains a widely unacknowledged contributor to the rich tradition of Christian realism, Blaise Pascal (1623–62).[50]

In his renowned *Pensees*, Pascal described the realm of earthly law and politics as irreparably tainted by sin and the lust for power.[51] Society went to great lengths to hide this scandal and pretend that human institutions, be they courts of law, kings, or ecclesiastical assemblies, were capable of meeting out true justice and acting with true wisdom divorced from self-interest. Elaborate rituals and exalted rhetoric were part of the effort to bestow sanctity and legitimacy on legal and political processes undeserving of them. Given this reality, Pascal argued, the appropriate response was to treat the claims to moral certainty by lawyers, philosophers, or politicians with a combination of detachment and irony. Privately, the true Christian only could smile with irony at such claims, well aware of the intrinsic sham behind it all. This emphasis on the role of irony in politics was another contribution by Pascal to later Christian existentialists such as Kierkegaard and Niebuhr.[52] From Niebuhr's perspective, even a small dose of such irony would not be amiss regarding some of the claims by contemporary just war conservatives on behalf of American foreign policy.

The Role of the United States in the World

Of all the Christian realists, George Kennan and Reinhold Niebuhr had the most to say about the United States and the relationship of democracy to the conduct of foreign affairs. Kennan has been described as intrinsically elitist and a Hamiltonian skeptic of modern American democracy.[53] He believed that modern popular democracy represented a decline from the founders' original vision of a republic ruled by men of merit, moderation, and virtue. Modern democracy tended to breed foreign policies based on popular enthusiasms and prejudices that were inevitably harmful to the country's long-term interests. The national interest required a skilled elite of foreign policy professionals who, like the fabled European diplomats of the eighteenth and nineteenth centuries, would conduct the nation's affairs with realism and pragmatism, and without allowing themselves to be carried away by the general public's penchant for moralism and self-righteousness. Kennan's eloquent plea against that recurrent staple of American political rhetoric, the idea of American "exceptionalism"—the notion that the United States is different from, and morally superior to, the rest of the world—was as powerful as it was prophetic:[54]

> I should make it clear that I am wholly and emphatically rejecting any and all messianic concepts of America's role in the world: rejecting, that is, the image of ourselves as teachers and redeemers to the rest of humanity, rejecting the illusions of unique and superior virtue on our part, the prattle about Manifest Destiny or the "American Century" —all those visions that have so richly commended themselves to Americans of all generations since, and even before, the foundation of our country. We are, for the love of God, only human beings, the descendants of human beings, the bearers, like our ancestors, of all the usual human frailties . . . no divine hand has ever reached down to make us, as a national community, anything more than what we are, or to elevate us in that

capacity over the remainder of mankind . . . if there were any qualities that lie within our ability to cultivate that might set us off from the rest of the world, these would be the virtues of modesty and humility; and of these we have never exhibited any exceptional abundance.

From Kennan's viewpoint, the country needed a skeptical "protesting minority" that would educate the public and its political leaders about the complex realities of international relations. Kennan was one of the harshest critics of the Wilsonian legacy in American foreign policy and of the country's tendency to embark on foreign crusades in the name of a misguided morality.[55] His model for America's role in the world came from John Quincy Adams, whose famous speech of July 4, 1821, was a ringing critique of the crusading spirit and the interventionism it bred, and a timeless call for limiting American foreign policy in the realm of morality to the power of example. The speech is worth quoting, not only for the light it sheds on Kennan's own thinking, but also for its refreshing contrast to much of the *hubris* that has pervaded American thinking on foreign policy in the last few years:[56]

> [I]f the wise and learned philosophers . . . should find their hearts disposed to enquire what has America done for the benefit of mankind? Let our answer be this: She has, in the lapse of nearly half a century, without a single exception, respected the independence of other nations while asserting and maintaining her own. . . . She has abstained from interference in the concerns of others, even when conflict has been for principles to which she clings, as to the last vital drop that visits the heart. . . . Wherever the standard of freedom and Independence has been or shall be unfurled, there will her heart, her benedictions, and her prayers be. . . . But she goes not abroad, in search of monsters to destroy. . . . She will commend the general cause by the countenance of her voice, and the benignant sympathy of her example. . . . She well knows that by once enlisting under other banners than her own, were they even the banners of foreign independence, she would involve herself beyond the power of extrication, in all the wars of interest and intrigue, of individual avarice, envy, and ambition, which assume the colors and usurp the standard of freedom. . . . The fundamental maxims of her policy would insensibly change from liberty to force. . . . She might become the dictatress of the world. She would be no longer the ruler of her own spirit. . . . [America's] glory is not dominion, but liberty. Her march is the march of the mind.

Unlike Kennan, Niebuhr was an uncompromising champion of democracy. For him, however, democracy was less a reflection of man's virtuous nature or potential for goodness than a necessity imposed by human sinfulness.[57] It was precisely because of man's corruptibility that democracy was necessary. In a world in which human beings were universally prone to put their self-interest above the common good, and in which human pretensions to disinterestedness invariably disguised, often unconsciously, egoistic aims, it was necessary to avoid concentrating power in the hands of a single individual or a small group of people. In this sense, democracy was a system of government best in keeping with the realities of original sin and the Fall, because it could lead to a fragmentation of power in such a way as to check some of the worst excesses of human egoism. Even so, Niebuhr was no starry-eyed apologist of democracy, and he believed that democratic societies were capable of great political sins and atrocities, often the result of their tendency to fall into self-righteousness.[58] In this, he very much agreed with Butterfield that the more filled with self-righteousness and a lofty sense of its mission in the world a nation was, the more likely it was to become blind to its own sins and to behave in a morally outrageous fashion. There is little doubt that Niebuhr, along with all the other Christian realists, would have been visibly troubled by the marked upsurge in American self-righteousness in the aftermath of September 11, particularly as articulated by the Bush administration and its supporters in academia and the religious world, both among evangelicals and conservative Roman Catholics. The abuses of power at Abu Ghraib, Guantanamo, and the myriad CIA prisons around the world; the morally ambiguous, if not downright destructive, consequences of the American occupation of Iraq four years after that country's invasion; and the sharp restrictions of civil liberties at home in the wake of September 11—all would have confirmed their concerns.

Few twentieth-century theological thinkers were as profoundly pro-American as Niebuhr was.[59] Deeply steeped in the country's historical traditions, he recognized the special character of the United States as a society of immigrant peoples founded explicitly on the ideals of liberty, equality, and democratic participation.[60] As with his devotion to democracy, his love for the United States was anything from uncritical. It was tempered by the knowledge that not far from the surface of American political life were strong millenarian and Wilsonian currents capable of carrying the country down the pursuit of quixotic foreign policy adventures involving the unmeasured and ultimately immoral, if well-intentioned, exercise of America's formidable power. For Niebuhr, the promise and the danger of America were inextricably intertwined.[61] The promise was embodied in the good America was capable of doing when it judiciously merged its self-interest with the interests of the rest of the world, as the country seemed to have done so skillfully at the end of World War II with the Marshall Plan, the creation of NATO, and the pursuit of an internationalist foreign policy bounded less by idealism than by prudence.[62] The danger was when America believed its own myth and forgot that it too was vulnerable to original sin and the corruption of power, as in Vietnam, or when it withdrew into a complacent idealism as it had done prior to World War II. In both cases, the United States neglected the concerns and interests of the rest of the world and allowed itself to be carried away by different versions of the notion that it was morally superior, purer, and wiser. Self-righteousness, the quintessential Achilles' heel of democracy, was one of the weaknesses of the United States.

Herbert Butterfield made a different kind of argument that is also highly relevant in the context of this discussion about American democracy, idealism, and foreign policy. In discussions about morality and international politics, most of the attention tended to focus on spectacular evildoers like Adolf Hitler and Joseph Stalin and their horrible misdeeds, but Butterfield pointed out that there was one peculiar issue that tended to get overlooked. It was what he called "the moderate cupidity of everyman" and its pernicious impact on the policies of individual governments and hence on the entire fabric of international relations.[63] The average "everyman" at the core of modern society—the typical citizen who, in a democratic society, might undo an elected government or, under an authoritarian system, might be courted by that regime to keep it in power—was not capable of conceiving, much less executing, evil on the scale of a Hitler or Stalin. His flaw was instead in his everyday moderate cupidity, his perpetual desire for a little more security, more material comforts, and a greater enjoyment of what Hobbes called "commodious living." In fact, there is a clear Hobbesian element to Butterfield's "everyman" because he lives in fear for his own and his country's security, and he is always desirous of increasing his own and his country's margins of security and prosperity. This "cupidity" of "everyman," when multiplied by millions of citizens, inexorably translates itself into foreign policies of nationalism, expansion, and an inability to put oneself in the shoes of one's competitors or adversaries. For Butterfield, this would have been as true of Wilhelmine Germany as of contemporary Russia, China, or the United States.

For the United States, Butterfield's focus on the cupidity of every man is a good antidote to general sentimental notions about the goodness of the American people serving as an effective check on domestic tyranny or the foreign policy misdeeds of the U.S. government. To the extent that the Iraq War was planned by a small group of government officials who then proceeded to sell the idea to the public, it seems an exception to Butterfield's warning. Yet some of the most significant international challenges to the United States across a whole range of issues involve devising foreign policies that, while true to the long-term interests of the United States, would run counter to the average, moderate "cupidity" of the American "everyman." One could note as examples of the problem the desire of many people to drive ever more commodious automobiles and their refusal to pay even a few cents more in gasoline taxes, leading to policy paralysis on global warming, energy security, and Middle East diplomacy; the average citizen's difficulty in empathizing with the plight of the world's poor, feeding Washington's reluctance to increase investment in international development assistance; and the seeming ease with which U.S. leaders, for the sake of pandering to public opinion in a simplistic way, can demonize entire foreign nations and promote correspondingly bellicose policies to deal with them, thereby harming long-term American diplomatic interests.

The Christian realists have been accused of undue pessimism and a supposedly harmful tendency to underestimate the possibilities open to the democratic impulse and morality to transform international relations in a positive direction.[64] Their reply was that human nature remains unchanged by democracy, and that democracy itself is as open to the corruptions of sin and power as any other political system.[65] At least for Western Europe and North America, democracy was preferable to its alternatives, not so much because democracy could overcome the human potential for evil, but because its institutions tended to divide and check power, thereby making it more difficult though not impossible for democracies to commit great evils. Indeed, some of the Christian realists like Kennan and Butterfield were positively horrified by the apparent relish with which the Western democracies had embraced nuclear weapons and not searched hard enough, in their view, for ways to abolish them or at least diminish their preeminent role in defense policy. In this regard, they curiously anticipated such different contemporary critics of nuclear weapons as former defense secretary Robert McNamara and the noted "just war classicists."[66]

The Christian realists also have been accused of being overly focused on diplomatic history and on the role of the "great man" or "great statesman" in history at the expense of larger systemic or structural questions.[67] This charge is certainly not true of Martin Wight, who has emerged as the most outstanding thinker in international relations theory on the history and practice of "state systems."[68] Wight's sophistication and breadth of historical perspective served as the inspiration to his colleague Adam Watson and his student Hedley Bull to do further pathbreaking work of their own in this field, covering the history and dynamics of state systems from ancient times to the modern day and spanning a wide range of diverse cultures and civilizations.[69]

Even with regard to Kennan and Butterfield, it must be said that they, too, focused on the balance of power, diplomacy, and the structures of particular

international systems as providing the context within which individual statesmen or leaders might carry out their work. Kennan's celebrated studies of
European diplomacy during the decades prior to World War I and
Butterfield's studies of eighteenth-century Europe bear this out.[70] As for the
charge itself, it begs the question of whether it may be appropriate sometimes
to focus on the individual statesman's role. Can anyone doubt that the course
of world history, and of respective countries' history, would have been different had Napoleon, Hitler, Stalin, or Mao never lived or had died early in their
youth? At a less cataclysmic level, can one deny the impact of Richard Nixon's
gambit to visit China in 1972, or Mikhail Gorbachev's bold policies in the
late 1980s, or George W. Bush's decision to invade Iraq in 2003? Other individuals in their place clearly might have made different choices.[71]

Herbert Butterfield emphasized the role that individual statesmen could
play in lowering tensions and even, in some instances, shifting the destructive
logic of what political scientists might call "zero-sum game" in international
politics to a more cooperative mode of interaction. Statesmen such as Otto
von Bismarck, Richard Nixon, Henry Kissinger, and Anwar Sadat did so by
taking bold but calculated gambles designed to offer incentives to an adver-
sary for a different kind of relationship based on mutual security instead of
relentless conflict. The individuals best suited to statesmanship were tough
but pragmatic realists who, through hard experience, had arrived at the conclusion that the old pattern of conflict could produce no useful results and
the time had come for a radical new departure based on mutual interests and
benefits.[72]

On balance, the Christian realists would counsel the United States today
to act with moderation, pragmatism, and what Butterfield would have called
a long-term view of history.[73] With its impressive economic and human assets
and its dynamic political and economic system, there was little reason, they
would have argued, for the United States to feel anxious about its future security or to act impatiently in its conduct of foreign policy, particularly with
regard to the dangers posed by radical Islamic fundamentalism and the spread
of nuclear weapons among states such as Iran. These threats could be managed patiently, with the support of allies and other states with common interests, while avoiding the unpredictable risks and unintended consequences
inevitably associated with war.

The Vastly Different World of the Twenty-First Century

Several trends define the world of the twenty-first century. First, it is truly a
global civilization, no longer dominated by Europe or even the West, although

the West's cultural, economic, and political influence is formidable and will remain so for the foreseeable future. In this global civilization, much to the surprise of those secular critics who in the 1960s were predicting the demise of religion in the wake of "modernization," religious traditions have reasserted themselves vigorously, mostly through the rise of fundamentalism in both the Christian West and the Islamic world.[74] China and India are also returning to the preeminence they once enjoyed (as late as 1860, they were the world's two largest economies), although they are doing so, not in isolation, but in the midst of a single global civilization tightly interconnected through trade, investment, communications, and the information revolution.[75] In spite of the rich diversity of this civilization, Martin Wight would have thought of it in terms of a single international system as well as—in the language of his student Hedley Bull—an international society increasingly bound by common norms of conduct embodied in international law and diplomacy.[76]

Second, the international system is neither bipolar, as it was during the second half of the twentieth century, nor dominated by Germany's struggle to achieve European hegemony, as was the case during the first half of that century. Instead, we live in a multipolar world in which a number of great powers, notably the United States, the European Union, China, Japan, India, and Russia, compete for influence and power within the context of certain restraints.[77] There is no great power anywhere in the world today aiming for continental hegemony as Germany did in Europe, and it is difficult to foresee in the near or even medium term a bipolar world arising again. The Christian realists' emphasis on moderation, diplomacy, an awareness of the balance of power, and the avoidance of wars of religion or ideology are as intensely relevant today as they were fifty years ago, in spite of the massive changes in the international system.

Third, the world is also confronting new challenges that the Christian realists, with the exception of Kennan in his later years, never imagined, especially with regard to the catastrophic damage being wrought by this new global civilization on the environment.[78] The perils of global warming, the pressures put by the world's relentless population growth on natural resources, the collapse of global fishing and wildlife stocks, the depletion of water resources in many parts of the globe, and the massive deterioration in the quality of the earth's soil, forests, water, and air are all new problems requiring fresh ways of thinking about international politics.[79] So are the dangers of potential pandemics and illnesses such as AIDS, which can devastate large regions of the world and leave millions of dead in their wake, in spite of the advances of modern science.[80]

One can make the argument that the Christian version of realism has more extensive resources than its secular Thucydidean counterpart with which to address these pressing problems of our contemporary world. Narrow notions of the national interest and a relentless preoccupation with extending the power of one's state, when coupled with an absence of faith in transcendent principles of morality, justice, or the common good, seem highly inadequate today for several reasons. Tackling some of the newer problems facing our world requires a notion of a common universal good that embraces but also goes beyond the self-interest of individual communities and states in the international system.[81] It also requires acceptance of the notion that some sacrifices in unilateral economic and military advantage may be necessary for the sake of the long-term security and well-being of the larger international system. Finally, it entails recognition that the pursuit of national aggrandizement through economic and military power needs to be balanced against larger concerns revolving around the values of international justice and morality. Christian realism, with its emphasis on a transcendent principle that ultimately stands in judgment above all human institutions and all human behavior, provides, if not a guarantee, at least a fruitful source and a persistent voice for these claims.

All the Christian realists were adamant in their warnings against utopianism.[82] For Niebuhr, some of the most outstanding achievements in international politics, such as the Marshall Plan, came from the marriage of morality to national self-interest, and not from the wholesale abandonment of the latter, which he believed was impossible anyway. George Kennan, rooted as he was in a Christian conception of human nature and politics that was essentially tragic, was a forceful critic of Woodrow Wilson and the utopian dimensions of his legacy. For him, the attempt to change the world in the name of the denial of self-interest ultimately led to self-serving policies that were morally and politically destructive. But, for all the Christian realists, the critique of utopianism did not mean the ultimate denial of a transcendent standard of justice, morality, and the common good. While this transcendent standard could not be applied directly to the harsh realities of international relations, it still served as a guidepost, as illumination, and as a potential source of human action, however much such action might be circumscribed.

The realists were neither pacifists nor advocates of collective suicide, but they believed that national self-interest, as defined narrowly within a Thucydidean universe, sometimes might have to be supplemented with a broader notion of the common good and of common global responsibilities. In their time, the closest they came to expressing this notion was with regard to nuclear weapons, toward which Kennan and Butterfield expressed an intense ambivalence if not outright rejection. In our own time, it is not difficult to see how they would have extended such a perspective to issues such as the protection of the world's environment, or the problem posed by that half of the world's population still living appallingly on less than two dollars a day.[83] Ultimately, whether in the twentieth century or in our own, Christian realism, for all its insistence on paying close attention to the realities of power politics and the tragic character of life in a fallen and sinful world, also carries within it the awareness that politics must remain subject, however tentatively and uneasily, to a higher transcendent standard embodied in the Christian revelation.

Notes

1. For some representative works, see Reinhold Niebuhr, *The Nature and Destiny of Man* (Boston: Prentice Hall, 1940); George Kennan, *Around the Cragged Hill* (New York: Norton, 1993); Martin Wight, *Systems of States* (Leicester, UK: Leicester University Press, 1977); and Herbert Butterfield, *Christianity, Diplomacy, and War* (London: Epworth, 1953). For two thoughtful critiques, see Joel Rosenthal, *Righteous Realists* (Baton Rouge: Louisiana State University Press, 1991); Michael Joseph Smith, *Realist Thought from Weber to Kissinger* (Baton Rouge: Louisiana State University Press, 1986).

2. "The most striking feature of the post–cold war world is its unipolarity. No doubt, multipolarity will come in time. In perhaps another generation or so there will be great powers coequal with the United States, and the world will, in structure, resemble the pre–World War I era. But we are not there yet, nor will we be for decades. Now is the unipolar moment." Charles Krauthammer, "The Unipolar Moment," *Foreign Affairs: America and the World* 70, no. 1, (1990/91), 23–34, quote from pp. 23–24.

3. See, for example, Reinhold Niebuhr, *The Structure of Nations and Empires* (New York: Scribner, 1959), 267–69, 281–86, cited in Reinhold Niebuhr, "Foreign Policy and World Responsibility," *Reinhold Niebuhr: On Politics* (New York: Scribner, 1960), 298–318. See also "Turn and Turn Again," *Economist*, March 1, 2007, p. 36.

4. "Gold from the Storm," *Economist*, June 30, 2007, p. 83–84.

5. "Breathing Fire," *Economist*, April 24, 2007, retrieved September 6, 2007, from http://www.economist.com/displayStory.cfm?story_id=9063414&fsrc=RS.

6. "Climbing Back," *Economist*, January 21, 2006, p. 69.

7. David Hume's classical description is particularly apt: "But whether we ascribe the shifting of sides . . . to jealous emulation or cautious politics, the effects were alike, and every prevailing power was sure to meet with a confederacy against it, and that often composed of its friends and allies." David Hume, "Of the Balance of Power," in *Essays Moral, Political, and Literary*, vol. I, pt. II, essay VII (1752),

ed. Eugene F. Miller (Library of Economics and Liberty, Liberty Fund, Inc., 1987), 349, accessed September 5, 2007, from http://www.econlib.org/Library/LFBooks/Hume/hmMPL30.html.

8. Butterfield, however, also wrote of the beneficial role that power can play: "[T]he world being constituted as it is, even power can perform a good function in society, when it imposes peace and establishes order over a wide region, thereby enabling the work of civilization to proceed and creating a field within which men may grow in reasonableness." Herbert Butterfield, *Man on His Past* (Cambridge: Cambridge University Press, 1955), 127–28.

9. Josef Joffe, "How America Does It," *Foreign Affairs*, September/October 1997, p. 13–27.

10. Ashton B. Carter, John D. Steinbruner, and William J. Perry, *A New Concept of Cooperative Security* (Washington, DC: Brookings Institution, January 1992).

11. The French foreign minister, Hubert Vedrine, was particularly adamant in his warnings about the dangers of the United States acting as a new "hyperpower." See "Hubert Vedrine, France's Clever Cockerel," *Economist*, February 28, 1998, p. 57.

12. For an early perspective on George W. Bush's foreign policy goals, see "George Bush and the Axis of Evil," *Economist*, February 2, 2002, p. 13–14. For the diagnosis five years later, see "The Hobbled Hegemon," *Economist*, June 30, 2007, p. 29–32.

13. "Our aim is to remind Americans of [the lessons of the twentieth century] and to draw their consequences for today. Here are four consequences: We need to increase defense spending significantly if we are to carry out our global responsibilities today and modernize our armed forces in the future; we need to strengthen our ties to democratic allies and to challenge regimes hostile to our interests and values; we need to promote the cause of political and economic freedom abroad; we need to accept responsibility for America's unique role in preserving and extending an international order friendly to our security, our prosperity, and our principles." Project for the New American Century, "Statement of Principles," June 3, 1997, http://www.newamericancentury.org/statementofprinciples.htm.

14. See, for example, the remarkable speech by one of the Athenian envoys: "Surely, Lacedaemonians, neither by the patriotism that we displayed at that crisis, nor by the wisdom of our counsels, do we merit our extreme unpopularity with the Hellenes, not at least unpopularity for our empire. That empire we acquired by no violent means, but because you were unwilling to prosecute to its conclusion the war against the barbarian, and because the allies attached themselves to us and spontaneously asked us to assume the command. And the nature of the case first compelled us to advance our empire to its present height; fear being our principal motive, though honor and interest afterwards came in. And at last, when almost all hated us, when some had already revolted and had been subdued, when you had ceased to be the friends that you once were, and had become objects of suspicion and dislike, it appeared no longer safe to give up our

empire; especially as all who left us would fall to you. And no one can quarrel with a people for making, in matters of tremendous risk, the best provision that it can for its interest." Thucydides *History of the Peloponnesian War* 1.76. See also, for example, Project for a New American Century, "Rebuilding America's Defenses: Strategy, Forces, and Resources for a New Century," September 2000, http://www.newamericancentury.org/RebuildingAmericasDefenses.pdf.

15. Herbert Butterfield, *The Discontinuities Between the Generations in History* (Rede Lecture 1971; London: Oxford University Press, 1972), 343.

16. See National Security Council, *The National Security Strategy of the United States of America*, September 2002, http:www.whitehouse.gov/nsc/nss.pdf.

17. See AEI-Brookings Joint Center, "Online Sensitivity Analysis: Iraq War Cost Estimator," http://aei-brookings.org/iraqcosts.

18. Stephen M. Walt, *Taming American Power: The Global Response to U.S. Primacy* (New York: Norton, 2005); "The View from Abroad," *Economist*, February 19, 2005, p. 24–26.

19. "Turn and Turn Again," *Economist*, March 3, 2007, p. 36.

20. See Carl von Clausewitz, *On War*, trans. and ed. Michael Howard and Peter Paret (Princeton, NJ: Princeton University Press, 1976), bk.1: 87. "If we keep in mind that war springs from some political purpose, it is natural that the prime cause of its existence will remain the supreme consideration in conducting it. That, however, does not imply that the political aim is a tyrant. It must adapt itself to its chosen means, a process which can radically change it; yet the political aim remains the first consideration. Policy, then, will permeate all military operations, and, insofar as their violent nature will admit, it will have a continuous influence on them." Sir Michael Howard, whose translation with Peter Paret of Clausewitz's *On War* remains the finest in the English language, had close ties of friendship and intellectual kinship with both Martin Wight and Herbert Butterfield.

21. Samuel P. Huntington, "The Clash of Civilizations?" *Foreign Affairs*, Summer 1993, p. 22–49.

22. George H. W. Bush and Brent Scowcroft, *A World Transformed* (New York: Knopf, 1998).

23. "If Germany is under judgment so are all of us—the whole of our existing order and the very fabric of our civilization . . . the judgment which lies in the structure of history gives none of us the right to act as judges over others, or to gloat over the misfortunes of the foreigner, or to scorn our neighbours as people under punishment. There is a sense in which all that we may say on this subject and all the moral verdicts that we may pass on human history are only valid in their application as self-judgments—only useful insofar as we bring them home to ourselves. When we are relating our personalities to the whole drama of human destiny, when we are learning to gain the right feeling for the intimate structure of history, we always come to regions where the most important truths only have inner reference and an inner ratification—as in the case of falling in love, when only we ourselves know our ultimate feelings, and these are hardly matter for

common discourse, even if they are capable of communication at all. In the privacy of this room I may say that Germany has come under judgment for what people call her Prussianism or for her adherence to a militaristic tradition. I know, however, that I have no *right* to say any such thing, and I very much doubt whether it would be within the competence of the technical historian to assert it. Here is the kind of truth which is only effective provided it is adopted and taken to heart by the nation concerned, as a matter between itself and God—we as outsiders, and third parties, are not entitled to presume upon it." Herbert Butterfield, *Christianity and History* (New York: Scribner, 1949), 52, 62–63.

24. "In our own day we encounter the problem of war in a new setting. The rapid development of weapons of mass destruction has enormously increased the destructive power in Soviet and Western hands. This has created a new dimension of catastrophe for any future global war. And because of the ramifications of the power blocs, and the tensions between them, there is grave danger that limited wars will become a global war. Obviously, the probability of tremendous, perhaps incalculable, destruction on both sides in a future war needs to be reckoned with when making calculations on the justifiability of any possible war." Reinhold Niebuhr, "The Hydrogen Bomb," *Christianity and Society* 15 (Spring 1950), 5–7, cited in Reinhold Niebuhr, "The Case Against Pacifism," *Reinhold Niebuhr: On Politics*, 145.

25. "The threat of atomic destruction has heightened the criminal irresponsibility of aggression, the employment of war as an instrument of national or bloc policy." Ibid.

26. Like the realists, Ramsey believed that just war analysis must begin with the assumption that force is a fact in political life that cannot be ignored. See Paul Ramsey, *The Just War* (New York: Scribner, 1968). Later in his life, Ramsey acknowledged he had been wrong about defending the Vietnam intervention on just war grounds.

27. See George Weigel, "The Just War Tradition and the World After September 11," *Logos: A Journal of Catholic Thought and Culture* 5, no. 3 (Summer 2002), 13–44.

28. In his description of "just war," Saint Augustine provided the following basic principles of conduct: The war is just in intent—there must be a high-minded reason to start the war; the war is just in disposition—hatred of the enemy is not an ingredient; the war is just in its auspices—a lawful authority has declared the war; and the war is just in its conduct—the means used are just and noncombatants are spared. Augustine, Saint, Bishop of Hippo [440]. *The City of God against the Pagans*, trans. R. W. Dyson (Cambridge: Cambridge University Press, 1998).

29. "In view of war's new dimension of annihilation, the justification for a defensive war of limited objectives, to prevent conquest and to force an end to hostilities, does not apply equally to the objectives of bringing an aggressor to unconditional surrender and punishment. Because the ultimate consequences of atomic warfare cannot be measured, only the most imperative demands of justice have a

clear sanction. For this reason, the occasions to which the concept of the just war can be rightly applied have become highly restricted." Niebuhr, "The Hydrogen Bomb," *Christianity and Society* 15 (Spring 1950), 5–7, cited in "The Case Against Pacifism," *Reinhold Niebuhr: On Politics*, 146.

30. For a historian's account of the Polish and Russian struggle against the Nazis, see, for example, John Keegan, *The Second World War* (New York: Viking, 1990). For a moving account by a young Polish Jew of his experiences fighting the Nazis across Eastern Europe after being drafted into the Red Army, see Gabriel Temkin, *My Just War: The Memoir of a Jewish Red Army Soldier in World War II* (Novato, CA: Presidio, 1997).

31. See, for example, James Turner Johnson, *Just War Tradition and the Restraint of War: A Moral and Historical Inquiry* (Princeton, NJ: Princeton University Press, 1981).

32. See, for example, Robert J. Sampson and Janet L. Lauritsen, "Racial and Ethnic Disparities in Crime and Criminal Justice in the United States," in *Crime and Justice: A Review of Research*, vol. 21, special volume entitled "Ethnicity, Crime, and Immigration: Comparative and Cross-National Perspectives," ed. Michael Tonry, 311–74 (University of Chicago Press).

33. See, for example, Roger Hood, "Capital Punishment: A Global Perspective," *Punishment & Society* 3, no. 3 (2001), 331–54.

34. See Michael Walzer, *Just and Unjust Wars: A Moral Argument with Historical Illustrations* (New York: Basic Books, 1977). For a response to some of Walzer's claims regarding the justifiability of targeting noncombatants, see Alex J. Bellamy, "Supreme Emergencies and the Protection of Noncombatants in War," *International Affairs* 80, no. 5 (October 2004), 829–50. For an attempt to reconcile just war theory and *jus in bello* to modern war, see James Turner Johnson, *Can Modern War Be Just?* (New Haven, CT: Yale University Press, 1986).

35. See, for example, Dieter Fleck, "International Accountability for Violations of the *Ius in Bello*: The Impact of the ICRC Study on Customary International Humanitarian Law," *Journal of Conflict and Security Law* 11, no. 2 (Summer 2006), 179–99.

36. For a revisionist account of the means used by the Allies during World War II, see Thomas J. Fleming, *The New Dealers' War: FDR and the War Within World War II* (New York: Basic Books, 2001).

37. See the Melian Dialogue, in which Thucydides records one of the Athenian speakers as claiming that "the end of our empire, if end it should, does not frighten us: A rival empire like Lacedaemon, even if Lacedaemon was our real antagonist, is not so terrible to the vanquished as subjects who by themselves attack and overpower their rulers. This, however, is a risk that we are content to take . . . we come here in the interest of our empire . . . and for the preservation of your country; as we would fain exercise that empire over you without trouble, and see you preserved for the good of us both." Thucydides, *Peloponnesian War* 5.

38. See, for example, Robert J. Myers, "Notes on the Just War Theory: Whose Justice, Which Wars?" *Ethics & International Affairs* 10 (1996), 115–30. Myers

ultimately validates "just war" theory's intention as well as its utility in coping with war. See also Simon Chesterman, *Just War or Just Peace? Humanitarian Intervention and International Law* (Oxford: Oxford University Press, 2001).

39. See Keegan, *The Second World War*; and Stanley Karnow, *Vietnam: A History* (New York: Viking, 1983).

40. William V. O'Brien, *The Conduct of Just and Limited War* (New York: Prager, 1981); George Weigel, "No Just War Possible?" in *The Catholic Difference*, Washington, DC, Ethics and Public Policy Center, April 2, 2003, http://www .eppc.org/news/newsID.1574/news_detail.asp; Keith Pavlischek, "Just and Unjust War in the Terrorist Age," *Intercollegiate Review* (Spring 2002), 24–32; Johnson, *Can Modern War Be Just*?

41. See William V. O'Brien, "The New Nations in International Law and Diplomacy," *Yearbook of World Polity: Volume III* (New York: Praeger, 1965).

42. For further analysis concerning nuclear deterrence and just war thinking, see Philip Acton, "The Just War Tradition and the Moral Character of Nuclear Deterrence," *Political Studies* 39, no. 1 (March 1991), 5–18.

43. John Finnis, Joseph Boyle, and Germain Grisez, *Nuclear Deterrence, Morality, and Realism* (Oxford: Oxford University Press, 1987).

44. See, for example, the warnings by John J. Mearsheimer and Stephen M. Walt, "An Unnecessary War," *Foreign Policy*, January/February 2003, pp. 51–59, and the subsequent analysis by a seasoned military professional, Lt. General Greg Newbold, USMC (Ret.), "Why Iraq Was a Mistake," *Time*, April 17, 2006, pp. 42–43.

45. "Based on the facts that are known to us, we continue to find it difficult to justify the resort to war against Iraq, lacking clear and adequate evidence of an imminent attack of a grave nature. With the Holy See and bishops from the Middle East and around the world, we fear that resort to war, under present circumstances and in light of current public information, would not meet the strict conditions in Catholic teaching for overriding the strong presumption against the use of military force." United States Conference of Catholic Bishops, "Bishops Express 'Serious Concerns and Questions' About Possible War with Iraq," news release, November 13, 2002. In contrast, see George Weigel, "Moral Clarity in a Time of War," *First Things*, January 2003, p. 20–29.

46. David Brooks, "Obama, Gospel, and Verse," *New York Times*, April 26, 2007, p. 25.

47. "So great are the perils of complete social disintegration, once violence is resorted to, that it is particularly necessary to oppose romantic appeals to violence on the part of the forces of radicalism. But this cannot be done successfully if absolutistic motifs are erroneously mixed with a pragmatic analysis of the political problem. The very essence of politics is the achievement of justice through an equilibrium of power. A balance of power is not conflict; but a tension between opposing forces underlies it. Where there is tension there is potential conflict, and where there is conflict there is potential violence. A responsible relationship to the political order, therefore, makes an unqualified disavowal of violence

impossible." Reinhold Niebuhr, *An Interpretation of Christian Ethics* (New York: Harper, 1935), 189, cited in "The Case Against Pacifism," *Reinhold Niebuhr: On Politics*, 143.

48. Of the unilateral disavowal of nuclear deterrence, Butterfield wrote that a "strong human affirmation . . . may be the only way of . . . deflecting the course of development to which we are now enslaved." Herbert Butterfield, *International Conflict in the Twentieth Century: A Christian View* (New York: Harper, 1960), 97.

49. "Our objective for the coming period ought obviously to be: first, the halting of the proliferation of nuclear weaponry; second, reduction of both Soviet and American arsenals to the minimum necessary to balance the greatest of the other arsenals; then heavy pressure for the further reduction of all these arsenals, with a view to the ultimate total elimination of this form of weaponry worldwide. Only when all that has occurred will we, and the rest of the world, be able to design defense policies directed to the realities of the postnuclear world. But a prerequisite for any real advance in those directions will be, of course, the abandonment by the U.S. government of the principle of first use, as well as any idea that it could expect the smaller powers to part with such weapons as they have while the United States and its European nuclear allies retain indefinitely their own." Kennan, *Around the Cragged Hill*, 215–16.

50. See Blaise Pascal, *Pensees*, trans. W. F. Trotter (New York: Dutton, 1958), a series of Pascal's reflections on God, man, and society.

51. "The nature of self-love and of this human Ego is to love self only and consider self only. But what will man do? He cannot prevent this object that he loves from being full of faults and wants. . . . He wants to be the object of love and esteem among men, and he sees that his faults merit only their hatred and contempt. This embarrassment in which he finds himself produces in him the most unrighteous and criminal passion that can be imagined; for he conceives a mortal enmity against that truth which reproves him, and which convinces him of his faults. He would annihilate it, but unable to destroy it in its essence, he destroys it as far as possible in his own knowledge and in that of others; that is to say, he devotes all his attention to hiding his faults both from others and from himself, and he cannot endure either that others should point them out to him, or that they should see them." Pascal, *Pensees*, 100.

52. "Irony may exhibit itself through a relation of opposition in a still more indirect fashion when it chooses the simplest and most limited human beings, not in order to mock them, but in order to mock the wise. In all these instances irony exhibits itself most nearly as conceiving the world, as attempting to mystify the surrounding world not so much in order to conceal itself as to induce others to reveal themselves. But irony may also manifest itself when the ironist seeks to lead the outside world astray respecting himself." Soren Kierkegaard, *The Concept of Irony* (Bloomington: Indiana University Press, 1968), 268.

53. See the insightful essay by David Mayers, "Diplomacy and the Politics of Amelioration: The Thought of George Kennan," *Virginia Quarterly Review*,

Spring 1991; and the obituary by J. Y. Smith, "Outsider Forged Cold War Strategy," *Washington Post*, March 18, 2005.

54. Kennan, *Around the Cragged Hill*, 182–83.

55. "I am disinclined to resume the rather fruitless discussion of the relationship between morality and foreign policy with which I have had so little luck in the past. . . . I would like to see this government conduct itself at all times in world affairs as befits a country of its size and importance. This, as I see it, would mean: that it would show patience, generosity, and a uniformly accommodating spirit in dealing with small countries and small matters; that it would observe reasonableness, consistency, and steady adherence to principle in dealings with large countries and large matters; that it would observe in all official exchanges with other governments a high tone of dignity, courtesy, and moderation of expression; that, while always bearing in mind that its first duty is to the national interest, it would never lose sight of the principle that the greatest service this country could render to the rest of the world would be to put its own house in order and to make of American civilization an example of decency, humanity, and societal success from which others could derive whatever they might find useful to their own purposes. If this be seen as immorality, let those of you who see it that way make the most of it." Kennan, *Around the Cragged Hill*, 209–10. See also George Kennan, "Morality and Foreign Policy," *Foreign Affairs*, Winter 1985/86; and George Kennan, "Foreign Policy and Christian Conscience," *Atlantic Monthly*, May 1959.

56. John Quincy Adams, speech on U.S. foreign policy, on July 4, 1821, to the U.S. House of Representatives.

57. "Man's capacity for justice makes democracy possible; but man's inclination to injustice makes democracy necessary." Reinhold Niebuhr, *The Children of Light and the Children of Darkness* (New York: Scribner, 1944), foreword.

58. "Another peril of democracy . . . is that we identify our particular brand of democracy with the ultimate values of life. . . . We must recognize the ambiguous and tragic character of a struggle in which a contest of power between two great blocs of power in the world obscures the moral issues involved in the struggle and creates a vicious circle of mutual fear, from which there is no easy escape. There must be a dimension of faith in which, whatever our loyalties and however justified our defense of them, we recognize the tragic character of the human drama, including the particular drama of our own day, and call upon the mercy of God to redeem us, not from the contemporary predicament of democracy, but from the perennial human predicament." Reinhold Niebuhr, "Democracy as a Religion," *Christianity and Crisis* 7 (August 4, 1947), 1–2, cited in "Government and the Strategy of Democracy," *Reinhold Niebuhr: On Politics*, 191–92.

59. "There is a fateful significance in the fact that America's coming of age coincides with that period of world history when the paramount problem is the creation of some kind of world community. The world must find a way of avoiding complete anarchy in its international life; and America must find a way of using its great power responsibly. These two needs are organically related; for the world

problem cannot be solved if America does not accept its full share of responsibility in solving it. From an ultimate standpoint this need not be regretted. For a nation which cannot save itself without at the same time saving a whole world has the possibility of achieving a concurrence between its own interests and 'the general welfare' which must be regarded as the highest form of virtue in man's collective life." Niebuhr, "American Power and World Responsibility," *Christianity and Crisis* 3 (April 5, 1943), 2, cited in "America's Precarious Eminence," *Reinhold Niebuhr: On Politics*, 280.

60. Reinhold Niebuhr, *The Irony of American History* (New York: Scribner, 1958).

61. For further analysis of Niebuhr's delineation of the inextricable entwinement of American destiny, Allied war aims, and national responsibility for world peace, see his essay "Anglo-Saxon Destiny and Responsibility," *Christianity and Crisis* 3, no. 16 (October 4, 1943), 3.

62. Reinhold Niebuhr, "The Marshall Plan," *Christianity and Crisis* 7, no. 17 (1947), 2.

63. "There could be a United States and a Russia standing at the top of the world, exactly equal in power, exactly equal in virtue, and each could fear with some justice that the other might steal a march on it, neither of them understanding for a moment—neither of them even crediting—the counter fear of the other. Each could be sure of its own good intentions, but might not trust the other, since one can never really pierce to the interior of anybody else. Mutual resentment would come to be doubled because, on the top of everything, each party felt that the other was withholding just the thing that would enable it to feel secure. This situation may never exist in its purity, but the essential predicament underlies international relations generally, making even simple problems sometimes insoluble." Herbert Butterfield, "The Moderate Cupidity of Everyman," *New York Times*, January 3, 1973, 39.

64. See, for example, Michael Smith, "Humanitarian Intervention: An Overview of the Ethical Issues," *Ethics and International Affairs*, ed. Joel Rosenthal (Washington, DC: Georgetown University Press, 1999), 271–95; Rosenthal, *Righteous Realists*; Michael G. Roskin, "National Interest: From Abstraction to Strategy," *Parameters*, Winter 1994, pp. 4–18.

65. Reinhold Niebuhr, *Christian Realism and Political Problems* (New York: Scribner, 1953).

66. For support for this proposition, see Campbell Craig, "The New Meaning of Modern War in the Thought of Reinhold Niebuhr," *Journal of the History of Ideas* 53, no. 4 (October–December 1992), 687–701.

67. For a closer analysis of this particular point, see, for example, Colin Elman and Miriam Fendius Elman, "Diplomatic History and International Relations Theory: Respecting Difference and Crossing Boundaries," *International Security* 22, no. 1 (Summer 1997), 5–21.

68. See, generally, Wight, *Systems of States*. (Leicester: Leicester University Press, 1977).

69. Adam Watson with Hedley Bull, *The Expansion of International Society* (Oxford: Oxford University Press, 1984).

70. George F. Kennan, *The Fateful Alliance: France, Russia, and the Coming of the First World War* (New York: Pantheon, 1984); Herbert Butterfield, *George III, Lord North and the People, 1779–80* (London: G. Bell and Sons, 1949); Herbert Butterfield, *Magna Carta in the Historiography of the Sixteenth and Seventeenth Centuries* (Stenton Lecture 1968; Reading: University of Reading Press, 1969).

71. "Wars may be caused, or empires fall, or civilizations decline, not necessarily through some colossal criminality in the first place, but from multitudinous cases of petty betrayal or individual neglect. . . . [A]ll of us must be able to recall occasions when our doing a trifle more or a trifle less than our duty has had a magnified effect, which we should never have calculated. Not only do little things become magnified, but big things, like our victory in the Second World War, sometimes appear to be achieved by so small a margin that we hold our breath at the memory of the hairbreadth escape." Herbert Butterfield, "The Role of the Individual in History," *History*, n.s., 40 (February–June 1955), 1–17.

72. "One could conceive the next step in progress to be one which would involve a crucial act of faith in human nature, in spite of all that has been said about the limitations of this latter. It would be a thing not without risk—a risk which itself would have to be a measure that could be achieved only by a state that would be acting from a position of power. It is not the young men or the academic people or the wishful-thinkers who would ever be able to measure the chances of it; and those who merely consider the struggle as a straight war of right against wrong would never entertain the idea at all. For such an object it would almost be better to confide all that one values to the good intentions of a Bismarck, in spite of all his offenses—confide it to a Bismarck at his best. There could be no higher act of statesmanship than this, and no act that could ever require a more creative statesmanship." Herbert Butterfield, "Morality and an International Order," in Brian Porter, ed., *International Politics 1919–1969: The Aberystnyth Papers*, 336, 355.

73. "It is of considerable advantage to acquire one's basic knowledge of politics from distant examples, where the controversy is over, the story completed, the passion spent. By this method, one gains a notion of the structure of political conflict, which one can never gain in the fever of one's own contemporary world. Then, when one returns to the present, one is able to see it more analytically. The alternative rather seduces one into carrying present-day passions into the past. Those who want to learn the anatomy of international warfare had better begin with something as dead as the War of Troy. Even the study of long periods and distant ranges of history may be important, producing a more flexible understanding of politics than short periods or recent events." Herbert Butterfield, *The Universities and Education Today* (London: Routledge and Kegan Paul, 1962).

74. See, for example, Michael O. Emerson and David Hartman, "The Rise of Religious Fundamentalism," *Annual Review of Sociology* 32 (August 2006), 127–44.

75. See David Shambaugh, *Power Shift: China and Asia's New Dynamics* (Berkeley and Los Angeles: University of California Press, 2005); "Smile Diplomacy," *Economist*, March 31, 2007, p. 7–10.

76. Hedley Bull, *The Anarchical Society* (New York: Columbia University Press, 1977).
77. See, for example, David Dollar, "Asian Century or Multipolar Century?" (paper prepared for the Global Development Network Annual Conference, Beijing, January 2007).
78. See the Intergovernmental Panel on Climate Change, Working Group III, "Mitigation of Climate Change," Fourth Assessment Report, pre-edited version, May 4, 2007.
79. See, for example, John Vogler, *The Environment and International Relations* (London: Routledge, 1986).
80. See Joint United Nations Programme on HIV/AIDS, "2006 Report on the Global AIDS Epidemic," May 2006; "Friendly Environment," *Economist*, June 8, 2007.
81. For a compelling presentation of this argument by a distinguished political philosopher outside the tradition of Christian realism, see Charles Beitz, *Political Theory and International Relations* (Princeton, NJ: Princeton University Press, 1979).
82. "There is a danger nowadays that one generation after another will be asked to lay itself on the altar for sacrifice, taught by the successive prophets of one utopia after another that this self-immolation will lead to a new heaven and new earth in the time, shall we say, of their great-grandchildren. And in such circumstances the sacrifice of the present generation of real live men is definitive and irretrievable, while the utopia which is supposed to serve as the compensation for it is hypothetical at best, since it is remote and depends on the concurrence of other favourable factors, too." Butterfield, *Christianity and History*, 103–4.
83. See, for example, G8 Okinawa Summit, "Global Poverty Report," July 2000.

CHAPTER 3

Reinhold Niebuhr, Christian Realism, and Just War Theory
A Critique

Keith Pavlischek

This chapter examines how Reinhold Niebuhr's Christian realism departs in fundamental and profound ways from the classical just war tradition and explains why this matters. In short, Niebuhrian realism proceeds from a liberal theology that rejects much of the theological and philosophical orthodoxy associated with the broad natural law tradition and its progeny just war theory, resulting in a worldview far different from that of early "Christian realists" like Augustine and Aquinas.

For brevity's sake, this paper defines "classical" or "traditional" just war theory as a theological-philosophical trajectory that runs from Ambrose and Augustine through medieval developments summarized by Aquinas, then reaffirmed by Calvin and the early modern just war theorists, such as Grotius, Vitoria, and Suarez. Contemporary proponents of classical just war theory include Paul Ramsey (who revived the tradition among Protestants following World War II), James Turner Johnson (Ramsey's student), Oliver O'Donovan, George Weigel, and more recently Darrell Cole.

An obvious question is whether this classical just war tradition, contrasted here against Niebuhr's Christian realism, is not also a form of Christian realism. The answer is "yes." Few would object to classifying two millennia of reflection as broadly "Christian realist" if what is meant is "not pacifist," if it takes seriously the Christian doctrine of original sin, and if it declares the inevitable influence of human fallenness in political life and international affairs. Indeed,

Niebuhrian realism shares with older Christian realisms—notably the just war tradition—concerns about power, justice, and the law of love in this world. However, while classical (Augustinian-Thomistic-Calvinistic) and Niebuhrian forms of Christian realism share a rejection of Christian pacifism of all varieties (with the exception of individual "vocational" pacifism), they differ so profoundly on fundamental issues of moral theology and political morality that one might wonder if the broad label "Christian realism" obscures more than it reveals. Perhaps it is more accurate to speak of two rival forms of Christian realism, one of which can be fairly labeled "classical" or "traditional" (just war) and the other Niebuhrian. This essay explores three major weaknesses of Niebuhrian realism when applied to the use of force: its pacifistic theological foundations, its dissolution of noncombatant immunity (jus in bello), and its overrestrictiveness when employing force (*jus ad bellum*) across the entire spectrum of conflict.

Christian Realists on Pacifism

Niebuhrian Realism and Pacifism: Shared Assumptions

Niebuhr rejected the Christian just war tradition and did so explicitly as part of a polemic against Roman Catholic natural law doctrine. This was largely because Niebuhr's own intellectual roots were firmly planted in the soil of theological liberalism. He took the classical doctrines of the Christian faith and reinterpreted them as allegories of the human condition. Of course, Niebuhr is famous for his rejection of the "idealism" associated with the Social Gospel, but he rejected its utopian expectations, not its progressive objectives. In fact, Niebuhr never left that side of the political spectrum in American politics, and he remained skeptical of orthodoxy and derisive of "biblical literalism" throughout his life. He wrote, "The biblical symbols cannot be taken literally because it is not possible for finite minds to comprehend that which transcends and fulfills history. . . . The symbols, which point towards the consummation within the temporal flux, cannot be exact in the scientific sense of the word."[1]

Niebuhr's rejection of classical just war thinking reflected part of his departure from a more traditional Christian realism grounded in natural law. At a superficial level, Niebuhr seemed to be aligned with classical just war theory due to his rejection of pacifism. However, the difference between Niebuhr and that broader classical tradition is evident, not so much in the rejection of pacifism *per se*, but rather in the form of that rejection. The point worth noting here is that although Niebuhr rejected the optimistic liberal pacifism of his early years, he nevertheless simply accepted the biblical exegetical premise of the liberal pacifist. That is, Niebuhr simply accepted the liberal Protestant (pacifist) understanding of the Sermon on the Mount, namely, that Jesus radically denounced all resort to force violence and coercion and expected his disciples to follow his example. For the Christian pacifist, the teaching and example of Jesus precludes Christians from the profession of arms and from participation in war. Niebuhr and his disciples conceded that the Gospel ethic, or the ethic of Jesus, is a pure ethic of love and nonviolence, but concluded that the perfect morality modeled by Jesus (and expected of his disciples) is not practical in human society and thus must be moderated by a pragmatic or realistic ethic of responsibility that requires a choice of lesser or necessary evils on behalf of the community.

Niebuhr's critique of pacifism is set forth in "Why the Church Is Not Pacifist." Originally published in 1939, Niebuhr's thesis is that "the refusal of the Christian Church to espouse pacifism is not apostasy and that most modern forms of pacifism are heresy."[2] The heretical form of pacifism was held by his liberal Protestant contemporaries, who have "reinterpreted the Christian Gospel in terms of the Renaissance faith in man. Modern pacifism is merely a final fruit of this Renaissance spirit, which has pervaded the whole of modern Protestantism. We have interpreted world history as a gradual ascent to the Kingdom of God which waits for the final triumph only upon the willingness of Christians 'to take Christ seriously.'"[3]

The nonheretical form was what Niebuhr identified historically as exemplified in medieval ascetic perfectionism and in "Protestant sectarian perfectionism." In these forms, "the effort to achieve a standard of perfect love in individual life was not presented as a political alternative. On the contrary, the political problem and task were specifically disavowed." Instead, "it was content to set up the most perfect and unselfish individual life as a symbol of the Kingdom of God."[4]

Niebuhr seems to have been referring to what may be called individual "vocational" pacifism, which is not heretical because it does not call upon all Christians or the entire church to embody the ideal of pacifism. However much that may have been the case with "medieval ascetic perfectionism," it reflects a serious misunderstanding of historic Mennonite Christian pacifism.

Niebuhr here is referring to the type of historic Christian pacifism as reflected in the Schleitheim Articles of 1527,[5] which are widely regarded as the theological consolidation of Anabaptist pacifism. The authors declared, "We are agreed as follows concerning the sword: The sword is ordained of God *outside the perfection of Christ*. It punishes and puts to death the wicked, and guards and protects the good. In the Law the sword was ordained for the punishment of the wicked and for their death, and the same [sword] is [now] ordained to be used by the worldly magistrates."

Here it is worth noting that the classical pacifist rejection of the profession of soldiering, or armed police work, goes hand in glove with the rejection of political authority for Christians, more generally.

> [I]t will be asked concerning the sword, Shall one be a magistrate if one should be chosen as such? The answer is as follows: They wished to make Christ king, but He fled and did not view it as the arrangement of His Father. Thus shall we do as He did, and follow Him, and so shall we not walk in darkness. . . . Also Peter says, Christ has suffered (not ruled) and left us an example, that ye should follow His steps. . . .
>
> Finally, it will be observed that it is not appropriate for a Christian to serve as a magistrate because of these points: The government magistracy is according to the flesh, but the Christian's is according to the Spirit; their houses and dwelling remain in this world, but the Christian's are in heaven; their citizenship is in this world, but the Christian's citizenship is in heaven; the weapons of their conflict and war are carnal and against the flesh only, but the Christian's weapons are spiritual, against the fortification of the devil. The worldlings are armed with steel and iron, but the Christians are armed with the armor of God, with truth, righteousness, peace, faith, salvation, and the Word of God.

This form of Christian pacifism is not a heresy, says Niebuhr, because "it is a reminder to the Christian community that the relative norms of social justice, which justify both coercion and resistance to coercion, are not final norms, and that Christians are in constant peril of forgetting their relative and tentative character and of making them too completely normative."[6] But that says more about Niebuhr than it does about how the early Mennonites or the "peace churches," more generally, justified their pacifism. Having not been instructed in the finer points of twentieth century dialectical theology, these early pacifists justified their dualism by a direct appeal to the life and teachings of Jesus. The teachings of Jesus, as they understood them, were taken as normative and therefore required faithful disciples of Jesus to forgo both the sword and political office. Strictly speaking, this was not "vocational" pacifism, for they were indeed calling all believers and the entire church to embody the ideal of pacifism.[7]

The point worth emphasizing is that Niebuhr seems to think these pacifists were right in their biblical interpretation and understanding. "It is," says Niebuhr, "very foolish to deny that the ethic of Jesus is an absolute and uncompromising ethic." The injunctions of the Sermon on the Mount are all (and here he quotes, approvingly, Ernst Troeltch) "uncompromising and absolute."

> Nothing is more futile and pathetic than the effort of some Christian theologians who find it necessary to become involved in the relativities of politics, in resistance to tyranny or in social conflict, to justify themselves by seeking to

prove that Christ was also involved in these relativities, that he used whips to drive the money-changers out of the Temple, or that he came "not to bring peace but a sword," or that he asked the disciples to sell a cloak and buy a sword. What could be more futile than to build a whole ethical structure upon the exegetical issue whether Jesus accepted the sword with the words: "It is enough" or whether he really meant: "Enough of this?"[8]

Niebuhr is partially on to something here. Exegetical attempts by liberal protestants to legitimate Christian political participation and to justify the use of force from these passages is, indeed, rather futile and pathetic. But the target of this passage is a straw man (as were so many of Niebuhr's polemical assaults on Thomists, Lutherans, Calvinists, and sectarian Protestants). The classical Christian tradition, which Niebuhr all too often held in contempt, had far greater exegetical and theological recourses at its disposal.

But still, Niebuhr and Niebuhrian realists are determined to repudiate the Christian pacifist's "absolutism" and his refusal to "get his hands dirty." So, somehow Niebuhr must figure how to compromise and relativize the "uncompromising and absolute" ethic of Jesus. He does so in a manner entirely consonant with his dialectical theology, by elevating that ethic to an impossible and transcendent ideal: "Those of us who regard the ethic of Jesus as finally and ultimately normative, but not as immediately applicable to the task of securing justice in a sinful world, are very foolish if we try to reduce the ethic so that it will cover and justify our prudential and relative standards and strategies."[9]

To act "responsibly," the Christian must be willing to engage in what, according to "the ethic of Jesus," would otherwise be considered vicious or blameworthy acts for the good of the community. Not to put too fine a point on it, because he accepts the pacifist interpretation of the meaning of the Sermon on the Mount, Christians become obliged to do evil (as understood by the ethic of Jesus) so that good may come. Christian support for the political application of lethal force, or the resort to war, may be a *necessary* evil, or it may be a *lesser* evil, but still Christians are expected to do evil so that good may come.

It is here that the modern Niebuhrian form of realism most obviously dissents from the classical form of Christian realism embodied in traditional just war theory. The classical just war tradition shares with the pacifist the belief that if Jesus condemns an action as vicious and otherwise prohibits his disciples from engaging in that action, or if Holy Scripture more generally prohibits an action, then Christians are obligated to refrain from that action. The classical Christian just war tradition agrees with Christian pacifists in their insistence that Christians ought not do evil so that good may come.

In this most fundamental issue, Niebuhr's exegetical strategy repudiates the interpretation of both classical Christian just war teaching and historic

Christian pacifism. Classical Christian just war theologians all explicitly reject the notion that the Sermon on the Mount embodied an "ideal ethic" for the Christian, insisting that Jesus intended to restrain personal or private vengeance, not to restrain the just employment of *political* force, which to the contrary, is understood as an agent of his Father's wrath and love (always citing the Pauline biblical text of Romans 13:1–7 as the *locus classicus*). Even the pacifists of the *Schleitheim* Confession believed that the sword is ordained by God, albeit "outside the perfection of Christ." The difference between this "sectarian" or "perfectionistic" pacifism and that of the magisterial Reformers was over whether a Christian could legitimately hold the office of soldier or exercise coercive political authority more generally and still be a faithful and obedient Christian. Classical Christian realism explicitly rejected the pacifist implication that the profession of soldiering is intrinsically evil or that fighting a just war is a lesser or necessary evil. To the contrary, for the classical Christian tradition, *failure* to employ discriminate and proportionate force, including lethal force, when required by demands of justice motivated by charity is blameworthy (or vicious) while the decision to fight in a just war is praiseworthy (or virtuous).

In dispensing with the classical just war tradition, Niebuhr seemed to believe that he was rejecting a political dogma unique to Roman Catholicism and specific to natural law doctrine. However, Niebuhr was actually jettisoning a far broader tradition of reflection on political authority, the use of force, and the ethics of war. Thus, in his classic book *We Hold These Truths*, John Courtney Murray captured nicely the extent to which Niebuhr's own brand of anti-pacifism was an intramural fight among American liberal Protestants and, more importantly, highlighted the central issue at stake between Niebuhr's realism and more traditional Christian thinking about force and political responsibility. The "old" Protestant morality, says Murray—referring to the social gospel liberalism against which Niebuhr infamously rebelled—wrongly equated personal with political ethics and therefore applied the simple commands of Jesus, particularly in the Sermon on the Mount, to the different world of national and international decision making. Murray shared this criticism of the "old" morality with Niebuhr. But Murray then turned his attack on the "new" Protestant moralist, what Murray labeled "ambiguist." While Murray does not mention him by name, he unmistakably has Niebuhr in particular and the Niebuhrian realists in general in his sights. Having shattered the simplistic illusions of the "old" morality, they have left a moral vacuum: "Against the absolutism of the old morality, in which the contingent facts got lost under insistence on the absolute precept, the new morality moves toward a situationalism, in which the absoluteness of principle tends to get lost amid the contingencies of fact. . . . Whereas the old morality saw things as so simple that moral judgment was always easy, the new morality sees things as so complicated that moral judgment becomes practically impossible."[10]

In arguing against Niebuhr's "theoretically false dilemmas" in favor of an understanding of the political order as having distinctive purposes and methods, Murray was not merely situating himself within a narrowly construed, specifically Catholic doctrine of natural law, but also solidly within a broader Catholic and Protestant political theology on political responsibility and the use of force. He knew that both theologically and philosophically, Niebuhr had radically departed from that tradition, as much as had the "older" tradition of liberal Social Gospel Protestantism.

The Classical Just War Critique of Pacifism

While it would be impossible to survey the entire range of the just war/classical realist position, it will be helpful to summarize a few representative views. As Darrell Cole notes, "Clement of Alexandria, Eusebius, Ambrose, and Augustine," to name just four very early Christian theologians, defended the just use of force unequivocally. Their various "defenses"—especially Augustine's—were the genesis of the Christian just war doctrine, a doctrine that insists that war can be the sort of thing Christians ought to support. Most important, according to Cole, "none of these early Christian approaches to war treated it as a necessary evil. Each held that the person who used just force was acting in a way consonant with God's wishes and was, though in a way less praiseworthy than bishops and clerics, following Christ. The just soldier's acts in war were thus thought to be positively good acts—acts that would shape him into the kind of person fit for beatitude with God."[11]

For Saint Augustine, the decision to go to war is never a decision between two evils. Hence, in *Contra Faustum* 22.74, Saint Augustine famously asks, "What is the evil in war?" He responds by rejecting the notion that war's evil is "the death of some who will soon die in any case," adding that "this is mere cowardly dislike, not any religious feeling." The real evil of war lies in any evil intent of the warriors or of the political authorities who wage war: "love of violence, revengeful cruelty, fierce and implacable hatred of the enemy, wild resistance, the lust of power, and such like." But Augustine immediately adds that "it is generally to punish these things, when force is required to inflict the punishment, that, in obedience to God or some lawful authority, *good men* undertake wars, when they find themselves in such a position as regards the conduct of human affairs that *right conduct* requires them to act, or to make others act in this way."

When Thomas Aquinas discusses just war in the *Summa Theologiae* (II–II.40), he does not do so in the section on justice, but rather in the section on charity—specifically, the love of God. He makes it clear that war is not necessarily a vice that is opposed to the love of God. On the contrary, warmaking, when just, can be a form of love. The short answer to his question, "Whether it is always sinful to wage war?" is "no." In agreement with just war theorists before and after him, Aquinas moves from the responsibility of political authorities to guard the peace domestically to their responsibility to protect the commonwealth from external threats. Concerning the former, Aquinas stressed the continuity between the Old and New Testaments. In discussing the New Law and its relationship to the Old Law, he says, "[T]he intention of the [Old] Law was that retaliation should be sought out of the love of justice . . . and this remains still in the New Law." Moreover, in his discussion of Paul's advice to the Romans concerning the governing authorities (Romans 13:1–7), Aquinas insists that it is not merely allowable but positively "meritorious for princes to exercise vindication of justice with zeal against evil people." Finally, Aquinas argued that it is both "praiseworthy and advantageous" for someone in proper authority to kill a person dangerous to the community. Therefore, it is not at all surprising to find that Aquinas argued that protecting the commonwealth from foreign threats is not intrinsically sinful, and then set forth the criteria required to justly wage war: legitimate authority, just cause, and right intention.

John Calvin was even more explicit with regard to the obligations (not mere permission) of the civil authority (what he called, in the language of the day, the "civil magistrate"). While "the law of the Lord forbids killing," Calvin observed, in order "that murderers may not go unpunished, the Lawgiver himself puts into the hands of his ministers a sword to be drawn against all murderers. . . ." Citing several biblical examples, Calvin argued that since the "true righteousness" of the civil magistrate is "to pursue the guilty and the impious with drawn sword," then if magistrates should rather "sheathe their sword and keep their hands clean of blood, while [in a passage most relevant to contemporary terrorism] abandoned men wickedly range about with slaughter and massacre, they will become guilty of the greatest impiety. . . ." Calvin is most pointed here because he is directly confronting the challenge of the early Anabaptists. But this view is not narrowly Calvinist or "Reformed," for Calvin is simply summarizing the Christian consensus that a virtuous statesman is obligated to use force not as a necessary or lesser evil, but as a positive obligation. To *refrain* from using proportionate and discriminate force in defense of justice, order and peace is to act impiously (or viciously). For Calvin (and here he is simply rearticulating the tradition), soldiering is a holy vocation, and to reprove this vocation is to blaspheme God. The chasm between Augustine, Aquinas, and Calvin, on the one hand, and the consequentialism or proportionalism of Niebuhr and his modern disciples is therefore quite profound, although it may appear seemingly superficial because of their mutual rejection of pacifism.

"Dirty Hands" Niebuhrian Realism and Noncombatant Immunity

In large measure, the revival of the just war theory following the Second World War was a reaction to the failure of Niebuhrian realism to address what in just war terms is referred to as *jus in bello* criteria of noncombatant immunity or the principle of discrimination. Both the *jus in bello* and international law, which had implicitly relied upon the just war tradition, expressly prohibited the direct and intentional targeting of noncombatants. This convention was explicitly challenged by the Allied strategy of terror bombing or obliteration bombing of German cities, which commenced early and continued throughout the war. But the most notable protest during the war came from a Jesuit priest, a natural law exponent of just war theory, John C. Ford, in an essay titled "The Morality of Obliteration Bombing."[12] As Michael Walzer recently commented, however, "Inside the government [both American and British], there seemed to be a ban on moral talk: there's no one here but us realists!" The debate over whether the goal of the Allies should be to kill as many German civilians as possible, so as to demoralize the enemy and shut down the economy, or whether their planes should aim only at military targets, was conducted entirely in the language of strategy. "The idea that civilians were innocent men and women, immune from direct attack, was never mentioned. Instead, the questions posed were radically 'realistic.'"[13]

Recovering the earlier just war emphasis on *jus in bello* would be central to Paul Ramsey's project, but Niebuhrian realism would also be challenged on this score by Catholic philosopher and theologian Elizabeth Anscombe. The distinction between Niebuhr's realism and traditional just war doctrine is most evident in her classic article "Mr. Truman's Degree."[14]

Anscombe begins with a standard natural law description of the prohibition against killing the innocent (e.g., murder): "For me to choose to kill the innocent as a means to my ends is always murder, and murder is one of the worst of human actions. So the prohibition on deliberately killing prisoners of war or the civilian population is not like the Queensberry Rules: its force does not depend on its promulgation as part of positive law, written down, agreed upon, and adhered to by the parties concerned."[15]

She then proceeds to denounce the contemporary tendency to obliterate the distinction between "killing" in war and "murder," stating famously, "It is characteristic nowadays to talk with horror of killing rather than of murder, and hence, since in war you have committed yourself to killing—for example, 'accepted an evil'—not to mind whom you kill. This seems largely to be the work of the devil."[16]

But, of course, Anscombe is not dodging responsibility with the caveat "the devil made me do it." Rather, Anscombe immediately sets her sights on *pacifist* arguments. This might seem odd at first glance, since her aim is to repudiate the "realist" defense of the direct and intentional attacks on civilians. However, pacifists, she argues, share much of the blame. "I also suspect that it is in part an effect of the existence of pacifism, as a doctrine which many people respect though they would not adopt it. This effect would not exist if people had a distinct notion of what makes pacifism a false doctrine," she wrote.[17]

For Anscombe, the just warrior's denunciation of the obliteration bombing campaign in Germany and her protest against the nuclear attacks on civilians at Hiroshima and Nagasaki against realist defenders (Christian or otherwise) goes hand in glove with a philosophical (e.g., natural law) and biblical-exegetical critique of pacifism. Anscombe warns us that those who reject pacifism for the wrong reason, whether out of a desire to dabble in international relations, foreign policy, and realpolitik, or perhaps out of an empirical realization that something had to be done to stop Hitler (the 1930s version of being "mugged by reality"), do not necessarily resort to the distinctions required by just war and natural law, but inevitably resort to some form of consequentialism or realism. Both the pacifist and the realist tend to reduce killing in war to the moral equivalent of murder. The pacifist considers all killing in war to be murder and against the requirements of the ethic of Jesus. The difference is that the pacifist wants to draw from it the conclusion that you should never kill, while the realist wants to draw from it the conclusion that sometimes you should regard yourself as being forced to murder. You have to get your hands dirty. But if your hands are dirty already, having been forced to kill, then why be concerned about traditional distinctions between combatants and noncombatants, especially if killing civilians might end the horror of war much more quickly and perhaps "save civilization" to boot?

Perhaps the *reductio ad absurdum* of this sort of "dirty hands realism" is the infamous statement of Curtis LeMay in defense of the terror bombing of Tokyo: "Killing Japanese didn't bother me very much at that time. . . . I suppose if I had lost the war, I would have been tried as a war criminal. . . . Every soldier thinks something of the moral aspects of what he is doing. But all war is immoral, and if you let that bother you, you're not a good soldier."

Niebuhrians will no doubt object to being identified with these senti-ments. Nevertheless, it is telling that, contrary to the rather profound reflec-tions of Catholic natural law thinkers Ford and Anscombe, Niebuhr could only muster the following reflection on the obliteration bombing campaign: "It is not possible to defeat a foe without causing innocent people to suffer with the guilty," he wrote. "It is not possible to engage in any act of collective opposition to collective evil without involving the innocent with the guilty. It is not possible to move in history without becoming tainted with guilt."[18]

This is precisely the "ambiguist" style of argumentation that Murray and Anscombe found so objectionable. As Darrell Cole observes, the problem from the classical just war perspective is not with the first two sentences. The just warrior knows that innocent people will suffer in even the most justly fought war, both because of unintended harm and because some soldiers, even in a just cause, will act viciously and harm noncombatants. That is why no war should be entered into lightly and why the resort to force needs to be justified (*jus ad bellum*). The just warrior's problem is with the third sentence. Cole calls attention to the regressive logic of what he calls "dirty hands think-ing," and it is worth quoting at length:

> Those responsible for the decision to fight in a just war and those who fight virtuously in war do not become necessarily tainted with guilt (i.e., there is nothing inherently evil about deciding to fight in a war or about fighting in war). Such virtuous people know that innocent people will suffer, but they do not intend this suffering and the success of their war-fighting plans are not in any way dependent upon the suffering of innocent people. The vicious persons responsible for the war are the ones necessarily tainted with guilt, as are those who, though fighting on the just side, fight unjustly. The Allies of World War II, for example, were not guilty of any suffering caused to the innocent people of Europe as long as they did not behave viciously in battle, that is to say, so long as they approximated the *jus in bello* as best they could. The Nazis were responsible for the suffering of the innocent people caught in a battlefield cre-ated by the Nazis, except of course the suffering caused by the Allies when they engaged in vicious practices like saturation bombing. The trouble is that, as soon as we start wringing our hands with self-imposed guilt, our own evil actions may follow . . . once we begin to believe we are acting viciously by the very nature of the case, then the temptation becomes to be a little more vicious and guarantee victory. Dirty hands thinking tells us that we have already crossed a moral threshold in fighting a war to begin with, and once having crossed that threshold, we may be tempted to make sure that it was worth it and guaranteed victory.[19]

One of Murray's criticisms of Niebuhr's realism was that it collapsed into a form of "situationalism." The problem is that Niebuhr habitually analyzed moral-political problems by recourse to the most general of considerations, such as the law of sacrificial love and the realities of sinfulness. Cole asks us to recall that a central tenet of Niebuhr's realism, contrary to Social Gospel liberalism, is that the life and work of Jesus do not offer us a social ethic; it was not, per Rauschenbusch and other liberal Protestants, a "simple possibility." Niebuhr argues that the ethic of Jesus was a personal ethic or individual ethic since Jesus meant to change the quality of the individual's life. Jesus offers us a pure ethic of love, an ethic too pure to be realized in this life, but an ideal toward which we must strive if we hope to act well.[20] This personal ethic of love is in need of a social ethic, because human beings don't love each other but themselves.

To the question, "Why does the Christian seek justice?" Niebuhr replies that love is the reason we seek earthly justice. While the Christian must admit that ethic of love taught by Jesus is an impossible ideal, the ideal is still essential if we want to achieve the worthwhile mundane goals of earthly justice. Moreover, human beings are not completely corrupted by self-interest, for they retain the law of love (or the law of our being), which is boundless self-giving. Between these two forces we formulate "ad hoc restraints," and this we can call natural law. The goal of law is justice, yet justice is related to love in that the law is both "an approximation of the law of love" and "an instrument of love."[21]

So, observes Cole, "Niebuhr's logic seems to lead us to claim that vicious acts in war [e.g., the direct and intentional targeting of innocent civilians] are sometimes needed to get the job done, but when we do such things, we do them out of love. In other words, Jesus' ethic of love impels us to do vicious things. There is something wrong about this." And Cole calls our attention to Timothy Luke Jackson's characterization of this logic as one in which love "claiming to transcend justice, actually falls below it in embracing too violent means for political ends."[22] Here, finally, the contrast between Niebuhr's realism and the just war tradition is most stark. For the just warrior, some vicious acts, such as deliberately and willfully killing innocent people, even in war, cannot be ascribed to anything like Jesus' ethic of love or as a "loving" act.

Niebuhrian Realism and *Jus Ad Bellum*

In large measure, it was the failure of Niebuhrian realism to address adequately the moral issues related to the *jus in bello* principle of noncombatant immunity that led to a revival of serious and sustained reflection on just war in the latter half of the twentieth century. Just as Niebuhrian realism tended to loosen restrictions on the *jus in bello* principle of noncombatant immunity, it has also been in large measure responsible for the conceptual problems and historical distortions associated with understanding just war theory as a form of cryptopacifism or as reflecting a so-called "presumption against force." I want to suggest that the Niebuhrian realist, to the extent that the resort to force is understood as a "controlled exception to pacifism," has contributed to the tendency in recent years to proliferate the "criteria" for the legitimate resort to force. The problem with regard to the *jus ad bellum* tends to be the precise opposite of the problem with the *jus in bello*. While the Niebuhrian realist tends to lower the moral bar where the just war tradition has set it high, the realist tends to render moralistic and restrictive what the *jus ad bellum* considers matters of political prudence.

The contemporary debate among Christian moral theologians and philosophers over whether the just war tradition incorporates a "presumption against violence," on the one hand, or whether it reflects a presumption for justice, on the other, can be understood as a debate between modern Niebuhrian Christian realists who, with no little irony, align themselves with neo-Anabaptist pacifists such as John Howard Yoder and Stanley Hauerwas against more traditional moral theologians who embrace the classical tradition. Modern Christian realists, at least to the extent that they follow Niehbuhr's lead, seem compelled to understand the resort to force as a controlled exception to general pacifism. And the neo-Anabaptist pacifists have found, despite their deep theological disagreements, common cause with Niebuhrian realists on the general prohibition against the use of force by Christians. The convergence of the neo-Anabaptists and the Christian realists on this point, despite their profound disagreements and sharp polemics, is perfectly understandable upon deeper reflection. Both share the belief that the life and teaching of Jesus require all Christians—the entire church—to be pacifists. The difference is that modern neo-Anabaptists are less willing than the Christian realists to compromise and do evil so that good may come. The difficulty becomes prominent when the neo-Anabaptists and the Christian realists together try to construct a "just war theory" generated out of a "presumption against violence."

The notion that just war theory grew out of a presumption against violence has had a profound influence on much of modern ecclesiastical and academic writing on issues of war and peace, from the Catholic bishops who embraced the idea in large measure as a compromise between Roman Catholic pacifists and just war traditionalists in their pastoral letter *The Challenge of Peace*, to the frequent and entirely predictable functional pacifist statements of mainline Protestantism, to a narrow but influential swath of American evangelical Christianity.[23]

Classical Christian just warriors, on the other hand, continue to insist that historically, just war theory did not arise out of nonviolent assumptions but out of assumptions of justice; more pointedly, out of the normative requirement that political authorities are responsible for justice. Contrary to the assertions on many contemporary pacifists, Darrell Cole insists rightly that assumptions of nonviolence have nothing to do with the genesis of Christian just war theory:

> Christian pacifists, of course, think that just war theory developed precisely because early Christians had to figure out a way to harmonize their nonviolent assumptions with the desire to aid their neighbors with acts of force. This is factually wrong. Pacifists cannot point to a single Church Father who helped develop the Christian just war doctrine out of "nonviolent assumptions." On the contrary, just war theory arose out of assumptions of justice and the virtue of charity. Assumptions of nonviolence had nothing to do with the genesis of Christian just war theory.[24]

The great theologians of the Christian church such as Augustine, Aquinas, and Calvin did not begin with a "presumption against war" but rather with a *presumption against injustice*, focused on the need for *political authority* to employ the responsible use of force to confront wrongdoing. Indeed, the criteria classified under *jus ad bellum* does nothing else than specify the terms under which those in political power are authorized to resort to force.[25]

But the problem with the presumption-against-war position or an understanding of the just war tradition as a controlled exception to pacifism is not merely historical. More important, it introduces a certain perverse logic into moral reflection on the use of military force, a perversity that helps account for the irrelevance of most recent academic and ecclesiastical teaching on the ethics of war. How does this happen? The resort to military force in the just war tradition has historically come to be defined through the following moral concepts: just cause, competent authority, right intention, reasonable hope of success, last resort, the goal of peace, and overall proportionality of good over harm. However, both historically and in terms of the inner logic of the just war idea, the criteria are not all of equal importance. Just cause, competent authority, and right intention, the "criteria" mentioned by Saint Thomas and drawn from Saint Augustine, have priority because they are immediately oriented to the fundamental political goods of justice, order, and peace. The remaining concerns (and the criteria often tend to proliferate)—last resort, proportionality, reasonable chance for success, and the prospects for peace— must be taken seriously; but being prudential tests, they are, as James Turner Johnson says, "of a qualitatively different character from the deontological criteria"[26] of the first three criteria. Contemporary writers advancing the presumption-against-war position, however, tend to invert these priorities so that prudential criteria such as last resort (probably the least helpful of the criteria) are presented as being at the center of the tradition.

To draw attention to this inversion of priorities is no mere splitting of academic hairs. By inverting the logical priority of the criteria, the presumption-against-war interpretation of the tradition ends up presenting just war as a jumbled collection of abstract moral ideals, or a "checklist" of pacifist-inspired requirements utterly disconnected from political and military judgment. Both historically and conceptually, however, the just war approach to the use of force is already in dialogue with the spheres of statecraft and military expertise. Indeed, just war reasoning belongs to, and properly resides with, military commanders and statesmen considering the use of force, not academics, activists, and certainly not ecclesiastical bureaucrats. In short, if the mere use of military force is conceived in the first instance as the "problem" (or the evil) to which avoidance is the preferred solution, then just war reasoning is reduced to little more than a moralistic checklist, or a set of hurdles that the "ethicists" put before the statesman, imported from the outside, as it were, from a realm external to the task of statecraft.

However, in almost every instance, the responsibility to make prudential judgments as to whether a military operation will be successful (the criterion of reasonable chance for success) or will result in greater good than harm (the principle of proportionality) rests with those who have the political authority and competence to render such judgments. This normally does not include bishops, theologians, and professors, who are no more competent on these questions than the average citizen, and usually less so. It is the disorienting inversion of logical priorities in the presumption-against-war teaching that explains why, in recent years, we confront the maddening spectacle of theologians who know virtually nothing about military strategy, force structure, and weapons capability holding forth confidently on the likely or unlikely success of a potential military operation. It accounts for the frequently heard assertion that pacifists and just warriors share a common commitment to military force as a "last resort," the only purported difference being that pacifists believe a last resort is never reached—as if that were a minor difference. It also explains how it can be that so many intellectuals can support the use of force in theory, but also always oppose it in practice.

Now, it is the case that modern Niebuhrians realists will, while modern Christian pacifists will not, justify exceptions to pacifist-generated strictures against the use of force. But because the moral baseline is pacifist, the exception to which is conceded to be sinful or evil, the bar for the permissible use of force tends to get raised to an almost impossible level. Hence, in the section of Niebuhr's *The Nature and Destiny of Man* devoted to the deficiencies of Catholic just war theory and natural law, one looks in vain for a careful consideration of just resort to force. However, we do get this comment: "The very same war which fails to yield an absolutely clear sense of 'justice' *may yet concern itself with the very life and death of civilizations and cultures*. Men do have to make important decisions in history upon the basis of certain norms, even though they must recognize that all historic norms are touched with both finiteness and sin; and that their sinfulness consists precisely in the bogus claim of finality which is made for them."[27]

Niebuhr, the former pacifist, came to justify the resort to war because the very life and death of civilization was at stake. We should be thankful for this, but it raises innumerable questions related to the just use of force across what the military calls the entire "spectrum of conflict," including issues related to the first use of force, military intervention for humanitarian reasons, counterinsurgency operations against nonstate actors, and every other potential use of military force short of the survival of "civilizations and cultures." Niebuhrian realism is too ambiguous to prove much help on this score.

Finally, Darrell Cole has called our attention to a feature of the classical just war tradition that distinguishes it from Niebuhrian realist and pacifist views alike: that a failure to engage in a just war is a failure of virtue, a failure to act well.

> An odd corollary of this conclusion is that it is a greater evil for Christians to fail to wage a just war than it is for unbelievers. When an unbeliever fails to go to war, the cause may be a lack of courage, prudence, or justice. He may be a coward or simply indifferent to evil. These are failures of natural moral virtue. When Christians (at least in the tradition of Aquinas and Calvin) fail to engage in just war, it may involve all of these natural failures as well, but it will also, and more significantly, involve a failure of charity. The Christian who fails to use force to aid his neighbor when prudence dictates that force is the best way to render that aid is an uncharitable Christian. Hence, Christians who willingly and knowingly refuse to engage in a just war do a vicious thing: they fail to show love toward their neighbor as well as toward God.[28]

Failure to engage is a just war is to act viciously. To fight a just war justly is an act of charity. Failure to fight it justly, by directly and intentionally attacking innocents, is to act viciously. Niebuhrian Christian realism is deficient to the extent that it is unable to make these moral distinctions or mitigates them under a cloud of ambiguity.

Conclusion

Classical just war theory is Christian and realistic. This venerable tradition has provided policy guidance to political and religious leaders for nearly two millennia and is founded on a moral view of human affairs that is also deeply conscious of the necessary prudential judgments that come with political and military responsibility. Hence, classical Christian realism asserts that there are times to employ violence in this world, but that such activities should be limited within the strictures laid out in the just war tradition. In contrast, Niebuhrian realism is rooted in the shallow soil of theological liberalism and therefore lacks an adequate worldview to provide a robust alternative to pacifism, guide the decision to engage military force (*jus ad bellum*), or limit the use of violence during conflict (*jus in bello*). What is needed today in facing the security threats associated with apocalyptic terrorism, powerful nonstate actors, and outlaw regimes is a robust theologically grounded Christian realism that is not quasi-pacifistic, but which utilizes rather the resources of the classical tradition in thoughtful policies working toward greater security and peace.

Notes

1. Reinhold Niebuhr, *The Nature and Destiny of Man*, vol. 2, *Human Destiny* (New York: Scribner, 1943), 289. Niebuhr's hostility to "biblical literalism" extended beyond a mere critique of Christian fundamentalism. Numerous critics have observed that Niebuhr's major work in systematic theology, *The Nature and Destiny of Man* was really an exercise in applied anthropology and that all the great doctrines of the Christian tradition get transformed into saying something about human nature or human hope. This was a consistent criticism of Niebuhr from more conservative Protestants but also from his closer colleagues. For example, Niebuhr's biographer, Richard Fox, tells us that Niebuhr was none too pleased when several academic and religious reviewers of his book *Beyond Tragedy* (1937), including his Union Seminary friends and colleagues, questioned his reduction of orthodox classic Christian doctrines to the status of "myth." His Union Seminary colleague Joseph Haroutunian responded to an angry letter from Niebuhr by defending his charge that he was a Platonist:

   I called you a Platonist because your God is primarily the ethical ideal which passes judgment upon us by its sheer unattainable excellence. The "tension" between the ideal and the real seems to me to be the essence of your religion. Your God does not perform miracles; never has and never will; hence to you the Incarnation and Resurrection of the dead are myths, not fantasies indeed (I never said so, nor made an "effort" to say so), and yet "trans-historical"—shall we say, unhistorical? Reiny, for truth's sake, tell me, just what do you do with Paul,

Augustine, Luther, for whom sin and death, *together* were what Christ saved us from? . . . Yours is a truncated Christianity, one that pushes aside the cry of the human heart for life with God in eternity.

In a most insightful comment on this exchange, Fox says that Niebuhr was particularly enraged at the critiques of his reviewers in part "because he was so committed emotionally to his self-image as a crusader *against* liberalism in theology." Fox rightly noted that Niebuhr's theological liberalism "ran deep, deeper than he ever understood" (Richard Fox, *Reinhold Niebuhr: A Biography* [Harper and Row, 1985], 183). Indeed, this is why Niebuhr could speak and defend the *idea* of the resurrection of Jesus, but could still write to Norman-Kemp Smith shortly after his Gifford Lectures that that he did not want to give comfort to the literalists, adding, "I have not the slightest interest in the empty tomb or physical resurrection (Fox, p. 215).

2. Niebuhr's essay on "Why the Church Is Not Pacifist" was recently reprinted in *The End of Illusions: Religious Leaders Confront Hitler's Gathering Storm*, ed. Joseph Loconte (Lanham, MD: Rowman and Littlefield, 2004), 135.

3. Niebuhr, "Why the Church Is Not Pacifist," in Loconte, *End of Illusions*, 141.

4. Ibid., 133.

5. The Schleitheim Confession can be found at http://www.anabaptists.org/history/schleith.html.

6. Niebuhr, "Why the Church Is Not Pacifist," 143–44.

7. Niebuhr's attitude toward the classic pacifist position seems ironic, but it comes at the expense of reinterpreting what the early Mennonites thought they were doing. In contrast, classical just war theory has respect for the pacifist position, although just war should be willing to call it heretical. It is heretical because it proscribes Christians from holding offices that Scripture does not prohibit Christians from holding. And it diminishes the role of the Christian magistrate from an honorable office to one that is intrinsically sinful. But at least the classic Christian just war position has the virtue of taking classic pacifists seriously on their own terms.

8. Niebuhr, "Why the Church Is Not Pacifist," 135.

9. Ibid.

10. John Courney Murray, S. J., *We Hold These Truths: Catholic Reflections on the American Proposition* (1960), 278.

11. Darrell Cole, "Good Wars," *First Things*, October 2001, 243.

12. John C. Ford's essay, "The Morality of Obliteration Bombing," was originally published in *Theological Studies* 5 (1944), 261–309.

13. Michael Walzer, "Can There Be a Moral Foreign Policy?" in *Liberty and Power: A Dialogue on Religion and U.S. Foreign Policy in an Unjust World*, by Brian J. Hehir et al. (Washington, DC: Brookings Institution, 2004).

14. G. E. M. Anscombe, "Mr. Truman's Degree," in *The Collected Philosophical Papers of G. E. M. Anscombe*, vol. III, *Ethics, Religion, and Politics* (Oxford: Blackwell, 1981), 10.

15. Anscombe, "Mr. Truman's Degree," 64.
16. Ibid., 67.
17. Ibid.
18. Reinhold Niebuhr, "The Bombing of Germany," in *Love and Justice: Selections from the Shorter Writings of Reinhold Niebuhr*, ed. D. B. Robertson (New York: Meridian Books, 1967), 222. This article was originally published in *Christianity and Society* (Summer 1943).
19. Darrell Cole, "Virtuous Warfare and the Just War: A Christian Approach" (PhD diss., University of Virginia, 2001), 111–12. See also Darrell Cole, *When God Says War Is Right* (New York: Waterbrook, 2002); and Darrell Cole and Alexander Webster, *The Virtue of War: Reclaiming the Classic Traditions East and West* (London: Regina Orthodox, 2004).
20. Cole, "Virtuous Warfare," 104.
21. Ibid., 105. The citation is from Reinhold Niebuhr's *Christian Realism and the Political Problem* (New York: Scribner, 1953), 171–72.
22. Cole, "Virtuous Warfare," 112–13. The citation is from Timothy Jackson's "Christian Love and Political Violence," in *The Love Commandments: Essays in Christian Ethics and Moral Philosophy*, ed. Edmund N. Santurri and William Werpehowski (Washington, DC: Georgetown University Press, 1992), 191.
23. For an excellent summary of the debate, see the exchange between Paul J. Griffiths and George Weigel, "Who Wants War? An Exchange," *First Things*, April 2005. Paul Ramsey addressed this issue as early as 1968 in "Can a Pacifist Tell a Just War?" in *The Just War: Force and Political Responsibility* (New York: Scribner, 1968).
24. Darrell Cole, "Listening to Pacifists," in *First Things* (August/September, 2002). Also accessible at http://www.firstthings.com/article.php3?id_article=2054.
25. It is also significant that Father Bryan Hehir, a central architect of the bishops' pastoral letter *The Challenge of Peace*, which argued that the tradition begins and ends with a presumption against force, has conceded the historical point in a review of James Turner Johnson's book *Morality and Contemporary Warfare* (Yale University Press, 1999). See Hehir's review in *Commonweal*, March 10, 2000.
26. James Turner Johnson, *Morality and Contemporary Warfare* (Yale University Press, 1999) p. 42.
27. Niebuhr, *Nature and Destiny*, 284.
28. Cole, "Virtuous Warfare," 93.

CHAPTER 4

Morality and U.S. Foreign Policy*

Ernest W. Lefever

It is too simple to attribute the pervasive moral confusion in America to our involvement in Iraq, though that protracted trauma doubtless has brought to a head our growing weariness with the burdens of power and disenchantment with what Denis Brogan once called "the illusion of American omnipotence."

Underlying the moral awakening and confusion has been a continuing struggle between two different ways of looking at history and politics, two streams of American thought that have vied for ascendancy, especially since the mid-nineteenth century. The late Reinhold Niebuhr called these inclinations "rational idealism" and "historical realism," each manifesting itself in diverging political attitudes, expectations, and behavior.

Rational idealism in essence is the child of the Enlightenment, and in its pure form it affirms the perfectibility, or at least improvability, of mankind and the possibility, if not inevitability, of progress in history. The diverse schools within this approach are united in their ultimate faith in the nobler nature of man. The earlier idealists saw reason as the redemptive agent that would save humanity and politics and eventually inaugurate an era of universal peace and brotherhood—the socialist paradise or the Kingdom of God on earth. The natural goodness of man, they believed, can be translated into the structures of politics. Poverty, injustice, and war can be eliminated. The rational idealists were supported by the views of men such as Tom Paine, Walt

* A version of this essay was first published in *Ethics and World Politics* (Baltimore: Johns Hopkins University Press, 1972) and was subsequently reprinted in *The Irony of Virtue: Ethics and American Power* (Boulder, CO: Westview, 1998). It is reprinted here in updated form with the permission of its author.

Whitman, and Walter Rauschenbusch, the articulate spokesman of the Protestant Social Gospel movement. Wilsonian idealism, the manifestation of rationalism in the international sphere, reached its zenith in 1928 with the signing of the Kellogg-Briand Pact outlawing war as an "instrument of national policy."

Historical realism, in contrast, emphasizes the moral limits of human nature and history and has its roots in Saint Augustine, John Calvin, Edmund Burke, James Madison, and most other classical Western thinkers. Rejecting all forms of religious and secular utopianism—including Fascism and Communism—the post-Versailles realists have included men as varied as Niebuhr, Carl L. Becker, Winston Churchill, and Dean Acheson. Noting that the extravagant expectations of the Wilsonians were not ratified by subsequent events, the self-designated realists hold that all political achievements are limited by man's dogged resistance to drastic reconstruction. With this recognition of "original sin," they argue that perfect peace, justice, security, and freedom are not possible in this world, though approximations of these lofty goals are not beyond man's grasp. To the rational idealist, the "impossible ideal" is achievable because it is rationally conceivable. To the historical realist, the "impossible ideal" is relevant because it lends humility without despair and hope without illusion.

In the real world, there are few wholly consistent adherents to either approach. Were Jefferson and Lincoln rational idealists or historical realists? Obviously, they were a combination of both—Jefferson leaning toward the idealist view, and Lincoln toward the realist. Like most Americans, they tended to be optimistic about the more distant future and at the same time were practical and realistic about immediate problems and possibilities.

Rational idealism and historical realism are not complete moral systems, but two different perspectives coexisting uneasily within the Western commitment to a political order of justice and freedom. As approaches, they are subject to certain limitations and weaknesses. In one sense, each tends to balance and correct the other. Most moral philosophers, political theorists, and statesmen tend toward one view or the other. On the practical level, virtually all political leaders have been realists, regardless of how idealistic their rhetoric may have been. I believe that the historical realist approach, particularly in its Christian realist form, is a more adequate reading of the Judeo-Christian tradition and a sounder guide to politics than its post-Enlightenment rival, but recognize that it, like rational idealism, is subject to corruption.

Idealists versus Realists

Both of these respectable philosophical approaches have been demeaned and distorted by emphasizing certain of their virtues to the neglect or exclusion of other elements in the larger body of Western normative thought. Each is vulnerable in its own way to the vices of political aloofness, on the one hand, and crusading arrogance, on the other. Rational idealists, frustrated by stubborn political realities, sometimes degenerate into sentimentalists whose strident demand for perfection becomes a substitute for responsible behavior. When personal purity becomes more important than political effectiveness, the resulting aloofness is virtually indistinguishable from that of cynical Machiavellians who insist that might alone makes right. The historical realist becomes irresponsible when his preoccupation with man's baser nature cuts the taproot of social concern and permits him to become a defender of injustice or tyranny.

A lopsided realist can come to hold that what is good for America is good for the rest of the world and that it is our "manifest destiny" to make other peoples over in our own image, by force if necessary. An equally lopsided idealist can support efforts to reshape other societies by more subtle, but not necessarily less reprehensible, means. Members of each approach can degenerate into cynical isolationists or overbearing crusaders. Seen in this light, the extremists in both groups have more in common with each other than with the mainstream of their own tradition.

The corruption of realism or idealism can be called moralism—the most popular rival and impostor of genuine morality. Morality or ethics (the Greek derivative with the same meaning) has to do with right or wrong behavior in all spheres. It is the discipline of relating ends and means. However primitive or sophisticated, all moral systems define normative ends and acceptable rules for achieving them. Moralism, on the other hand, is a sham morality, a partial ethic. Often it is expressed in self-righteous rhetoric or manipulative symbols designed to justify, enlist, condemn, or deceive rather than to inform, inspire, or serve the cause of justice. The moralism of the naïve and well intentioned may be sincere. The moralism of the ambitious and sophisticated is likely to be dishonest. Intellectually flabby and morally undisciplined, moralism tends to focus on private interests rather than the public good, on the immediate at the expense of the future, and on sentiment rather than reason. Morality is a synonym for responsibility. Moralism is a conscious or unconscious escape from accountability.

Soft and Hard Moralism

The varieties of moralism flowing from the corruption of the two approaches always subvert honest political dialogue and responsible behavior, but at the present point in American history, soft moralism of the sentimental idealists is a greater threat than hard moralism of the power realists. The views of the hard cynics—the extreme Machiavellis and gung-ho imperialists—find little hospitality in the university, the church, the press, or in the public generally. The small voice of the hard moralists is barely audible. In sharp contrast, the soft moralism of the rational idealists has had increasing appeal because many Americans are wearied by the burdens of power—the cost of nuclear deterrence and the perplexities of helping to keep the peace in distant places.

Today, the rational idealistic approach—in its religious and secular versions—and the various corruptions of this stance find wide acceptance among certain articulate leaders in the church and university, and are actively promoted by a segment of the mass media. Given the high level of moral turbulence and uncertainty, it is important to take critical note of this more pervasive manifestation of American moralism, acknowledging that some of its attributes are also similar to those of hard moralism.

Moralism, soft or hard, tends toward a single-factor approach to political problems, while mainstream Western morality emphasizes multiple causation, multiple ends, and multiple responsibilities. Many Americans have demanded peace (often simplistically defined as the absence of war) with insufficient regard for the other two great social ends, justice and freedom. If one of the valued goals—peace, justice, or freedom—becomes the supreme political end, the other two are bound to suffer. Peace (or order) without justice and freedom is tyranny. Justice without freedom is another form of tyranny.

The statesman has a mandate to use the resources at his command to maintain a tolerable balance among the competing claims of order, justice, and freedom, though in grave crises he may be compelled to sacrifice one temporarily to save the other two. Confronted with the infamy of Pearl Harbor, the American people sacrificed peace in the interests of security and were prepared to accept limitations on their freedom for the same end. Any political community must enjoy minimal security before it can develop the discipline of justice and the safeguards of freedom.

The Sovereign State

The soft moralistic view tends to distrust the state, especially its coercive power, while Western ethical thought affirms the necessity of the state and insists on the responsible use of its power. Absolute power may corrupt absolutely, as Lord Acton asserted, but less-than-absolute power may or may not corrupt those who exercise it. There is little evidence that Lincoln, Churchill, or Truman were corrupted by power; they may even have been ennobled by it. Hitler, Stalin, and Mao were doubtless corrupted before they gained power. Power is amoral. It can be enlisted to liberate or enslave, to guarantee security or take it away. There is a vast difference between the Germany of Adolf Hitler and the Germany of Angela Merkel.

A state government must possess a monopoly on the legitimate use of violence within its domain. As the sovereign authority over a given territory—whether city, country, or empire—the government is the ultimate agency for resolving internal conflicts of power and interest. Were it not for the state, Saint Augustine said, men would devour one another as fishes. Martin Luther asserted that the central task of the state was to protect the innocent by restraining evildoers. Of the modern democratic state, Reinhold Niebuhr famously said, "Man's capacity for justice makes democracy possible; but man's inclination to injustice makes democracy necessary." The problem is not to eliminate the state, the professed goal of utopians and anarchists alike, but to make political power accountable to its citizens by a system that permits them peaceably to give or withhold consent and, if necessary, to throw the rascals out. If a government becomes tyrannical and all peaceful means for redressing grievances have been exhausted, the people, said Lincoln, have the right to rebel by violent means. The acceptance of Lincoln's view on the right of revolution does not negate the essential character of the responsible state. It is the fundamental agency for "insuring domestic tranquility, providing for the common defense, promoting the general welfare, and securing the blessings of liberty." In serving these central social objectives there is no substitute for the state, the sovereign political community. In a democratic and pluralistic society, however, other agencies, such as the university, the church, and economic organizations, have a positive role to play.

American Military Power

Soft moralism is highly critical of the exercise of American military power, except in self-defense, and even this is often narrowly defined. Classical moralists reject both the arbitrary abstention from power and its unrestrained use, and insist that the United States has a responsibility for international peace and order commensurate with its capacity to affect external events. Our military power—as a deterrent, a threat, or an active force—should be limited to dealing with real and present dangers to world peace. A workable international order can only rest on a propitious balance of force among the great powers. U.S. military might, including its nuclear arsenal, is an essential factor in preventing a shift in the balance of forces that could lead to war or the capitulation of friendly states.

Intervention and Reform

Some soft American moralists actively call for interventionist foreign policies designed to reshape the internal customs and institutions of other states. At the same time, they often degrade or even deprecate the primary security role of foreign policy. This strange combination of reform-intervention and security-isolation turns foreign policy on its head. In the classical view, the first task of domestic policy is order and justice. The reform interventionists, soft or hard, blur the salient distinction between what can and ought to be done by a government for its own people, and what can and ought to be done in the vast external realm over which it has no legal jurisdiction and where its moral and political mandate is severely limited. The insistence that the U.S. government employ extraordinary and sometimes coercive means to reshape the internal political, economic, or social structures in other sovereign communities is morally arrogant; it flies in the face of the most basic international law that, in the words of the United Nations Charter, prohibits intervention "in matters which are essentially within the domestic jurisdiction of any state."

Western morality respects the right of each political community to develop in its own way at its own pace, as long as it does not impinge coercively on other political communities. President Nixon's words in Romania in 1969 were a refreshing restatement of this principle: "We seek normal relations with all countries, regardless of their domestic systems"; each state has the right to "preserve its national institutions." His trip to China underscored his words. Ignoring this self-constraint, moralistic voices keep urging the government to withhold security or economic aid in order to force domestic changes within friendly states whose structure or policies do not accord with the critics' preferences.

This peculiar American penchant to export our virtue reached a high-water mark, at least in rhetoric, under President Kennedy and found belated legislative sanction in 1966 in Title IX of the Foreign Assistance Act. This act declared that all U.S. economic aid programs should encourage the development of "democratic private and local governmental institutions" in the recipient countries by using their "intellectual resources" to stimulate "economic and social progress" and by supporting "civic education and training skills required for effective participation in governmental and political processes essential to self-government." Still, this intrusive sally into other people's affairs, however naïve or wrongheaded, does not compare to the breathtaking sweep or moral pretension of the Communist Manifesto with its strident call to the workers of the world (read self-appointed elect) to redeem societies everywhere without regard to state frontiers. The same can be said of the militant Islamic fundamentalism associated with Al Qaeda. Arrogance is the chief sin. Civilized human beings, observed Leopold Tyrmand, should "agree not to burden each other" with their "excessive humanity."

Viewing U.S. foreign policy as an instrument for reform rather than of stability is not only arrogant; it also overlooks the severely limited capacity of any external agency to influence and reshape alien cultures. Any government has the right to request American economic or technical assistance. By the same token, Washington has the right to accept or turn down the request. The provision of economic or military aid that serves the interests of both parties presents few problems. It is wrong, however, for the donor government to give, withhold, or modify aid to force significant domestic changes unacceptable to the recipient regime and unrelated to the efficient use of the assistance.

The crusading impulse to reform should be clearly distinguished from the humanitarian motive that has prompted the U.S. government over the years to do more for the foreign victims of hunger, disease, and war than any other government in history. Such relief is not designed to restructure institutions, overthrow regimes, or promote "free elections."

The Weak and the Powerful

Soft moralism tends to associate virtue with weakness, just as it associates vice with power. Western morality affirms the fundamental worth of the poor and the weak and recognizes that they are less able to defend their rights than the rich and powerful. Further, under the rubric of noblesse oblige, men privileged by wealth or station are duty-bound to protect and assist the lowly. But this does not automatically endow the weak with innocence or virtue, whether they are deprived by nature, sloth, exploitation, or other circumstances.

The behavior of all states, great and small, must be judged by the same moral yardstick, recognizing that the degree of responsibility is commensurate with the capacity to act. "He who has much given to him will have much required of him." Yet there is a widespread tendency among moralistic Americans to regard the developing world with a kind of perverse paternalism that excuses childish, demanding, and otherwise irresponsible behavior.

Neither the weak nor the strong are immune from error or corruption. The much confessed "arrogance of power" should not blind us to the arrogance of weakness, which may express itself in simple claims of virtue, insistence on unjustified "reparations," or demands for minority control, all calculated to exploit a pervasive sense of guilt in the American character. As Churchill pointed out, we Anglo-Saxons tend to feel guilty because we possess power. However, it is not only the powerful that exhibit conceit. For instance, in a speech to the United Nations in 1960, Premier Saeb Salaam of Lebanon said: "We, the small, uncommitted nations, can perhaps take a more objective view of the world situation. We can judge international issues with comparatively greater detachment and impartiality; in a sense, the small uncommitted nations can be said to represent the unbiased conscience of humanity."

Recent official Swedish statements reflect this moralistic tendency. Though espousing neutrality, Swedish officials have been quick to condemn the behavior of the big powers, particularly the United States, and to take "moral" stands on a variety of international issues. It is morally easy for politicians or religious leaders to cheer or condemn from the sidelines when they have no responsibility and are unwilling to become committed. With studied hyperbole John P. Roche makes the point: "Power corrupts. And the absence of power corrupts absolutely."

Preoccupation with the Present

The moralistic approach tends to be preoccupied with the present, neglectful of the past, and nonchalant about the future. Impatient with imperfection, the new romantics indulge in what Elton Trueblood has called the "sin of contemporaneity." It may be argued that enchantment with the chronological now represents a positive contribution drawn from the existential emphasis on the present tense imperative, but it may be an escape from the eternal now that binds the past and future in an endless chain of responsibility. Humans are creatures of history, a product of the past, an actor in the present, and an influence for the future. To reject the past, as so many radicals do, is to reject the fabric of human continuity that gives moral meaning to the present.

Many university students today show no interest in the developments that had the most dramatic impact on the political outlook of their parents. If events like Pearl Harbor, the Vietnam War, and the fall of the Berlin Wall are not known nor have no common meaning, how can the two generations communicate? The understanding of recent history is vital, even if earlier eras must be shortchanged. This suggests the advisability of teaching history backward, starting with today's newspaper and covering the past decade before moving to the more distant past.

The Devil-Theory

Some of the more extreme American moralists, baffled by complexity and impatient with the untidy state of the world, sometimes adopt what amounts to a devil-theory of politics. They attempt to identify the central flaw, the fatal error, the demonic force underlying our present plight.

The earlier rational idealists discovered a series of plausible devils that, separately or in combination, were held responsible for war, injustice, poverty, and many other human afflictions. Each was fatally vulnerable to its rational and righteous counterpart. Capitalism, the prince of darkness, could be slain by socialism. The confusion of tongues, the cause of international misunderstanding and conflict, could be cured by the United Nations. Nationalism could be exorcised by world government. The military and the "merchants of death" could be abolished by the renunciation of war. The idealists and their ideal solutions failed. The Wilsonians, it has been said, reached for utopia and gave us hell.

The devil-theory approach lends itself to an apocalyptic interpretation of politics. The whole world is polarized and the golden mean, the vital center, and orderly change are thrown to the winds. The forces of good (read progressive or revolutionary) at home and abroad are arrayed against the forces of evil (read status quo or reactionary) and there is no compromise. The "establishment" will be crushed and "the people" will prevail. It is only a matter of time and dedication.

Limits of Moral Reasoning

Most American moralists have an inadequate understanding of the limits and possibilities of logic, rationality, and calculation. According to classical Western norms, moral reasoning is a possibility, indeed a necessity. Humans are reasoning creatures. Within the limits of circumstance, they can plan, devise, calculate, though they can rarely control or determine events. Circumstances are too complex, precise prediction is impossible, and risk is never absent.

To acknowledge the serious limits of rational calculation is not to depreciate reason, or the necessity to marshal relevant facts, or the desirability of projecting the probable consequences of competing lines of action. Politics is more an art than a science, but the scientific discipline of weighing evidence is a compelling moral obligation. To ignore evidence, to disdain logic, or to overlook empirical data is to retreat into blind emotion that spawns illusions. If the romantics fail to discipline their desires with data and persist in their illusions, they become almost indistinguishable from cynics or nihilists.

Just as contemporary sentimentalists expect too little from reason, the earlier rational idealists expected too much. Reason provides the capacity to behave responsibly. Reason is not an independent human agency that transcends the self, but rather a servant of the self with all its pride and prejudice. A morally sensitive statesman can enlist reason in the pursuit of wise and prudent policies. A morally corrupt politician can likewise enlist reason for his ignoble ends. The old utopians believed that reason and goodwill, unaided by power, would transform politics, but the new romantics seem to despair of reason altogether.

Western morality, in sum, affirms the dignity of the individual and the necessity for the state. It is precisely because the individual is finite and inclined to pursue his selfish desires at the expense of his neighbor that structures of order and justice are needed. The responsible state alone is capable of insuring that basic human rights will not be trampled underfoot. These objects are shared by both classical and contemporary Christian realism.

The great majority of American people, by temperament and their respect for law, are committed to a domestic order rooted in a prudent balance of justice and freedom, and to an international order that is safe for diversity and peaceful change. Movement toward these political goals at home and abroad requires a working combination of the "impossible ideal" and an appreciation of political limitations. A man's aim should exceed his grasp, but not by too much. Our times call for idealism without illusion and realism without despair.

CHAPTER 5

War Within Reason
A Romantic Epistle
to the Christians[1]

Charles A. Jones

The just war tradition provides a robust and comprehensive framework for arguing about war. It offers guidance on the declaration and conduct of war and has exerted a profound and beneficent influence on the law of armed conflict. In addition, it has been remarkably resourceful in accommodating new and complex moral choices arising out of irregular warfare, nuclear weapons, humanitarian intervention, and precision-guided munitions. Most of all, today it appears to offer an arena within which those of many faiths and of none can meet on equal terms. The tradition is no more than that: a tradition and not a theory. Standing to one side of the mid-twentieth-century current of thought conventionally known as Christian realism, it has generally inclined toward legalism and occasionally lapsed into zealotry. Yet, properly understood, the just war tradition deserves renewed consideration by Christian realists, rooted—as it is—in a modest Christian worldview profoundly aware of temporal power and the state. Marked disagreements persist within the tradition on particular questions, including the identification of legitimate authority, double effect, and conditional deterrence. It is all too often reduced to a mere box-ticking exercise to justify some specific instance of resort to force or military episode, when it ought rather to be thought of as a space for moral reflection. But at least the parameters of debate are secure, with pacifists and advocates of the unconstrained use of force consigned to the fringes.

Something along these lines appears to be the dominant view in the United States and Britain. It is mistaken. Indeed, it is more than that; it is pernicious, not in itself but by its narrowness. It is a view that encourages complacency and shuts the door on a wide range of moral experience, both personal and collective, intrinsic to modern warfare. It leaves the Christian churches with some of their biggest guns in fixed emplacements and pointing the wrong way. It encourages the secular mind to ride in the slipstream of the Christian juggernaut, seemingly absolved from any need for profound consideration of its dire moral predicament. It allows pacifists and nihilists alike too easy a dismissal of rational approaches to warfare. So, if those engaged in the planning, authorization, and conduct of contemporary armed conflict are to limit the moral harm to which they—let alone their enemies—are exposed, just as they now routinely seek to address psychological and physical damage, then the silken warp of love, justice, and authority with which just war discourse has traditionally been woven needs an altogether tougher weft, spun from the full range of modern political and military experience and imagination rather than the more limited range of concerns that preoccupied Saint Thomas Aquinas at the dawn of the modern international system.

For it is in a version substantially indebted to Aquinas and his Spanish Dominican successors that the just war tradition is most often presented.[2] They wrote at a time—broadly between 1200 and 1650—when the monarchs of France, England, Spain, and several other European countries were steadily establishing sovereign authority over consolidated territories at the expense of Pope and Emperor. The discovery, in the second half of this period, of orderly political communities in the Americas that had neither accepted nor—like the Turks—rejected the gospel merely aggravated the position by confirming the autonomy of international relations from any single faith and its technical anarchy, or lack of any supreme temporal authority capable of arbitrating between princes.[3] In these circumstances, a doctrine of how armed conflict between sovereigns could be contained within the moral realm was sorely needed, and this is what the later scholastic theologians attempted.

Reduced to its bare bones, the doctrine runs like this. Justified resort to war requires a formal declaration of hostilities—all other remedies having been exhausted—by a proper authority with a reasonable prospect of victory and moved by right intention to make good an injury or wrong of sufficient importance to outweigh the unavoidable evils that must result from the conduct of hostilities. Once engaged in warfare, combatants are enjoined not to attack noncombatants and to use no more force than is needed to achieve their objectives.

Some of the bread-and-butter debates that constitute contemporary debate within the tradition leap readily from the page, like fishes eager for

Saint Peter's wise words. Questions about legitimate authority, collateral damage, and right intention are daily on our lips. Where does legitimate authority reside in a world where many states have long since lost control of large tracts of their territory while armed groups flourish without any clear political program or aspiration either to secede from or gain control of the state? Where does legitimate authority reside at a time when permanent alliances or regional unions such as NATO or the European Union begin to acquire a measure of autonomy, even from their most powerful members, and uncertainty about the authority of the United Nations Security Council is aggravated by the pretensions of the United States of America to a quasi-imperial regulatory role? How are we to regard collateral damage? Is it justified by the outcome of a military operation, or must it be the unintended outcome of attack upon a legitimate target, as demanded by the scholastic doctrine of double effect? Again, does a successful outcome cancel out the evil of a war undertaken for unjustifiable reasons? Regime change, as such, was not and could not have been the moral or legal basis for our recent invasion of Iraq, but we were all glad to see the back of Saddam Hussein. Is this good enough? And what of nuclear deterrence? May it be right to threaten to do wrong if, by so doing, one minimizes the chance of ever having to carry out the threat? Or do the long years of preparedness of all those in the command structures responsible for nuclear weapons inevitably corrupt those charged with our defense, required—as they are—to will what is almost certainly morally indefensible?[4]

The Limits of Secularization

Legitimate authority, double effect, conditional threat: It is here, or hereabouts, that the first step of a critique of the tradition might be taken. For Saint Thomas, the very idea of legitimate authority was embedded in an Aristotelian concept of perfect political community.[5] By this, he did not mean a polity without error, but one that was complete, in that it provided the conditions for individuals to live the good life. Within such a polity every adult had responsibility, by the exercise of prudence, for the conformity of behavior to natural law; but the prudence of the prince in this respect was uniquely important, for he alone was not subject to the regulatory check of positive law and he alone took responsibility for the whole polity rather than just a household, estate, or city. Few people today think in quite this way, and it is not at all clear that modern forms of representative democracy provide quite the same authority to heads of state that Aquinas provided for late-medieval princes.

Double effect and conditional threat raise further problems, at least for the secular mind. Christian thought about moral issues has always been more concerned with intention than outcome. War is no exception. Right intention, as much as just cause, is a condition of justifiable resort to force. There is more. Saint Thomas and Saint Augustine treated war in very different ways. Yet both located their discussion of armed conflict within a broader discussion of spiritual love or *caritas*. Oliver O'Donovan puts it most succinctly: "In the context of war we find in its sharpest and most paradoxical form the thought that love can sometimes smite, and even slay."[6]

In short, legitimate authority and right intention, central concepts in the just war tradition, are deeply embedded in Christian theology, and in one very specific, albeit central, strand of Catholic theology. So, even as Western liberalism consigns religious belief to the private realm, the trace of religion remains when legitimate authority is sought in the secular state or the United Nations, while the law of armed conflict deriving from the just war tradition has become universally applicable through a series of international conventions.

Thus, the grounding of contemporary thought about war in Christianity prompts two urgent questions—"Can the tradition be successfully salvaged?" and "Is this all the Church has to say about war?" Each is addressed to a distinct group: the first to believers and unbelievers alike, and the second rather more exclusively to the faithful. In offering a tentatively positive answer to the first of these questions, this paper also suggests that the just war tradition by no means exhausts the resources of Christianity for thinking about war.

Natural law theorists may reason their way to a view of common morality, universal in incidence, providing a ground for the regulation of warfare.[7] But for those who cannot quite swallow a secular version of legal naturalism there is a second, more secular route, which is to ground value in community, whether it be the national community or a universal community of humankind. The trouble with such views is that they seem constantly to be seeking some substitute for the divine authority that was once held to underpin political authority, whether it be through Hegelian recognition or organic nationalism; and such attempts look ever less palatable in the face of Nietzschean and postmodern critiques of metaphysics and social constructivist exposures of the imagined or invented character of supposedly organic or primordial nations. Worst of all, the vision of a single global community that might harbor a secular ethics of armed conflict is inchoate and poorly institutionalized, while any lesser form of communitarianism (such as that of Michael Walzer, whose *Just and Unjust Wars* has deservedly been the most enduring secular contribution to the tradition) can hardly avoid privileging the state of which one is oneself a citizen, thereby admitting arguments from national interest or supreme emergency that run counter to the spirit of Augustine and Aquinas and pave the way for preemptive military action or exemplary displays of force.[8]

Even if the problem of legitimate authority and political community can be solved, the secular thinker faces a second problem: the balance between intentions and outcomes. Recall Augustine's chilling maxim: "Love; and do what you will!"[9] If a Christian accepts this injunction, it is in the belief that social life is so uncertain that any form of consequentialism is almost certain to mislead, in the manner of the reassurances of Macbeth's witches or the notoriously ambiguous utterances of the oracle at Delphi. My soul is my responsibility; perhaps God will, in some way, take care of the consequences? For the nonbeliever, by contrast, consequences may seem to be just about all there is, and they are certainly not to be disregarded lightly. Conversely, there is no Lord to know the secrets of our hearts. Yet analysis of risk (as the product of probability and harm), let alone its application to policy, is fraught with difficulties, as is all too clear from any objective assessment of the opportunity cost of applying the precautionary principle in the face of terrorism.[10] Once again, then, separation of the tradition from its implicit theology poses problems.

Aquinas and Augustine: Liberals and Neocons

The question faced by the secular thinker wishing to deliberate within the just war tradition is how long the locomotive will go on running once the tender has been uncoupled. Will it reach some convenient downward slope where gravity takes over? Is there any prospect of developing some alternative source of motive power? (What kind of buffers lie ahead?) Is it possible, as Nick Rengger has argued, for even nonbelievers to avoid starting from scratch or regrounding, in the manner of Walzer, a tradition that is, after all, as much "Western" and Aristotelian as Christian?[11]

The question addressed to the Christian is very different and may be answered in two ways. It might be argued that what the Church has to say about war can be amplified or even rectified simply by shifting the weight of the tradition from Aquinas to Augustine. Alternatively, it can be argued that there is a case for exploiting the broader resources of the Church in the quest to comprehend warfare and retain it within a Christian moral framework. To continue the railway metaphor, the Christian has a choice of locomotives—Aquinas or Augustine—yet also needs to consider whether it might not be prudent to send some goods by way of branch lines rather than entrust the whole lot to the express, just in case the main line gets blocked. For Christianity has many other resources for thinking about war besides the high discourse of justice and charity. Two of these will be considered in due course: pilgrimage and the Passion.

The problem with Aquinas, it may be argued, is that his tendency toward codification and his attachment to the modern state have laid him open to lawyers and liberals. Codification leads to ever finer formulations of humanitarian law and a baffling profusion of rules of engagement. Some years ago, Human Rights Watch found that warring factions in Colombia, whether representing the state, quasi-state, or anti-state, all conduct training for their troops, with varying degrees of efficiency, in the law of armed conflict and military ethics.[12] While this is to be applauded, it has not prevented widespread offenses by all parties in recent years. Legalism, when taken to extremes, gets out of sync with reality. At the same time, the Thomistic tradition may be thought too conservatively statist in a world where unipolarity, nonstate military organizations, and the United Nations compromise the legal equality of states and their singular role in relation to public violence. So, in two distinct ways, the Thomistic strand of the just war, once realist, may be thought to have slipped into an idealist world of aspiration and denial.

Can the tradition be rebuilt on an Augustinian chassis? The trouble with this proposal is the ease with which Augustinian versions of the just war—resolutely realist in their treatment of power—lend themselves to an idealistic identification of power with justice. Augustine himself was wonderfully free of this sin.[13] When Christians of his day asked how it was that God could permit the Roman Empire, once having adopted Christianity as its official religion, to be defeated in battle, he replied that all civilizations, Christian as much as pagan, were bound to suffer catastrophe, and that the history of the postlapsarian world (the *civitas terrene*) was a process of human suffering and a part of the divine plan through which redemption from original sin might finally be achieved. Following the Fall, he argued, the *civitas terrene* was inhabited by two kinds of people, the elect and the reprobate. Both were sinful, but the elect were in receipt from God of what Augustine termed "efficacious grace." The reprobate were motivated entirely by self-regarding love or cupidity. The elect, because of efficacious grace, were able, even in an imperfect world, freely to choose the lesser of any two evils by an effort of the will.

Taken together with Augustine's radically deontological belief that the entire moral worth of action rests in intention, and not in outcomes, this distinction between reprobates and the elect leads to the conclusion that defeat in war is a source of purification and strength to the elect, while even victory will turn the reprobate toward further sin by stoking their self-righteousness and arrogance. So Augustine reasoned that a war declared with right intention by the Christian leader of a relatively uncorrupted political community could be justified. Indeed, here war consisted in the punishment of aggressive behavior by others: Christian sovereigns had a duty to act by choosing violence with the intention of achieving a just peace.[14] In this way, men might will peace while engaging in war and, provided the intention was pure, no amount of incidental harm would outweigh it. Fought "with love in one's heart," war might be conducted with savage disregard for the rules of *jus in bello* and was likely to prove "a grim and horrible necessity," bringing unavoidable harm to noncombatants.[15]

This interpretation of Augustine owes much to Herbert Deane, who may, in 1963, have been overly concerned with the possibility that the then government of the United States might resort to the (loving!) use of nuclear weapons. By contrast, Deane's British contemporary, Herbert Butterfield, found in Augustine the resources for a more quietistic renunciation of the false righteousness of moralistic politics, and a trust that God and the Church must outlast tyranny. Yet if it *is* a distortion, it is a distortion that captures the apocalyptic tone occasionally to be found in the correspondence of Arnold Toynbee and finds echoes in some strands of contemporary U.S. thought.[16] Who, one must ask, are the elect, and how are we to know them?

If the Thomistic and Augustinian traditions are liable to collapse, respectively, into liberal and neoconservative forms of political idealism, there remains the question, raised earlier, of the broader resources of Christianity as expressed in narratives of pilgrimage and the Passion, and the witnessing of these. Rather than develop this strand of the argument in abstract terms, it may be more helpful to do so through a third form of political realism rooted neither in state-centrism nor in power.

Cultural Realism: Representations of War

Close study of the ethical assumptions and implications of war, and of their more or less conscious use as weapons, offers a method of investigating the morality of armed conflict that is every bit as realistic as state-centrism or an undue privileging of conflict. Such a strategy offers a first step along the road to a new ethic of warfare, encompassing a wider range of experience, both political and personal, than the just war tradition. It draws on those representations of warfare—in histories and memoirs, in the novel and other literary genres, in cinema, and in graphic art—through which modern creativity has sought to express the emotional and moral experience of warfare and combat. To interrogate modern culture is to encounter a wider range of virtues and vices and broader matters of value—such as secrecy, alienation, metamorphosis, and personal identity—than is customarily considered in contemporary debate about the ethics of war.

As an empirical method, study of the representation of war is neutral in principle. It offers resources to both the religious and the secular thinker. To those who dismiss such an approach as no more than heuristic or throw up their hands and say that it is mere social constructivism, and that war cannot be reduced to ideas, the answer comes in two stages. First must come some form of pragmatism. The study of representations is nothing less than the study of attempts by those who have engaged in war more or less directly to express the experience. It does not simply reflect or directly correspond to the phenomenon itself. To paraphrase Richard Rorty, it is not the mirror of war. Instead, it offers—resorting for a moment to Kantian terminology—an empirical method for feeling out the contours of the noumenal world of war-in-itself. For while battle is deceptively visible, war—as a condition of the whole of society—is necessarily invisible, only to be grasped by transcendental or pragmatic methods. Second, and more mundanely, it happens that, by good fortune, very few of my generation in Western Europe, and not so very many even in the United States, have had direct experience of battle. Even those who have can only convey it by adopting some genre or other, as is evident from narratives of the Bosnian War.[17] A study of the "imaginarie" of war is therefore necessary both for those who lack direct experience and for those who cannot convey that experience except through forms of mediation.[18]

Epistemological and methodological niceties aside, this approach to the morality of war must remain lifeless on the page without some illustration, however brief, of the kinds of resources that may help reason arrive at fresh terms with modern warfare and extend the moral vocabulary available to deal with it.

The Christian might well begin by considering just two texts, the first very widely known, the second less so, but based on a third, once universally familiar text in the English-speaking world. Gillo Pontecorvo's film *The Battle of Algiers* uses a quasi-documentary style to tell the story of the insurgency organized by the National Liberation Front (FLN) in the city of Algiers during the 1950s.[19] Easily read as a neo-Marxist tract with a dialectical structure of exclusion and transgression synthesized as complicity, this Italian-Algerian coproduction is also a Christian Passion narrative that casts the audience quite explicitly in the role of witnesses to the sufferings, torture, and death of the rebels and their metaphorical resurrection in the spontaneous and ultimately successful revival of the revolution a few years later.[20] There is nothing accidental or subliminal about this point of view. We know that

Pontecorvo chose music with care, and by opening the film with a scene of torture backed by the first chorus of Bach's *St. Matthew Passion*—with its chorale line "Come, ye daughters of Zion!"—he leaves no room for doubt, even though he stops before the choir enters.[21] The audience is immediately implicated in the narrative as chorus or witnesses, as are the mass of Arabs, and most of all Arab women—those daughters of Zion, ululating from the rooftops of the Casbah—who will finally complete the revolution—or, should we say, constitute the nation, the metaphorical church—when the blood sacrifice of the founders has been accomplished.

Then there is John Buchan, best known for the first of his Richard Hannay adventures, the twice-filmed *Thirty-Nine Steps*.[22] Buchan had serious political ambitions, served as a member of Parliament, and was later to die in office as governor-general of Canada, responsible in large measure for restoring the prestige of the monarchy, thereby bringing Canada into the Second World War.

Buchan wrote the third of the Hannay novels as World War I, and his warwork as a propagandist in the British Ministry of Information, drew to a close. *Mr. Standfast* takes its name from a character in John Bunyan's *Pilgrim's Progress*, one of the most widely read narratives in English during the eighteenth and into the nineteenth century, though soon to be eclipsed by Scott and Dickens.[23] The central argument of *Mr. Standfast* is that the outcome of conflict is now determined through the secret and shameful war of espionage and deception, rather than the open and honorable war of the battlefield. The narrative device he employs to press home this message is the modeling, of what presents superficially as a thriller, on Bunyan's devotional text. In *Pilgrim's Progress*, Pilgrim himself first leaves home and family to travel through a world of temptations and dangers to salvation. In the second half of the book, his wife and children follow. Adopting the same two-part structure and playing with the stereotypes of his day, Buchan embarks on a game of Romantic inversions worthy of his literary hero, Sir Walter Scott, in which the Pilgrim figure (Hannay), a brigadier in the British army, is adrift, *incognito*, and emasculated in the feminine secret world in the first half of the book, while his male yet feminized opponent, a German spy, proves unable to survive in the masculine world of the battlefield in the second half of the story.

The Realism of Romanticism: Scott and His Heirs

Reference to Sir Walter Scott very conveniently leads the way back to the beginnings of the modern secular tradition of thought about warfare, which can be located quite firmly in the Romantic movement of the early-nineteenth century. One or two anticipations aside, notably Laurence Sterne and Denis Diderot in literature and Goya in graphic art, it was to be Scott who created the Romantic sensibility to warfare that constitutes the primary secular tradition to rival the just war in modern times. He took the world by storm with his first novel, *Waverley*.[24]

Romanticism is often depicted as a conservative, counter-Enlightenment impulse. It is beyond question that the movement was implicated in the restoration of hereditary monarchy and the authority of the Church following the final defeat of Napoleon. But there is a second and equally plausible account of romanticism that better accounts for the durability of the movement and its peculiar suitability to speak of war, and this explanation centers on the tension between binary pairs, such as authority and violence, masculinity and femininity, deduction and narrative, rationality and authenticity, fantasy and fiction, and, indeed, classicism and romanticism. Here is a process that in some ways mimics war itself and finds (Romantic) expression in Clausewitz's contrast between escalation and friction, anticipating the textual no-man's-land between truth and make-believe in which John le Carré, Anthony Swofford, and Charles Mackey rub shoulders. Which is the most truthful? Which is closest to the reality of contemporary warfare?[25]

One of the primary differences between classical and Romantic music is the manner in which the Romantics move into ever more remote keys, deferring resolution further and further as the century progresses. In much the same way, Scott sets up binary oppositions of sanity and madness, preface and narrative, fact and fiction, gender, and degrees of civility, and then toys with his reader by doubling and folding these oppositions against one another, not unlike an angler by turns playing out and reeling in the line. His novels are inhabited by honest outlaws, effeminate generals, and corrupt magistrates, and the general effect is to put in question the very binaries that provided the point of departure.[26]

Scott has more to say and more profound things to say about war than any other novelist of the nineteenth century writing in English, and he is at his best when writing of armed conflicts that hover uneasily between rebellion and war proper, as when he writes of the Stuart risings against the Hanoverian kings of 1715 and 1745, or the gradual modernization of the Scottish highlands at the expense of the traditional clan society. Thus Waverley, eponymous hero of the first of the Waverley Novels, is a British army officer who finds himself, almost inadvertently, in company with highlanders as the 1745 uprising gets under way, hardly realizing the compromise of his original loyalties or the threat to his own identity and safety until, on the battlefield of Preston Pans, he hears the familiar voice of the colonel of his own regiment from the opposing lines, looks around, and notes, as though seeing for the first time, the rough clothing, the unintelligible Gaelic, the sheer foreignness of those with whom, a moment before, he had felt such solidarity.[27] In Scott, then, the issue of justice between established authorities that once spurred Aquinas is no longer central. In its place are those matters of contingency, irony, and solidarity that have long inhabited and continue to pervade so many of the conflicts that have only lately, belatedly, come to be referred to as New Wars.

James Fenimore Cooper, very much aware of the model provided by Scott, performs a similar task in North America, ostensibly writing of the incompatibility of three understandings of the ethics of public violence: those of the indigenous peoples of the Americas, the colonists, and the regular European forces.[28] Cooper's description of the slaughter that follows the retreat from Fort William Henry—far more massacre than battle—remains one of the most powerful passages ever written about warfare, all the more so because it speaks, like *Waverley*, of a predicament where war is being waged without shared ground rules, as once between Spaniards and the Aztec and Inca hosts.[29]

War Within Reason

One more theme in romanticism, broadly understood, which is central to evolving nineteenth- and twentieth-century understandings of war, is reason itself. Haunted by the sequence of Enlightenment, Revolution, and Terror in France, romanticism has been less trustful than earlier generations of any account of practical reason patterned strictly on theoretic reason, understood as a quasi-deductive process based on self-evident principles. Here, it becomes apparent that my central argument, that we, today, had better adopt a skeptical posture of this kind toward the just war tradition and the varying interpretations to which it is open, is at heart a Romantic argument.

Well before Freud, before Darwin, and even before Marx, Romantics—and some of their eighteenth-century heralds—were aware of the cunning of reason and the multiplicity of incommensurate rationales. Much later, in Stephen Crane's path-breaking *Red Badge of Courage*, repetitions—both verbal and narrative—abound, and the implication of the great central repetition of two successive attacks seems to be that war is complex in the modern sense, with small variations in initial conditions leading to very large variations in outcome.[30] Once again, reason itself is the target of Joseph Heller's first and finest novel, *Catch-22*, where the market rationale of Milo Mindbender's logistical system for the officers' mess leads quite naturally to

the USAF bombing their own base as subcontractors for their German enemies, who, following Milo's miscalculated cornering of the Egyptian cotton
crop, have become their creditors as well.[31] Reason is the target of Kurt
Vonnegut in a critique of total war that is even more devastating than
Heller's, where time and space are entirely disturbed.[32]

Buchan and Pontecorvo wanted to show that war will not permit any single authoritative narrative and that war puts in question not only life but personal and political identity; Scott, Heller, and Vonnegut show that any
attempt to contain war within practical reason as traditionally understood
must fail. Alongside issues of authority, identity, complicity, and virtue sits
the grandest of themes: war as analogue of reason itself. Together, these
authors provide only the merest indication of the hoard of material that lies
barely touched by those historians, strategists, and ethicists who study war
professionally, and that has yet to inform the peculiarly limited and literally
scholastic public discourse on war with which we are trying to steer our way
through dangerous times. It begins to be clear that the project of retaining
war within reason runs willy-nilly into that of determining the scope and
capabilities of reason itself, and that war within reason denotes a struggle for
the soul of reason: a secular *Paradise Lost*.

There are signs that the ground is moving. Theodor Meron advanced within
the space of a few years from a naïve and legalistic reading of *Henry V* to a subtle and multifaceted understanding of warfare throughout Shakespeare's
work.[33] George Fletcher's intriguing study, *Romantics at War*, finds a U.S.
international lawyer grappling with the foreignness of collective guilt, collective responsibility, and collective punishment as they enter the American legal
system after 9/11.[34] More recently, a dissident strand of military history has
emerged, most notably in John Grenier's 2004 *The First American Way of War*,
which contests Russell Weigley's Clausewitzian high-conflict offshore view of
U.S. military culture and attempts to put in its stead a vision in which *petite
guerre* operations in North America, characterized by annihilation and deliberately disproportionate force, are foremost.[35] Writing as a serving Air Force
officer in the United States, Grenier casts My Lai as a marker on the road to
Fallujah. And now, Fred Anderson, whose brilliant account of the Seven Years
War, *Crucible of War*, so very closely shadowed Cooper's account in its attention to indigenous auxiliary forces, seems to have added his voice to that of
Grenier.[36]

Lately, too, officers and defense officials in the United States and the
British Isles have been watching *The Battle of Algiers*. What do they make of
it? To some, at least, it will seem to depict breaches of the legal and moral constraints within which they aspire to operate, but cannot. Yet the film's tortur-
ers and tortured, its terrorists and soldiers, do not stand outside the moral

realm. Their dilemmas are those of policymakers and soldiers today, caught between conscience and an ever more complex web of rules of engagement, joint operations, and sheer technique, and stripped almost bare of the rituals of declaration, surrender, victory, and group loyalty that once sustained them. If the objections of self-styled realists who throw up their hands and claim that all's fair in love and war are to be overcome, and war brought more firmly within reason, then a return to the form of realism outlined here—to a realism that is defined by closeness to lived experience—is required. Only in this way can the imaginative resources of modernity, both religious and secular, be effectively deployed to bring to heel a once-realist just war tradition, now gone astray, perhaps to supplement or perhaps, ultimately, to replace it.

The provisional conclusion of this argument is therefore cautious and even conservative, somewhat on the lines of Pascal's wager. If God does not exist, Pascal reasoned, then little is to be lost by believing. If he does exist, then disbelief carries a heavy penalty.[37] Belief seems the rational option. In much the same spirit, I am very far from suggesting that we dump the hard-won law of armed conflict forthwith, but I would suggest that we are close to the point where that law, and the just war tradition of moral deliberation that underpins it, may be overwhelmed by a host of anomalies. If there is, at that point, no alternative paradigm to take its place, the consequences for international relations may be bleak and deplorable. In such circumstances, an orderly withdrawal and regrouping seems the most prudent strategy.

Notes

1. I am grateful for the comments and suggestions of participants in the Christian Realism panel at the annual meeting of the American Political Science Association in Philadelphia on September 2, 2006, and for the input of Stuart Kaufmann and his colleagues at the University of Delaware. An earlier draft of the first part of the paper appeared in *Cambridge: The Magazine of the Cambridge Society* 57 (New Year 2006), 8–10.

2. William P. Baumgarth and Richard J. Regan, S. J., eds., *Saint Thomas Aquinas on Law, Morality, and Politics* (Indianapolis: Hackett, 1988); J. A. Fernández-Santamaria, *The State, War, and Peace: Spanish Political Thought in the Renaissance, 1516–1559* (Cambridge: Cambridge University Press, 1977).

3. Bernice Hamilton, *Political Thought in Sixteenth-Century Spain: A Study of the Political Ideas of Vitoria, De Soto, Suarez, and Molina* (Oxford: Clarendon, 1963).

4. I have dealt with some of these bread-and-butter issues in a reexamination of Hedley Bull's ideas about war that lays particular emphasis on the implications of unipolarity for an international society approach. Charles A. Jones, "War in the Twenty-First Century: An Institution in Crisis," in *The Anarchical Society in*

     a Globalized World, ed. Richard Little and John Williams (Houndmills: Palgrave 2006), 162–88.

5. This topic is treated in greater detail in Charles A. Jones, "Prudence," *Social Epistemology* I, no. 3 (Fall 1987), a paper rendered all but nonsensical by the editors' failure to offer proofs for correction.

6. Oliver O'Donovan, *The Just War Revisited* (Cambridge: Cambridge University Press, 2003), 9.

7. This is the argument advanced in J. M. Finnis, Joseph Boyle, and Germain Grisez, *Nuclear Deterrence, Morality, and Realism* (Oxford: Clarendon, 1987).

8. Michael Walzer, *Just and Unjust Wars* (New York: Basic Books, 1977).

9. Butterfield quotes Augustine slightly differently: "[L]ove God and do what you like." Herbert Butterfield, "Christianity and Human Relationships," in Herbert Butterfield, *History and Human Relations* (London: Collins, 1951), 43. I owe the refinement to Gareth McCaughan.

10. Timothy Roach, "The Politics of Risk: Implications for the UK's Management of International Terrorism"(MA diss., Cambridge, July 2006).

11. Nicholas Rengger, "On the Just War Tradition in the Twenty-First Century," *International Affairs* 78, no. 2 (April 2002), 362–63.

12. Human Rights Watch, *War Without Quarter: Colombia and International Human Rights War* (New York, Human Rights Watch: 1998).

13. In what follows I have relied on an earlier paper: Charles A. Jones, "Christian Realism and the Foundations of the English School," *International Relations* 17, no. 3 (September 2003), 371–87.

14. Herbert A. Deane, *The Political and Social Ideas of St. Augustine* (New York: Columbia University Press, 1963), 159.

15. Deane, *Ideas of St. Augustine*, 156n32.

16. On Toynbee, see Jones, "Christian Realism," 376–77. For an example of what seems to a notably intemperate approach to the just war, see Alexander F. C. Webster and Darrell Cole, *The Virtue of War: Reclaiming the Classic Christian Traditions East and West* (Salisbury, MA: Regina Orthodox, 2004).

17. Joel Dowling, "British Media, Parliamentary, and Military Accounts of the War in Bosnia, 1992–95" (PhD diss., Cambridge, 2004).

18. Many people dislike the now conventional use of *imaginary* as a noun, indicating the sum of what can be imagined. I propose the neologism—*imaginarie*—partly to appease (or perhaps to provoke) them by drawing a distinction, and partly for its resonance with "menagerie."

19. *The Battle of Algiers*, dir. Gillo Pontecorvo, Igor Film / Casbah Film, 1966, DVD (Argent Films Ltd, 2003: AGTD001).

20. I offer a more extended treatment of *The Battle of Algiers* in "Dialectic and Passion in Pontecorvo's The Battle of Algiers," *Millennium: Journal of International Studies* 35, no.2 (2007), 445–52.

21. For the care that Pontecorvo devoted to the choice of music for the soundtrack, see Irene Bignardi, "The Making of *The Battle of Algiers*," *Cineaste* 25, no. 2

(2000), 18–19; and Joan Mellen, *Filmguide to* The Battle of Algiers (Bloomington and London: Indiana University Press, 1973), 13–14 and 24–28. Mellen makes this point very strongly but has little to say about the specific choice of the first chorus of the *St. Matthew Passion*, which she refers to only as "the hymnal music of the first sequence" (26).

22. Andrew Lownie, *John Buchan: The Presbyterian Cavalier* (London: Constable, 1995).

23. John Buchan, *Mr. Standfast* (London: Hodder and Stoughton, 1919); John Bunyan, *The Pilgrim's Progress* (1678–84; repr., New York: New American Library, 1964).

24. Sir Walter Scott, *Waverley* (1814; repr., Oxford: Oxford University Press, 1986).

25. Karl Kroeber, "Frictional Fiction: Walter Scott in the Light of von Clausewitz's *On War*," in *English and German Romanticism: Cross-Currents and Controversies*, ed. James Pipkin (Heidelberg: Carl Winter, 1985). See also John le Carré, *Absolute Friends* (New York: Little, Brown, 2004); Anthony Swofford, *Jarhead* (New York: Scribner, 2003); and Chris Mackey with Greg Miller, *The Interrogator's War: Inside the Secret War Against Al Qaeda* (New York: Little, Brown, 2004). In all these works, ghosts of one sort or another abound.

26. Charles A. Jones, "Sir Walter Goes to War," *Cambridge Review of International Affairs* 12, no. 1 (Summer/Fall 1998). Illustrative of the new wave of Scott criticism more generally are some of the essays in J. H. Alexander and David Hewitt, eds., *Scott in Carnival* (Aberdeen: Association for Scottish Literary Studies, 1993).

27. Scott, *Waverley* (Edinburgh: Adam and Charles Black, 1877), II, 162.

28. James Fenimore Cooper, *The Last of the Mohicans* (1826; repr., Harmondsworth: Penguin, 1992).

29. Cooper, *Mohicans*, 206ff.; and on the Spanish encounters, see Charles A. Jones, "The Americas," in *The Balance of Power in World History*, ed. Stuart Kauffman and William Wohlforth (Houndmills: Palgrave, 2006).

30. Stephen Crane, *The Red Badge of Courage* (1895; repr., London: Oxford University Press, 1969).

31. Joseph Heller, *Catch-22* (1961; repr., London: David Campbell, 1995).

32. Kurt Vonnegut, *Slaughterhouse 5* (New York: Delacorte, 1969).

33. Theodor Meron "Shakespeare's Henry V and the Law of War," *American Journal of International Law* 86, no. 1 (January 1992), 1–45; Theodor Meron, *Henry's Wars and Shakespeare's Laws: Perspectives on the Law of War in the Later Middle Ages* (Oxford: Clarendon, 1993); Theodor Meron, *Bloody Constraint: War and Chivalry in Shakespeare* (New York and Oxford: Oxford University Press, 1998).

34. George Fletcher, *Romantics at War: Glory and Guilt in the Age of Terrorism* (Princeton, NJ: Princeton University Press, 2002).

35. John Grenier, *The First American Way of War: American War Making on the Frontier, 1607–1814* (Cambridge: Cambridge University Press, 2005); Russell F. Weigley, *The American Way of War: A History of U.S. Military Strategy and Policy* (New York: Macmillan, 1973).

36. Fred Anderson and Andrew Clayton, *The Dominion of War: Empire and Liberty in North America, 1500–2000* (New York: Viking, 2005).
37. From one of my students, who is more familiar with rational choice theory than I am, comes the delightful variation that if *they* exist, belief in one (and not the others) may be more hazardous than evenhanded agnosticism. Roach, "Politics of Risk."

CHAPTER 6

Christian Realism and the International Economy[1]

John Lunn

The Christian realism of Niebuhr and others had primarily a political cast, with discussions of military or ideological conflicts at the center. Many of the issues raised today in the political arena are more related to economic questions than traditional military considerations. The European Union has entailed both economic and political integration, while numerous other agreements, such as the North American Free Trade Agreement (NAFTA), envisage increased economic but low political integration. Even in trade agreements, however, nation-states voluntarily yield some sovereignty to institutions established to monitor the agreements. Meetings of the World Trade Organization involve protesters from many organizations who are concerned about the operations of the international economic order. In this chapter, I will attempt to relate and apply the principles associated with Christian realism to the economist's vision of how market economies operate. There will be a particular focus on international issues, including globalization.

Christian Realism and Economics

Classical (or traditional) Christian realism is associated with thinkers such as ethicist Reinhold Niebuhr, historian Herbert Butterfield, international relations scholar Martin Wight, theologian John C. Bennett, and diplomat John Foster Dulles. It was a reaction to the political and religious idealisms (e.g.,

Social Gospel, pacifism, Wilsonian liberalism) that characterized Western political and religious thought in the first decades of the twentieth century. Christian realism reminds us that there is moral content to political life, but that we must recognize the prominence of self-interest, pride, and power dynamics in politics. A reading of some of the classical Christian realists, especially Niebuhr and Bennett, shows that they were very critical of the capitalist system and the operation of the national economies and the international economy of their day. Others, such as Wight and later Kenneth Thompson, were less critical. An example of the capitalism critique can be found in Niebuhr's *Moral Man and Immoral Society*, which both criticized capitalism and often utilized a Marxian framework.[2] His animus toward capitalism is evident also in *The Nature and Destiny of Man*.[3] In short, the claim cannot be made that the most famous Christian realist, Niebuhr, was an outright supporter of the economic system of the United States or other Western nations. Ironically, however, Michael Novak and other neoconservatives have appropriated some of Niebuhr's ideas.[4]

David McCreary illustrates that the Christian realist who outlived Niebuhr and many others by a quarter of a century, John Coleman Bennett, offered a mixed view of this appropriation: "Indeed, Bennett was more sympathetic to liberation theology than he was to its detractors in wealthy countries. Bennett observes, 'More recently some neoconservatives claim Niebuhr as one of themselves. Michael Novak in his able book, *The Spirit of Democratic Capitalism*, claims to be inspired by Niebuhr. His picture of Democratic capitalism is not so bad, but his complacency about what it is like in this country today and about its being the best road for all countries is fatuous.'"[5]

Like Novak, I will not claim that Neibuhr or the other Christian realists would embrace either capitalism as practiced in the United States or the process of globalization were they alive today. Instead, I will examine the approach taken by the Christian realists to see whether an economic order based on market systems is consistent with that approach. First, though, I will address some specific criticisms Niebuhr had regarding market systems, and discuss the evolution from personal markets to impersonal markets.

Niebuhr defines the ultimate sin as pride, and considers three specific types—pride of power, pride of knowledge, and pride of virtue. Under pride of power he includes greed, writing: "Greed as a form of the will-to-power has been a particularly flagrant sin in the modern era because modern technology has tempted contemporary man to overestimate the possibility and the value of eliminating his insecurity in nature. Greed has thus become the besetting sin of a bourgeois culture."[6]

Niebuhr also identified a key problem with human beings as self-interest. He noted that even altruism tends to be tainted by self-interest.[7] For those who accept the simplistic characterization of capitalism as a system where "Greed is good," or who perceive the economic system as run merely on self-ishness, the illegitimacy of capitalism appears obvious. Perhaps Niebuhr thought in these terms about capitalism. However, capitalism does not require that people be greedy for the system to operate. As Deirdre McCloskey notes, even if people were less materialistic and more altruistic, markets would still be the best way to organize the economic order.[8] The market system allows people to be materialistic, selfish, and greedy, but it also permits people to meet their physical needs in less time than was true in previous centuries, allowing them to engage in activities they believe will benefit society or others.[9] Indeed, there is far more opportunity for people to deliberately choose Golden Rule activities (philanthropy) in a market economy than in a command system.

Niebuhr criticizes also the destruction of true individuality in modern commercial life, although the same arguments could be applied to any industrial society, regardless of the nature of the economic system. He writes:

> Modern industrialism pushes the logic of impersonal money and credit relationships to its final conclusion. The processes of production and exchange, which remain imbedded in the texture of personal relationships in a simpler economy, are gradually emancipated and established as a realm of automatic and rationalized relations in which the individual is subordinated to the process. The same historical dynamic, which corrodes the traditional social unities, loyalties, and inertias of medieval agrarianism and thus allows the business man to emerge and assume a creative role in history, continues the process of corrosion until communities and nations are bound together primarily by ties of mechanical interdependence and tempted to conflict by the frictions which this interdependence entails.
>
> Inevitably the early vision of capitalistic philosophers (Adam Smith) of a process of production and exchange which would make for automatic harmony of interests is not realized. Man controls this process just enough to disturb its harmony. The men who control and own the machines become the wielders of social power on a vaster scale and of more dynamic quality than previous history has known. They cannot resist the temptations of power any more than the older oligarchies of history. But they differ from previous oligarchies in that their injustices are more immediately destructive of the very basis of their society than the injustices of a less dynamic age. Modern society is consequently involved in processes of friction and decay which threaten the whole world with disaster and which seem to develop by a kind of inexorable logic of their own, defying all human efforts to arrest the decay.[10]

Niebuhr observed that production and exchange in industrial economies are no longer embedded in personal relationships as they were prior to the industrial revolution.[11] This is certainly true. However, most contemporary economists would argue that the movement to impersonal exchange is necessary for economic growth and prosperity. Douglass North states that economic growth of the kind that the developed nations experienced over the last 250 years requires the development of institutions that permit impersonal exchange over time and distance. He adds that "most societies throughout history got 'stuck' in an institutional matrix that did not evolve into the impersonal exchange essential to capturing the productivity gains that came from the specialization of labor that have produced the Wealth of Nations."[12]

A farm family in the sixteenth century may have produced most of their necessities themselves, obtaining goods and services they didn't produce themselves from people they knew; but the contemporary family relies on the actions of thousands of people they do not know to provide them with the goods and services they require. Specialization of labor is so productive that thousands of people scattered in many geographic locations may have been involved in the production and distribution of even fairly simple goods. For people to obtain the benefits of specialization they have to participate in an economic system that is complex and impersonal.

As the economic system becomes more complex, the coordination problem becomes more acute. Specialization of labor implies that people make things they do not plan on consuming and consume things they do not make. The actions of millions of people need to be coordinated in some way. The possible ways to coordinate the economic order are limited. In much of human history, a combination of tradition and command was used to coordinate economic activity, such as the Greek estate in the times of Aristotle or a medieval manor. An important question that has to be solved is how to generate and utilize important information. The more dynamic the economy, the more important it becomes to solve the information and coordination problems. Tradition and command fail to coordinate adequately the activities of millions of people and suffer from serious information problems.

The market system relies on individuals to make decisions without a central organizing mechanism. Instead, coordination is done by the price mechanism. People observe prices and price changes and alter their behavior in certain ways. Consumers tend to buy less of a good when its price rises, and suppliers try to produce more. An increase in price indicates the good has become relatively scarcer, either due to an increase in demand by consumers or a reduction in supply by producers. The price changes provide both a signal and an incentive for people to economize on the relatively more scarce good and to try to find ways to provide more of it to the marketplace. Whereas command systems tend to rely on decision-making processes that are hierarchical and employ force rather than incentives, decision making is more diffused under a market system. What is needed is a way to utilize important knowledge that is often local and dispersed. Markets are a relatively efficient way of doing so.[13]

It is important to recognize the incredible increase in wealth and living standards that took place as a result of the rise of capitalism and of industrialization. Angus Maddison has provided data to show the increases from 1820 to 1992.[14] Real per capita income increased almost twenty times in the Western nations during that time period, while life expectancy increased from thirty-five years to seventy-seven years. Furthermore, the life expectancies increased much more for poorer people than richer people, at least in Great Britain, where comparable data are available.[15] McCloskey illustrates how incredible these gains are by writing, "If you do not find this figure impressive, I suggest you are not grasping it. It is utterly unprecedented. It dwarfs the impact of the invention of agriculture. It means that your great-great-great-grandmother had one dress for church, and one for the week, if she were not in rags. Her children did not attend school, and probably could not read. She and her husband worked eighty hours a week for a diet of bread and milk (they were four inches shorter than you are). The scope of human life was radically narrowed."[16]

Market systems have developed as a solution to the coordination problem generated by an extensive division of labor. They can be seen as institutional responses to human finitude and incomplete knowledge. They are able to function effectively because they provide ways of economizing on information. The corrosive effects on social relations to which Niebuhr refers may be a part of the cost society pays for the increased productivity of utilizing increased specialization, but the corrosive effects may be due as much to complexity and the much larger size of society today as to the specific economic system. That is, if a society is made up of three hundred million people who are engaged in very specialized tasks, is it possible to have any economic order that would not be impersonal? The alternative appears to be to return to a simpler economy, but one that also would provide many fewer goods and services and a lower material quality of life.

The impersonal nature of exchange does not imply that all of life has to be impersonal. Individuals still live in families and neighborhoods, work on teams, volunteer to help others, pray, and play face-to-face. In fact, their capacity to do good with their time and money is greater now than ever before because of rising productivity and incomes made possible by impersonal and competitive global markets.

Themes of Christian Realism and Their Application to Economics

A Constrained or Unconstrained Vision of Human Beings

Thomas Sowell discusses two conflicting visions that people have about the nature of human beings.[17] He labels one vision the *unconstrained vision*, and people with this vision see human beings as inherently good. Sowell uses William Godwin's *Enquiry Concerning Political Justice* as an example of the unconstrained vision, in which people did not need incentives to do things, but simply needed to develop a higher sense of social duty. With better education and training, humanity could create a thriving and just society. The opposing vision Sowell labels the *constrained vision*. Exemplars of the constrained vision include Adam Smith and the authors of the *Federalist Papers*. "Instead of regarding man's nature as something that could or should be changed, Smith attempted to determine how the moral and social benefits desired could be produced in the most efficient way, *within* that constraint."[18]

Sowell identifies some "hybrid" visions that prevent an easy identification of the constrained vision with the political right and the unconstrained vision with the political left. In fact, he says that the constrained vision is not compatible with the atomism of extreme libertarianism: "In the constrained vision, the individual is allowed great freedom precisely in order to serve *social ends*—which may be no part of the individual's purposes. Property rights, for example, are justified within the constrained vision not by any morally superior claims of the individual over society, but precisely by claims for the efficiency or expediency of making social decisions through the systematic incentives of market processes rather than by central planning."[19]

Sowell's discussion does not include more recent religious figures, but it is easy to see that the idealists Niebuhr opposed held the unconstrained vision, while the Christian realists would fit more into the constrained vision classification. Niebuhr emphasized original sin when discussing what human beings were capable of doing. Niebuhr acknowledged that Scripture identifies human beings as created in the image of God, yet also as sinners. He writes:

> Man is a sinner. His sin is defined as rebellion against God. The Christian estimate of human evil is so serious precisely because it places evil at the very center of human personality: in the will. This evil cannot be regarded complacently as the inevitable consequence of his finiteness or the fruit of his involvement in the contingencies and necessities of nature. Sin is occasioned

precisely by the fact that man refuses to admit his "creatureliness" and to acknowledge himself as merely a member of a total unity of life. He pretends to be more than he is.[20]

Niebuhr saw human beings as constrained by sin and unable to bring about utopia on their own.

Sin and Other Limitations

Sin is one factor that supports a constrained view of humanity, but it is not the only thing. For instance, extremely incomplete knowledge is another real-world limitation. In an economy involving hundreds of millions of people, there is no way for centralized decision makers to obtain, interpret, and respond to the information needed in order to give the right commands about who is to produce what and how the goods are to be transported and distributed. It would be impossible even if society were relatively static, with a fixed supply of people and resources. The reality is much more complex, with changes in population due to births and deaths, as well as migration; changes in the age distribution of the population; discoveries of new sources of supply of some raw materials as well as depletions of other sources; and changes in technology that affect the uses to which a resource can be applied. Once again, the institutional frameworks that have evolved over time to economize greatly on knowledge, and that allow people with specific and relevant local knowledge to act on their own, are needed to coordinate the billions of economic decisions made each day. The best and brightest experts in the country cannot come close to accomplishing what is accomplished by the market system.

A Christian realist position is consistent with the constrained vision discussed by Sowell. As noted above, the constrained vision includes human limitations that are not due to sin—such as ignorance and finitude. We can identify at least two reasons why a complex economic order requires diffused decision-making processes. The first is the inability of even very intelligent and gifted people to acquire, analyze, and act on information that is widely diffused. Second, original sin suggests that human beings cannot handle the power that would come with control of the economy. Just as the businessperson cannot be trusted to always act in the best interests of society, so the politician and the government bureaucrat cannot be trusted to always act in the best interests of society. The businessperson and the government official are both human beings, and subject to the consequences of human finitude and human sin.

Power

A second theme of the Christian realists was power. The Christian realists recognized a tension with respect to power. On the one hand, power can be used to bring about good things—peace, stability, and even justice. On the other hand, power can be used and turned into tyranny and injustice. Power is needed to avoid the perils of anarchy, but power must be constrained to avoid tyranny. In discussing ethical messianism, Niebuhr wrote, "It recognizes that injustice flows from the same source from which justice comes, from the historical organization of life."[21] He described anarchy and tyranny as "the Scylla and Charybdis between which the frail bark of social justice must sail."[22]

Niebuhr argued that power is necessary, but power must also be constrained. In political realms, important constraints involve democratic institutions and separation of powers. For the United States, these constraints include federalism, which involves delineating areas where states take precedence and areas where the federal government overrides state decisions, along with the three branches of the federal government constraining one another.

There remains the question of power in the economic arena. This question is complicated by the increasing importance of the international arena. Even if the international arena is ignored, economic power entails several dimensions. First, there is the power the wealthy have relative to those who are not wealthy, especially relative to the poor.[23] Second, there is the power that may be associated with industrial concentration. Third, there is the power of the government to regulate and control the behavior of economic agents, but also the power of the government to favor some groups at the expense of others. Economic power and political power are interrelated. In many situations the wealthy do not have the power to coerce others unless government abets the process. However, government often aids the wealthy because of the wealth they have. Niebuhr noted that it is erroneous to think that economic power is always the most basic form, although it may be the most basic form in modern industrial democracies.[24]

With reference to market economies, the questions of concentration and monopoly are central. The prevailing view of economists when Niebuhr was writing was that industrial concentration implied great power on the part of the large corporations, and that power was only partially offset by unions and government. Competition had constrained producers from an ability to exercise power in earlier times, when production processes still permitted small-scale production. The modern corporation, however, was not effectively constrained by competition. Often economists would compare some behavior of real-world firms with an ideal situation—the model of perfect competition. When the real world fell short of the ideal, a solution whereby government could correct the market failure would be proposed.[25] In many of these cases, monopoly behavior was presumed when the firm behaved differently from the model of perfect competition.

The view of contemporary economists is quite different. Competition is a powerful constraint on the behavior of firms, although competition is not just price competition. In a dynamic economy, a firm may develop a new product or process that gives it an advantage, enabling the firm to earn substantial profits, but competitive behavior over time usually attenuates the power of the firm and its profits. A firm that epitomized corporate power in Niebuhr's day was General Motors. Today, GM epitomizes the decline of American industrial dominance and has been overtaken by Toyota as the world's largest carmaker. In a world of imperfect information and transaction costs, many of the behaviors of real-world firms can be explained without resorting to monopoly power or to market failure.[26] Contemporary economists also recognize the existence of "government failure," or situations in which the root of a problem is the government, or situations in which the solution to a market failure is as bad as, or worse than, the market failure itself.

Competition is the most important constraint on power in a market economy. When competition is weak, government is capable of limiting economic power, but it is a question as to whether it actually does. An important constraint on the power of domestic firms is competition from foreign firms. The improved quality of American-made cars over the last two-and-a-half decades is due more to competition from Japanese carmakers than from government action. Competition comes in many forms. Competition can occur with respect to price, quality, location, advertising, warranties, service, convenience, novelty, durability, reputation, and so on. Technological change creates new industries, altering old industries and revamping the production processes of firms. The most obvious examples involve the communications and information industries relating to computers, cell phones, BlackBerry devices, fax machines, GPS, Internet, e-mail, camera phones, and so on. The computer chip did not just change the computer industry. Computer chips are embedded in automobiles, cell phones, and household appliances. Companies that make cash registers used to hire mechanical engineers. They hire different types of engineers today because the cash register is a computer. The development of container boxes revolutionized shipping whether by truck, train, or ship. For much of American business today, the dynamism in the economy makes any monopoly power short-lived.

Markets are a way of dispersing economic power. This does not imply that some firms do not have a lot of power, especially for a period of time. However, the search for opportunities by other firms or would-be entrepreneurs tends to erode market power held by any one firm over time. This process of competition, combined with the fact that competition can take many forms, provides a constraint on the economic power of firms. The decentralized, competitive process appears to be consistent with Niebuhr's views concerning the necessity for multiple loci of power competing and balancing one another.

There is another dimension of power that may be of concern—the greater power of owners of firms relative to their employees. Even here, though, it is easy to overstate the power of firms relative to workers. If pay or job conditions are poor at one firm, workers can move to work for other firms. At one time in history, there were a large number of company towns where a firm dominated a local area and the firm had monopsony power—power over the wages of the workers. However, improvements in transportation, infrastructure, communications, and education have eliminated most of these situations in contemporary industrial countries.[27] Over time, fluctuations in employment and real wages will reflect shifts in demand and supply of the various kinds of workers in the economy.

At a more micro level, there are asymmetries that can become important. If demand shifts so that a particular skill or occupation is not as valued as before, workers can retrain and alter their skills to be more attractive. However, the retraining is more difficult for some workers—those who are older or who are less educated. It is often difficult to know what skills to try to develop. Furthermore, the skills may be in demand in different locations than the workers facing reduced employment opportunities. After working for one firm for many years, workers may find it difficult to find new employment if the firm has to lay them off. A factor that should still be considered is that the cause of the layoffs may be reduced demand for the product of the firm due to the competitive vicissitudes in the economy overall. That is, the firm may be behaving as it is because it lacks power in its product market.

Another type of power is the power to influence government decision making so as to obtain favors or avoid penalties from the government. Industry groups raise funds to contribute to campaigns to be able to influence government decision making. Of course, so do many other groups, including labor unions, environmental groups, the NRA, the Religious Right, and the National Council of Churches. Once again, there is competition among interest groups for government favors, and it is rare that any group obtains everything it wants.[28] Even though the United States is primarily an industrial and service-oriented economy, farmers tend to receive substantial subsidies from the government. The same is true in Europe.[29] In fact, a highly contentious issue in international trade negotiations is the subsidies the developed nations provide their farmers, at the expense of farmers in the poorer nations of the world. I will address international issues in the next section.

Power in International Markets and Globalization

The arguments for market systems based on the constrained vision discussed above apply also to international markets, so I will not repeat those arguments, other than to say that the greater degree of complexity associated with the global economy relative to any domestic economy makes it even more difficult to imagine a centralized authority directing international exchange. Instead, I will focus on power issues in international markets. The most important international economic institutions were created, developed, and run by the developed nations of the world. Many economists would argue that the governing institutions of international trade and finance have operated to benefit the developed nations, often at the expense of the developing nations. In particular, the International Monetary Fund (IMF) has faced criticism for imposing stringent requirements on developing nations for them to obtain help from the IMF.

A brief historical review may place things in perspective. In the latter part of the nineteenth century the world, or at least the Western world, was on a path of increased international economic integration. Reductions in transportation costs had turned many local markets into national and even international markets. O'Rourke and Williamson show that differences in grain prices narrowed sharply across Europe and between Europe and the United States from 1870 to 1910,[30] which implies that the markets were become more integrated. Both labor and capital moved in large quantities across borders, especially as Europeans continued to migrate to the Americas. However, changes in American policy sharply curtailed immigration into the country in the first several decades of the twentieth century. Furthermore, many other immigrant nations also curtailed immigration during this time.[31]

International trade flows dropped during World War I, picked up after the war, and then dropped again due to the Great Depression and World War II. During the depression, nations engaged in beggar-thy-neighbor policies, such as increasing tariffs to reduce imports and stimulate domestic production and exports. The cumulative effect was to make everyone worse off. During World War II, the Allies began work on constructing an international economy that would avoid the mistakes of the previous several decades. The International Monetary Fund was created to stabilize the foreign exchange markets, and a framework for reducing trade restrictions was created—the General Agreement on Tariffs and Trade (GATT). Several features of GATT were installed to encourage all signers of the agreement to lower tariffs and other trade restrictions.[32] One was a focus on multilateral instead of bilateral negotiations. A second was the most-favored nation clause.[33] Each country was to lower tariffs on a particular commodity to the lowest rate applied to imports of that commodity from any other country. That is, if the tariff in the United States on steel from Great Britain was 5 percent and the tariff rate on steel from other countries was greater than 5 percent, then these rates were to be cut to 5 percent. The early rounds of negotiations led to a substantial lowering of tariffs among many of the countries of the world, an increase in trade, and economic growth.

The institutions developed during the war and established after the war seem to be consistent with the focus of the Christian realists. They involved multilateral negotiations and trade-offs. The negotiators tried to avoid mistakes of the past and applied neither a utopian approach nor a defeatist approach to the institutions. The negotiations recognized the self-interest of nations, but also the fact that all could be better off if they cooperated to reduce trade barriers.

After World War II, the West returned to the path of greater integration that had existed prior to World War I. Globalization is not really a new phenomenon, although the pace of it and some of the characteristics of it are new. Even in the nineteenth century there were firms that had production facilities in more than one country and therefore were multinational firms. After World War II, the number of multinationals grew rapidly, and by the mid-1970s it was common for firms headquartered in other countries to have production facilities in the United States. The change that has happened in more recent years is that the entire production process has been internationalized, with firms taking portions of their supply chain and having some part of it done in other countries, sometimes in facilities the company owns and other times utilizing separate firms.[34] At one time businesses thought globally only in terms of customers. Today, they think globally in terms of markets, capital, and production, and some firms even are beginning to think globally in terms of personnel.

Another major change in recent years has been due to political changes—the collapse of the Soviet Union and the movement to markets for many countries that had operated under a command system for forty years or more. Furthermore, China has opened up and is part of the integrated world economy today, and India has moved away from its history of autarky. For low-skilled workers in the wealthy countries of the West, these changes have affected them as much as globalization or outsourcing. As Richard Freeman notes, the inclusion of the former Soviet Union, China, and India into the world economy has virtually doubled the world's labor force.[35] Since these countries are much more labor intensive than the developed nations, the supply of labor has risen much more than the supply of capital, resulting in downward pressure on wages. Freeman summarizes his argument as follows:

I argue that the expansion of global capitalism to China, India, and the former Soviet bloc has initiated a critical transition period for workers around the world. Pressures of low-wage competition from the new giants will battle with the growth of world productivity and the lower prices from those countries to determine the well-being of workers in higher income economies as the low-income countries catch up with the advanced countries. While U.S. wages will not be "set in Beijing," how workers fare in China and India and other rapidly developing low wage countries will become critical to the position of labor worldwide.[36]

The question of economic power under the current form of globalization is complex. On the one hand, there is increased competition among firms from numerous countries so that the market power of any one firm is usually limited. As Freeman noted above, the competitive position of labor worldwide has fallen relative to capital with the entry of China, India, and others into the world economic system. The resulting decline in wages for low-skilled labor in developed countries is due to this phenomenon rather than firms' market power.[37] To attract investment, some countries may be susceptible to demands from a firm for special favors if it is to invest in the country, reducing the gains to the host country. The larger concern is whether the international institutional system, which still is dominated by the United States and Western Europe, will respond to the interests of the developing world. To some extent, powerful firms in the developed world try to influence governments to restrict imports from developing countries, but other forces at work include labor unions and citizens in the developed nations. There remains a danger that political forces in many countries could bring about a stop to the greater integration of economies, leading to beggar-thy-neighbor policies that harm all. As O'Rourke and Williamson note, the process of economic integration that took place in the nineteenth century and early in the twentieth century was stopped by anti-immigrant legislation and steep increases in trade barriers.[38]

The current international economy is the result of economic and political forces. Globalization is not strictly a capitalist process unaffected by governments. While it is true that there is not a global government that can regulate the behavior of multinational firms, national governments are not without tools that can affect the behavior of these firms. Furthermore, the institutions that emerge from negotiations among national governments also can affect firm behavior. The degree of control at the international level is not as great as the degree of control over domestic firms at the national level. However, it also must be recognized that government regulations do not always derive from concerns for the common good.

What approach to an issue like globalization would be consistent with Christian realism? I think that an acceptance of globalization would be in order, bearing in mind that we are dealing with an evolutionary process that involves both people and firms responding to changing incentives, as well as governments in negotiation with one another. The effects of globalization are neither strictly positive nor strictly negative. Tens of millions of Chinese and Indians have moved out of poverty over the last two decades, but the relative wages of low-skilled workers in the United States and other developed nations have been flat or declining. The two results are related. To protect the wages of low-skilled workers in the United States would harm the workers in China and India.[39] Since American politicians are going to focus more on their constituencies than on Chinese or Indian workers, pressure for trade protectionism will continue.

As developing nations such as China and India grow, they will exercise more power in the world economy. That is, we will see a dispersion of power instead of power residing strictly in the Western economies. Power in the international economy will become more balanced and less asymmetrical than it has been in recent years. This is not to say that such change is free of painful adjustments. The growth of China and India may cause great problems for other developing nations that were able to compete in markets like textiles before China entered the world market.[40] Furthermore, Africa remains unconnected in significant ways with the world economy and therefore benefits less from globalization.

The economic problems that remain cannot be solved by resorting to ideological appeals, such as unfettered capitalism or state control of economies. Much of the developed world, especially Africa, needs large investments in infrastructure, health care, and education—areas that usually require substantial government activity. However, Africa is also a prime example of how state control is no guarantee that citizens will benefit. Some of the most corrupt governments are located there. Realism, as defined by the Christian realists, is needed if policy solutions are to be developed that actually generate improvements in the lives of the world's poor.

Conclusion

I cannot claim that any of the Christian realists would accept the analysis above were they alive today. However, to the extent that they relied on the results of political scientists or other social scientists in their analysis of public policy, it is at least possible that they would be less antagonistic to market economies than their writings might indicate. Much of their analysis relating to economic issues was consistent with the prevailing view of economists of their day, but the prevailing view of economists today is quite different.

In this paper, I have tried to take a couple of key themes of the Christian realists and show that they are consistent with the operations of market economies. Furthermore, the contemporary international economy and the process of globalization are also consistent with these themes. The current situation is the result of deliberate political negotiations and the independent decisions of billions of people operating within a world economy that relies heavily on specialization of labor and impersonal economic exchanges. Given both human nature and human limitations, market systems are needed to coordinate the actions of these billions of people. There are several factors that limit the power of any one institution, be it a firm or a nation. They include competition, multilateral negotiations, and a type of balance of power that is gradually shifting away from the West.

In the last couple of decades we have witnessed the escape from poverty of millions of people, especially in China, India, and other parts of Asia. There are reasons to be hopeful that the next several decades will see even more people escape poverty. If this happens, it will be through a realistic approach that recognizes the need for incentives and finds ways to constrain those who have power. There is room for optimism but not for utopianism.

Notes

1. I thank Robin Klay, Jeff Polet, and Eric Patterson for helpful comments on earlier drafts. Any remaining errors are mine alone.
2. Reinhold Niebuhr, *Moral Man and Immoral Society: A Study in Ethics and Politics* (London: SCM, 1963), 113–68. John Milbank, *The World Made Strange: Theology, Language, Culture* (Oxford: Blackwell, 1997), 234.
3. Reinhold Niebuhr, *The Nature and Destiny of Man*, vol. 1, *Human Nature* (New York: Scribner, 1941), 66–67.
4. Michael Novak, *The Spirit of Democratic Capitalism* (New York: American Enterprise Institute/Simon & Schuster, 1982); Michael Novak, "Reinhold Niebuhr: Model for Neoconservatives," *The Christian Century*, January 22, 1986, 69–71.
5. David McCreary, "John Coleman Bennett in Contemporary Context," in *The Christian Realists: Reassessing the Contributions of Niebuhr and His Contemporaries*, ed. Eric Patterson (Lanham, MD: University Press of America, 2003), 139.
6. Niebuhr, *Nature and Destiny*, vol. 1, 191.
7. Niebuhr, *Moral Man*, 55.

8. Deirdre McCloskey, "Avarice, Prudence, and the Bourgeois Virtues," in *Having: Property and Possession in Religious and Social Life*, ed. William Schweiker and Charles Mathewes (Grand Rapids, MI: Eerdmans, 2004), 321–22.
9. This is not to say that only during one's free time can one be of service to others. Instead, many people serve others through their work by helping to provide goods and services that people want. Furthermore, someone who develops a product that people value, employs people, and pays taxes is doing good.
10. Niebuhr, *Nature and Destiny*, vol. 1, 66–67.
11. For a discussion of why the ethical approaches used by many theologians fail to adequately consider the differences between personal exchange and impersonal exchange, see Peter J. Hill and John Lunn, "Markets and Morality: Things Ethicists Should Consider When Evaluating Market Exchange" *Journal of Religious Ethics*, forthcoming.
12. Douglass North, "Economic Performance Through Time," *American Economic Review* 84 (1994), 364.
13. The seminal article dealing with the question of how knowledge is used is F. A. Hayek, "The Use of Knowledge in Society," *American Economic Review* 35 (1945), 519–30. See also Michael Polanyi, *The Tacit Dimension* (Glouster, MA: Peter Smith, 1966), and Thomas Sowell, *Knowledge and Decisions* (New York: Basic Books, 1980). On the importance of impersonal exchange, see the three volumes by F. A. Hayek, *Law Legislation and Liberty*, vol. 1, *Rules and Order* (Chicago: University of Chicago Press, 1973), vol. 2, *The Mirage of Social Justice* (Chicago: University of Chicago Press, 1976), and vol. 3, *The Political Order of a Free People* (Chicago: University of Chicago Press, 1979). See also F. A. Hayek, *The Fatal Conceit: The Errors of Socialism* (Chicago: University of Chicago Press, 1988).
14. Angus Maddison, *Monitoring the World Economy, 1820–1992* (Washington, DC: Organization for Economic Cooperation and Development, 1995).
15. Robert William Fogel, *The Escape from Hunger and Premature Death, 1700–2100: Europe, America, and the Third World* (Cambridge: Cambridge University Press, 2004), 36–37.
16. McCloskey, "Avarice," 327.
17. Thomas Sowell, *A Conflict of Visions* (New York: William Morrow, 1987).
18. Sowell, *Conflict*, 21 (italics in the original).
19. Ibid., 116 (italics in the original).
20. Niebuhr, *Nature and Destiny*, vol. 1, 16.
21. Reinhold Niebuhr, *The Nature and Destiny of Man*, vol. 2, *Human Destiny* (New York: Scribner, 1943), 21.
22. Niebuhr, *Nature and Destiny*, vol. 2, 258.
23. See John Lunn, "On Riches in the Bible and in the West Today," *Faith and Economics* 39 (2002), 14–22, for a discussion of what it means to be wealthy enough to influence governmental decisions.
24. Niebuhr, *Nature and Destiny*, vol. 2, 261–62.

25. Market failures exist when even perfectly competitive markets fail to achieve an efficient equilibrium. The traditional market failures are monopoly, externalities, and public goods. Harold Demsetz discusses this tendency, dubbing it the "nirvana approach," and argues that a comparative analysis between the behavior of real-world firms and the behavior of real-world governments in "correcting" the market failure is needed; see Demsetz, "Information and Efficiency: Another Viewpoint," *Journal of Law and Economics* 12 (1969), 1–22.

26. Since imperfect information is one of the sources of market failure, technically market failure still exists. But imperfect information is part of the human condition, applying to economic agents as well as political agents.

27. Classroom examples of monopsony today tend to use examples from sports—baseball when it had the reserve clause or the NCAA's restrictions on paying student-athletes. Monopsonistic situations are much more likely to exist in poorer and more rural nations.

28. See Sam Peltzman, "Toward a More General Theory of Regulation," *Journal of Law and Economics* 19 (1976), 211–40; Gary S. Becker, "A Theory of Competition Among Pressure Groups," *Quarterly Journal of Economics* 98 (1983), 371–400; Joseph Kalt and Mark A. Zupan, "Capture and Ideology in the Economic Theory of Politics," *American Economic Review* 74 (1984), 279–300; and Sam Peltzman, "The Economic Theory of Regulation After a Decade of Deregulation," in *Brookings Papers on Economic Activity: Microeconomics 1989*, ed. Martin Neil Baily and Clifford Winston (Washington, DC: Brookings Institution, 1989).

29. Furthermore, poor and more rural countries tend to subsidize industry instead of agriculture. These empirical observations are predicted by Becker's model cited in the previous footnote.

30. Kevin H. O'Rourke and Jeffrey G. Williamson, *Globalization and History: The Evolution of the Nineteenth-Century Atlantic Economy* (Cambridge, MA: MIT Press, 1999), 43–53.

31. O'Rourke and Williamson, *Globalization and History*, 185–206.

32. Especially in the early decades of the GATT negotiations, the focus was on tariffs. Nontariff barriers have proved more difficult to reduce.

33. Eventually the United States began using most-favored nation status as a political bargaining tool, granting it to the Soviet Union when détente was pursued.

34. This situation is referred to as fragmentation in the international trade literature. For an analysis, see Ronald W. Jones, *Globalization and the Theory of Input Trade* (Cambridge, MA: MIT Press, 2000), and Alan Deardorff, "Fragmentation in Simple Trade Models," *North American Journal of Economics and Finance* 12 (2001), 121–37.

35. Richard B. Freeman, "Labor Market Imbalances: Shortages, or Surpluses, or Fish Stories?" (paper presented at the Boston Federal Reserve Economic Conference, "Global Imbalances: As Giants Evolve," Chatham, MA, June 14–16, 2006), 9.

36. Freeman, "Labor Market Imbalances," 4.

37. The huge increase in the labor supply has strengthened the bargaining position of firms, though.

38. O'Rourke and Williamson, *Globalization and History*, 286–87.

39. For a discussion of policies to help the poor, see Albino Barrera, *Economic Compulsion and Christian Ethics* (Cambridge: Cambridge University Press, 2005).

40. See Pietra Rivoli, *The Travels of a T-Shirt in the Global Economy: An Economist Examines the Markets, Power, and Politics of World Trade* (Hoboken, NJ: Wiley, 2005), 164–72, for some discussion of the impact as China has been permitted to import more textiles and clothing into the United States.

CHAPTER 7

Reinhold Niebuhr's Christian Realism and the Bush Doctrine

Mark. R. Amstutz

As is well known, 9/11 marked a radical turning point in the Bush administration's foreign policy. The shift became apparent early on in the tone, content, and moral clarity of the president's rhetoric, evidenced in his major speeches following the attacks. Building on the themes and principles articulated earlier, the Bush administration released in September 2002 a new National Security Strategy (NSS), representing a codification of the post-9/11 foreign policy of the United States. This new orientation, which subsequently came to be called the Bush doctrine, has received significant criticism both domestically and internationally, especially for integrating moral language with security concerns. As I argue in this paper, however, the Bush policy of muscular idealism combines the competing traditions of American foreign policy[1] and can contribute toward a more stable and humane global order.

I propose to assess the Bush doctrine from a perspective rooted in Christian realism. I do so for two reasons: First, because the president himself has acknowledged that the Christian faith has profoundly affected not only his personal life but also his understanding of vocation as a public servant; and second, because some of the key elements of the Bush doctrine have been defined and justified in moral and biblical language.

Reinhold Niebuhr, whom Arthur Schlesinger, Jr., once called the "the father of us all," was the preeminent twentieth century American political ethicist. He, more than any other religious thinker, helped restore Protestantism's political credibility after progressive idealists had all but eliminated from religious discourse traditional theological concepts of sin, repentance, grace, and redemption. Niebuhr not only challenged the sentimental idealism of mainline clergy, but also encouraged vigorous engagement with existing domestic social problems and international political issues. Although his domestic political sympathies were associated with liberal causes, internationally he was a staunch defender of the balance of power theory and, in particular, the use of political power to restrain evil and foster global order. For him, justice within and among nations was best pursued by managing power in the service of the common good rather than by simply devising ideal plans to improve the world. Indeed, Niebuhr's influence on domestic and international political ethics was due to his championing of a principled realism that integrated power with morality and caution with hope. According to McGeorge Bundy, Niebuhr was "probably the single most influential mind in the development of American attitudes which combine moral purpose with a sense of political reality."[2]

Niebuhr's Christian realism provides an appropriate framework from which to assess the morality-based diplomacy of George W. Bush. To begin with, Niebuhrian political ethics provide a sophisticated, biblically informed approach to political thought and action. Niebuhr takes seriously both politics and religion, while also seeking to understand the complex intersection of spiritual and temporal authority. Following the Augustinian model, he attempts to define and distinguish the nature and demands of the City of God and the earthly city and to illuminate the challenges of Christian politics.

Niebuhr's realism affords a comprehensive Christian ethical framework that builds on the major contending theological perspectives within Christian thought. In particular, Niebuhr bases his Christian political ethics on the Augustinian-Lutheran view of sin and grace, the Reformed perspective on Christian vocation, and the Catholic emphasis on the pursuit of the common good. But because of the frailty of reason and the pervasiveness of sin, Niebuhrian realism is skeptical that justice can be secured. At the same time, because people bear the image of God and can be agents of grace, they can contribute to the common good by the responsible use of their freedom. People, in short, are both creatures and creators, sinful yet capable of self-giving love. This paradoxical, dialectical perspective of persons is captured in one of Niebuhr's most famous aphorisms: "Man's capacity for justice makes democracy possible; but man's inclination to injustice makes democracy necessary."[3]

This paper is divided into three parts. In the first section, I describe key elements of Niebuhr's political ethics, generally referred to as Christian realism. The second section describes major elements of the Bush doctrine, focusing on the integration of moral ideals with the realistic demands of power politics. In the third section, I assess the Bush doctrine using the Niebuhrian framework. The aim is not to analyze the doctrine's efficacy, but to assess its moral legitimacy using the Christian realist perspective.

Niebuhr's Christian Realism

For Niebuhr, the only adequate account of the limits and possibilities of just and humane politics depended on a religious conception of history and life. The Christian faith was not an impediment to political action but was its foundation. Two core presuppositions that pervaded Niebuhr's political thought were his conception of human sin and his view of human nature.[4]

Following Augustine, Niebuhr regarded sin as universal and comprehensive, affecting all persons and every aspect of human life. No person was exempt from sin and no human action could successfully overcome self-love. Since reason itself could be tainted by sin, reliance on moral principles could provide only a proximate guide to ethical action. Given the proclivity to self-interest and self-righteousness, the most effective way of advancing the common good was not by identifying justice per se but by restraining self-interest.

A second core assumption was Niebuhr's conception of human nature. Niebuhr accepted the biblical account that humans are created in the image of God. Because of this, he believed that persons had the capacity to love others, pursue the common good, and use freedom responsibly in promoting justice, provided they acknowledged their finiteness, self-love, and pride. Because of the ubiquity and persistence of sin, however, humans could never love God and their neighbor fully. Self-love was always lurking in the background. Niebuhr's idea of human nature thus consisted of two dimensions—one leading to self-giving love and the other leading to self-interest. The first dimension equipped humans to participate as creators in the ongoing task of redemption, while the second impaired justice by enthroning self-interest in disregard for, or at the expense of, the interests of others. Thus, self-love and self-giving love were two sides of the same coin.

Based on these two core assumptions coupled with other theological resources, Niebuhr devised a sophisticated framework of political ethics. This Christian realist political architecture was characterized by five distinctive features: the priority of power, the moral limits of political action, the need for humility, the inconclusive nature of human initiatives, and the need for responsible political action.

(1) An important theme in Niebuhr's political ethics is the necessity of power to promote and maintain a humane communal order. Although love is an absolute ethic for believers, Niebuhr did not think that Jesus' morality was

applicable to the task of creating and sustaining a humane political order. Since voluntary human cooperation on a large scale is impossible, political society needs government to ensure compliance and to confront the brutal realities of self-interest. The problem of communal order at the international level is even more problematic because no central authority exists to resolve conflicts among sovereign states. As a result, Niebuhr argued that the only way of pursuing international order was by maintaining a fundamental balance of power among states.

Since power is essential in preventing conflict and maintaining peace, Niebuhr was a staunch opponent of pacifism as a strategy to peacemaking. He was supportive of believers who sought to model an alternative lifestyle based on the ethic of Jesus, provided they did not use this approach as a political tactic. What Niebuhr opposed were pacifists who considered their nonviolent approach not only morally superior but also more efficacious in confronting the problems of aggression and tyranny. According to Niebuhr, Christian idealists who are so concerned with avoiding violence are likely to end up supporting "the peace of tyranny as if it were nearer to the peace of the Kingdom of God than war."[5]

(2) A second Niebuhrian principle is the inadequacy of all human initiatives. Because of the universality of sin, all political decisions—indeed, all human actions—will necessarily involve partiality and self-interest. While the quest for the common good is often impaired by insufficient knowledge, the primary reason for the inadequacy of collective moral action, according to Niebuhr, is the inability to identify moral ideals dispassionately and then faithfully implement them. This is difficult because partiality and pride cloud perception and impair implementation. Since sin distorts all human initiatives, controlling the future is impossible. Niebuhr wrote, "The illusions about the possibility of managing historical destiny from any particular standpoint in history always involve . . . miscalculations about both the power and the wisdom of the managers and of the weakness and the manageability of the historical 'stuff' which is to be managed."[6]

Given the inadequacy of all human initiatives, political action needs to be limited and modest in scope. Modesty is important because human action, even when inspired by the loftiest ideals, is always compromised by human sin. Indeed, injustices are likely to increase when decisions are justified in moral terms without acknowledging the limits of reason and the partiality of behavior. According to Niebuhr, evil is likely to increase the most when leaders forget that they are "creatures" and pretend that they have virtue, wisdom, and power that is beyond their competence.[7] Pretension, not wrong action or improper judgment, is therefore the chief source of injustice.[8]

(3) A third Niebuhrian political norm is the need for humility in political affairs. Since understanding is always partial and human action is always tainted by sin, government leaders must avoid triumphalism in their political initiatives and programs. Such awareness, however, does not mean that moral judgments are impossible. On the contrary, people must use their knowledge and moral faculties to assess alternatives and then implement actions that are most consistent with the available information. Although the Pauline assertion that "all have sinned and come short of the glory of God" can be interpreted to inhibit all moral judgment, Niebuhr argued that partial judgments are not only possible but also necessary in life. He wrote that while conflicts between enemies should disappear at the "ultimate religious level of judgment," it is quite appropriate to advocate distinct policy preferences, on a provisional basis, when confronting important political challenges.[9]

One of the major dangers in pursuing moral action internationally is that it can lead to self-righteousness and pride. Since sin is ever present in all initiatives, public policies should be defined with care and pursued with humility. Moralistic language, and in particular Manichean dualism, should be avoided. "The Christian faith ought to persuade us," wrote Niebuhr, "that political controversies are always conflicts between sinners and not between righteous men and sinners."[10] As a result, the task of moral politics was not to set up Christ's Kingdom on earth, but to pursue proximate justice by promoting peaceful coexistence, public order, and human liberty, while mitigating the effects of excessive self-interest. In this task, the Christian faith could provide important resources—such as truth telling, contrition, repentance, and forgiveness—that could play an important role in inhibiting the spirit of vengeance and in promoting communal justice. In particular, the Christian religion might serve as the foundation of a free society by reinforcing humility, without which political tolerance is impossible.

(4) A fourth element of Niebuhrian political ethics is the need to advance goals with caution and tentativeness. Caution was necessary because moral action could result in arrogant, self-righteous action. While moral ideals were desirable to chart and inspire collective action, Niebuhr believed that great care needed to be taken to ensure that the pursuit of such ideals would not be compromised by self-interest.

Niebuhr also advocated tentativeness because he opposed reducing political ethics to a single moral value. Since most issues and problems in international politics involve multiple moral norms, some of them in conflict with each other, simple moral verdicts are impossible in public affairs. The ethical task is therefore to identify relevant moral norms, critically assess them in light of an issue or problem, and then identify the course of action that is likely to advance the common good most effectively. For Niebuhr, there is no single, overarching value that should guide political thought. Rather, he uses the Christian faith as a foundation to derive multiple values that he seeks to integrate in tentative and proximate ways to specific challenges. Kenneth Thompson writes that Niebuhr was conspicuous among theologians by his insistence that there was no single overarching norm for judging international affairs. He refused to see freedom, security, or justice as the controlling objective of American foreign policy. He agreed with the claim of Justice Oliver Wendell Holmes that "people are always extolling the man of principle, but the superior man is the one who knows he must find his way in the maze of principles."[11]

(5) Finally, while Niebuhr cautioned against overambitious, self-righteous political initiatives, he was equally concerned with the dangers of inaction resulting from an ethic of perfectionism. Some moralists were so concerned with their own moral purity that they refused to confront injustice and tyranny because such action would result in compromising the ideal of love. But Niebuhr, following Augustine, argued that the only way that a stable and partially humane world could be sustained was by harnessing power in the service of public justice, not by individually modeling Jesus' love ethic. For Christian realism, the quest for a just international peace necessitated morally inspired, courageous political action.

Although it is important that Niebuhr reminded us not to expect too much from political initiatives, he also stressed the importance of collective action in the service of freedom and justice. As Robin Lovin notes, "[W]e do need a Niebuhrian Realism that will reconnect politics with the vital center of human activity."[12] Such a cause demands a collective strategy that seeks to build and sustain free, democratic societies and a stable international order that inhibits aggression and tyranny. Niebuhr demonstrated this political engagement by his vigorous participation in public life. Through his sermons, speeches, and writings, he repeatedly and courageously sought to advance measures of relative justice that would contribute to a more stable and humane political order. For Niebuhr, the great danger was not erroneous action but simply inaction. This is why he observed at the outset of World War II that the fundamental source of immorality was "the evasion or denial of moral responsibility."[13]

The Bush Doctrine

There is a broad consensus that a new national security paradigm emerged in the aftermath of the September 11, 2001, attacks. The core ideas of this new paradigm, known as the Bush doctrine (BD), were first expressed in the president's declarations and speeches and then in the September 2002 National Security Strategy of the United States. While the new NSS repeated a number of themes emphasized in previous NSS reports (e.g., the importance of cooperation with allies, the need for a robust military power to deter and prevail, and the need for a liberal international economic order), the 2002 statement was noteworthy for its emphasis on promoting human dignity and democracy, maintaining military supremacy, responding to unconventional threats with preemptive force, and the willingness to act unilaterally, when necessary. Following the issuance of the 2002 NSS, President Bush continued emphasizing the BD's core themes by highlighting the need to pursue security with an integrated strategy rooted in power and morality that contributed to "a balance of power favoring freedom." Two of the most important subsequent expressions of the doctrine were the second inaugural address on January 20, 2005, and the revised NSS, released in March 2006.

Scholars differ on which elements constitute the BD. Some thinkers view the doctrine chiefly in terms of power and security, while others regard it as an exercise in Wilsonian idealism.[14] Still others emphasize the unique relationship of the United States to Israel.[15] For the purposes of this analysis, I regard the doctrine as an expression of principled realism in which security threats are addressed by both power and morality. The doctrine, as defined here, has four distinct elements:

1. Belief that unipolarity is conducive to peace and that a preponderance of American power can contribute to a peaceful and prosperous world order
2. The need for multilateralism to advance peace, freedom, and security, but a willingness to act unilaterally when necessary
3. Belief that the United Sates must be willing to use preemptive and preventive force to confront terrorist groups and rogue states with weapons of mass destruction (WMD)
4. The need for the United States to champion human rights and help foster political democracy

Of the doctrine's four features, the first three are based on power and are concerned with security, world order, and the international management of power. The fourth element, by contrast, is based on political morality and is chiefly concerned with fostering human dignity through the expansion of free societies. The doctrine's dimensions of power and morality, realism and idealism, are thus integrated in the conviction that democracies are inherently pacific and "have common interests in building a benign international environment that is congenial to American interests and ideals."[16]

Most of the criticism of and commentary on the BD has focused on the shortcomings of unilateralism and the dangers in shifting strategy from deterrence toward preemption.[17] But most of these criticisms have exaggerated the alleged changes. Both the 2002 and 2006 NSS, for example, emphasize the need for coalition building and call for unilateral action only as a last resort. Moreover, the idea that preemption is a new doctrine is without foundation, for states have always possessed an inherent right of anticipatory self-defense. What is clear is that the emergence of international terrorism, especially when coupled with access to WMD, poses an unprecedented security threat. Given the widespread criticism precipitated by the claim of preemption, the NSS 2006 introduced the following qualification: "The United States will not resort to force in all cases to preempt emerging threats. Our preference is that nonmilitary actions succeed. And no country should ever use preemption as a pretext for aggression."

Although most of the opposition to the BD has focused on its military dimensions, the most noteworthy feature of the BD is its emphasis on moral values. Indeed, Norman Podhoretz claims that the power of the BD is its "incandescent moral clarity."[18] Political morality is used not only to champion human dignity and self-government, but also to justify the cause of freedom. In the 2002 NSS, for example, the term *freedom* is used at least forty-six times, while the notions of democracy and liberty appear, respectively, thirteen and eleven times. Nowhere is the role of political morality more evident than in the president's second inaugural address. In that noteworthy speech, Bush states the moral basis of American foreign policy as follows:

> From the day of our founding, we have proclaimed that every man and woman on this earth has rights, and dignity, and matchless value, because they bear the image of the maker of heaven and earth. Across the generations, we have proclaimed the imperative of self-government because no one is fit to be a master and no one deserves to be a slave. Advancing these ideals is the mission that created our nation. It is the honorable achievement of our fathers. Now it is the urgent requirement of our nation's security and the calling of our time. So it is the policy of the United States to seek and support the growth of democratic movements and institutions in every nation and culture, with the ultimate goal of ending tyranny in the world.

Historically, foreign policy has been regarded as the pursuit of vital interests, with moral values playing a subsidiary role, if at all. Challenging this traditional conception of foreign policy, the president boldly announces that

"America's vital interests and our deepest beliefs are now one." Historian John Lewis Gaddis regards this conflation of ideals and interests as a major shift in the Bush strategy. No longer is freedom simply the aim and aspiration of American foreign policy, but it is now the strategy itself.[19]

Of course, the emphasis on right and wrong, good and evil, can be deeply disturbing not only to those who do not share a belief in transcendent morality but also to those who differ with the claimed normative judgments.[20] Since reliance on moral norms presents a direct challenge to the prevailing moral relativism common in contemporary discourse, Podhoretz argues that the emergence of a strategic vision rooted in morality was not a "happy circumstance" for some foreign policy pundits. He writes:

> Given its dangers, who but an ignoramus and a simpleton—or a religious fanatic of the very type with whom Bush was going to war—would resort to archaic moral absolutes like "good" and "evil"? And then, who but a fool could bring himself to believe, as Bush (like Reagan before him) evidently had done in complete and ingenuous sincerity, that the United States represented the "good"? Surely only a virtual illiterate could be oblivious of all the innumerable crimes committed by America both at home and abroad—crimes that the country's own leading intellectuals had so richly documented in the by-now standard academic view of its history?[21]

Philip Zelikow similarly suggests that Bush's political ethics were likely to be troubling to leftist moralists, who like their American predecessors in the 1920s and 1930s, preferred isolation to passing judgment on foreign injustice.[22] For such thinkers and leaders, some of them religious officials of mainline Protestant denominations, it was often preferable to focus on the imperfections of the United States than to confront oppression, injustice, and egregious human rights abuses in other countries.

A Niebuhrian Assessment of the Bush Doctrine

In this final section, I assess the political ethics of the BD using Niebuhrian principles. I first identify areas where the BD and Niebuhrian ethics coalesce and then explore where the two perspectives diverge.

Coalescence

A Common Framework
Undoubtedly, the most important similarity between Niebuhr's Christian realism and President Bush's principled realism is the reliance on a common

approach that integrates morality and power. Recall that Niebuhr regarded politics as an arena that should be informed by the ideals of justice while recognizing that Jesus' ethics could not be transposed directly onto domestic, and especially international, politics. Because of excessive self-interest, the law of love could never be fulfilled in temporal communities. Indeed, because people misuse freedom, conflict and injustice are inevitable in human community and can only be tentatively and imperfectly resolved through the coercive power of government. Nevertheless, it was important for human beings, who bear the image of God, to pursue proximate justice and an imperfect common good, knowing that the definition and implementation of moral ideals would always be compromised by human finiteness and partiality.

Like Niebuhr's political ethics, the Bush foreign policy also relies on the integration of moral ideals and power politics. In his 2003 address at Whitehall Palace in London, Bush described the Anglo-American approach as "our alliance of conviction and might." After observing that the British and the American people have "an alliance of values," the president declared, "The deepest beliefs of our nations set the direction of our foreign policy. We value our own civil rights, so we stand for the human rights of others. We affirm the God-given dignity of every person, so we are moved to action by poverty and oppression and famine and disease."

President Bush's second inaugural address, as well as the NSS 2006, similarly express the principled realism of the BD. Although the doctrine is never explained or justified in theological or philosophical terms, its fundamental assertion is premised on an alliance of moral values and political power—an idealism celebrating human dignity and a realism demanding world order based on power. Indeed, in his covering letter to the NSS 2006, Bush stated that idealism will inform the national goals of American foreign policy while realism will provide the means to achieve them.

It needs to be stressed that the claim of coalescence between Niebuhrian thought and Bush's idealistic realism is predicated on the view that the BD is based upon political morality. Since some thinkers interpret the rise of the doctrine as a response to America's monopoly of power, such a perspective does not take transcendent morality seriously. For example, Jonathan Monten views the emergence of the BD as a response to the rise of American power. Following the logic of realism, he claims that since "states rarely decline opportunities to expand power in the absence of countervailing force," the Bush administration chose to use its preponderant power by setting forth a unilateralist doctrine rooted in progressive thought.[23] In short, the material world, not moral values, explains the rise of the BD. Moreover, other critics claim that the doctrine is simply an expression of American exceptionalism, not the affirmation of universal political morality.

The Necessity of Power

As noted earlier, a distinctive feature of Niebuhrian realism is its belief that evil in politics could only be contained through countervailing power. Unlike the religious idealists of his day, Niebuhr did not think that Hitler's threat to world order could be mitigated through rational dialogue or economic engagement. Rather, it had to be confronted with power.

The Bush administration foreign policy shares with Niebuhrian realism the conviction that a humane global order can only be sustained through the management of power. Accordingly, the central premise of the BD is to create "a balance of power favoring freedom." Since democracies are inherently more peaceful than autocracies, the BD integrates the quest for national and international security by seeking to expand democratic governance in the world. Although administration leaders recognize that democracies can only develop from indigenous values and institutions, the BD assumes that the United States, collaborating with other major free societies, can create an environment that is conducive to the expansion of humane, participatory regimes, while simultaneously challenging the power of rogue states and terrorist networks with its considerable power.

Politics Rooted in a Christian Anthropology

A third common feature of Niebuhrian political ethics and the BD is the shared conception of a dualistic human nature—one that emphasizes the dignity and sinfulness of persons, the universal claim of human dignity, as well as the capacity for injustice. For Niebuhr, the foundation of this approach is a Christian view of persons and history. As noted earlier, Niebuhr assumed that a biblical anthropology was dualistic and paradoxical in that it was based on both the glory and sinfulness of persons. Because humans were created in the image of God, they had the capacity to be creators; but because their nature was corrupted by sin, they misused their freedom by denying their status as creatures.

Bush, a staunch evangelical, also bases his political perspectives and judgments on a Christian view of human nature. Like Niebuhr, he regards human nature as dualistic—capable of great good when freedom is used responsibly and also capable of great injustice when evil is triumphant over the good. Although he frequently acknowledges the moral frailty of humans and the suffering arising from political injustice, the president repeatedly celebrates the inherent dignity of all persons, claiming that human rights are God's gift to all persons, not rights granted by a government.

Although both Niebuhr and Bush affirm a dualistic conception of persons, it is clear that Niebuhr, as a theological ethicist, provides a more comprehensive and nuanced political ethic. As a result, Niebuhr's paradoxical anthropology leads to far more tentativeness and circumspection. For Bush, by contrast, moral language is used to set forth ideals rather than to chart dangers, thereby leading to a more confident proclamation of moral claims.

The Priority of Freedom and Democracy

Finally, both Niebuhr and Bush share a profound appreciation for political and economic freedom and, more generally, for the desirability of political democracy. Niebuhr claimed that freedom was indispensable in order for humans to use their gifts and abilities to carry out creative labor. He also argued that democracy was the most effective system to balance the demands of freedom and order. "It happens," he wrote, "that democracy is probably that form of society in which both freedom and order are brought most successfully in support of each other."[24] At the same time, Niebuhr cautioned against those who would regard democracy as a perfect resolution to the problem of community. To be sure, he thought democracy was the best alternative regime, which merited our "qualified loyalty." At the same time, democracy was not, and could not be, the final fulfillment of life given the inherent moral limitations of all political initiatives. Indeed, religious faith played an important role in illuminating the tragic character of all human struggles, thereby contributing to a more balanced perspective about politics in general and democracy in particular. Niebuhr claimed that biblical faith not only reminded believers of the limitations of all temporal institutions and initiatives, but also encouraged people to call on the mercy of God in their quest to develop and sustain "proximate solutions for insoluble problems."[25]

A central premise of the BD is the need to expand democratic government. The expansion of free societies was necessary, according to the president, not only because such regimes were more effective in promoting international peace, but also because freedom was necessary for people to realize their full creative potential. In his second inaugural—the president's most expansive call for global democratization—Bush declared that human dignity will be the central guide of American foreign policy. He stated, "We will persistently clarify the choice before every ruler and every nation. The moral choice between oppression, which is always wrong, and freedom, which is eternally right." Lest the inaugural be viewed simply as the product of zealous and expansive speechwriting, the global campaign for freedom was restated boldly again a year later in the 2006 NSS. The revised NSS declares that the United States must "defend liberty and justice because these principles are right and true for all people everywhere," and then declares that it will do so by "leading an international effort to end tyranny and to promote effective democracy." Bush readily acknowledges that the quest for freedom will take time ("it is the concentrated work of generations") and will be expressed in different ways in different societies. The United States, he states, will not impose our version of democracy on other countries. Rather, the aim of U.S. foreign policy is "to help others find their own voice, attain their own freedom, and make their own way."

Thus, both Niebuhr and Bush call for democracy and freedom, but they do so with different levels of confidence and triumphalism. For Niebuhr, democratic government is the best regime to provide human beings with both community and freedom. But such a regime provides no simple resolution to the problems of world order or the ongoing challenges of finding a proximate balance between social order and individual freedom. For Bush, by contrast, freedom is the road to political development, providing the foundation for a humane domestic political society and a stable and peaceful international society.

Divergence

From the perspective of Niebuhrian realism, the BD fails to appreciate sufficiently the inadequacies of human action in advancing moral purposes. To highlight the tensions and inconsistencies between Niebuhrian ethics and the BD, I focus on four doctrinal excesses. These excesses relate to the scope of action, the confidence about historical change, the use of moralistic language, and the self-confidence in achieving desired outcomes.

Excessive Social Engineering

The first inconsistency between the BD and Niebuhrian ethics lies in the scope of political reform. Since Niebuhr regarded sin as pervasive and inevitable in all of life, political action was always tainted by excessive self-interest. Modest reform was therefore preferable to grandiose projects. Moreover, since sin had even more deleterious effects in the anarchic international community than in domestic society, Niebuhr tended to be pessimistic about improving the human condition through radical reforms. This skepticism was evidenced by his strong opposition to solving the problem of war through world federalism. Given his preference for limited and modest political initiatives, the campaign for democratic expansion would no doubt have baffled him. Not only would he have regarded the goal of ending tyranny in the world as overambitious, but he also would have considered the campaign for democratic expansion as excessively simplistic. Even in the cold war years, when the major superpower conflict pitted totalitarian Communism against democratic capitalism, Niebuhr thought it unwise to view democracy in ideological or religious terms. Promoting a free society was desirable, but it should be done with modesty and based on a Christian view of persons.[26]

The Bush initiative to expand freedom is an ambitious, all-encompassing global project. The campaign for freedom—to end tyranny by helping to replace oppressive regimes with democracies—is a truly expansive initiative. In a historic address on liberty in November 2003, Bush stated, "The advance of freedom is the calling of our time; it is the calling of our country. . . . We believe that liberty is the design of nature; we believe that liberty is the direction of history. We believe that human fulfillment and excellence come in the responsible exercise of liberty. We believe that freedom—the freedom we prize—is not for us alone; it is the right and the capacity of all mankind." Thus, whereas Bush is confident in proclaiming the need for democratic expansion, Niebuhr is more cautious and circumspect in advocating political change.

Excessive Optimism About Historical Change
A second tension between the BD and Niebuhrian ethics relates to the doctrine's optimistic, progressive nature. Niebuhr was a staunch critic of the religious, moralistic thought of the 1920s and 1930s. He regarded progressive ideologies as based on illusory and sentimental aspirations. Given the power and pervasive influence of sin, there could be no such confidence in the improvement of the human condition. As he noted in his study on *The Irony of American History*, "The illusions about the possibility of managing historical destiny from any particular standpoint in history, always involve . . . miscalculations about both the power and the wisdom of the managers and of the weakness and the manageability of the historical 'stuff' which is to be managed."[27]

Since the course of history was unknown, and because leaders could never devise strategies to achieve a just peace on earth, political reforms needed to be modest and circumspect. Moreover, there could be no confidence in human progress. History would always remain inconclusive and indeterminate.

In contrast to the Niebuhrian uncertainties about historical change, Bush exudes confidence about the future, especially the cause of freedom. While acknowledging the uncertainties of life and indeterminate nature of history, his moral rhetoric in his post-9/11 speeches is confident, if not triumphalistic. In describing the threat posed by "terrorist networks" in his address to Congress immediately after the 9/11 attacks, the president expressed this confidence as follows: "The course of this conflict [war on terror] is not known, yet its outcome is certain. Freedom and fear, justice and cruelty, have always been at war, and we know that God is not neutral between them."

Bush's optimistic vision is perhaps best expressed in his second inaugural address, which ends on the following triumphant note: "We go forward with complete confidence in the eventual triumph of freedom. Not because history runs on the wheels of inevitability; it is human choices that move events. Not because we consider ourselves a chosen nation; God moves and chooses as He wills. We have confidence because freedom is the permanent hope of mankind, the hunger in dark places, the longing of the soul."

Excessive Moralism

A third tension between Niebuhrian ethics and the BD lies in the latter's use of expansive moral rhetoric. Although Niebuhrian political ethics involved the integration of moral values and power, Niebuhr was reluctant to frame political issues solely in moral or religious terms. Rather, he relied on a dialectical and at times paradoxical ethical framework that maintained competing moral values in tension. For Niebuhr, simple moral verdicts were not possible in politics.

By contrast, President Bush has been far more prone to apply moral values to public affairs and to reduce complex issues to simple moral verdicts. In particular, he has been eager to highlight the divine source of human dignity and freedom, claiming, for example, that the liberty the United States has sought to advance in the world "is not America's gift to the world, it is God's gift to humanity." Moreover, unlike Niebuhr's paradoxical ethics, Bush has tended to frame foreign policy concerns using dichotomous categories of justice and injustice, good and evil. The tendency to reduce to simple moral categories is illustrated in his 2002 West Point commencement address: "Some worry that it is somehow undiplomatic or impolite to speak the language of right and wrong. I disagree. Different circumstances require different methods, but not different moralities. Moral truth is the same in every culture, in every time, and in every place. . . . We are in a conflict between good and evil, and America will call evil by its name."[28]

Undoubtedly, the boldest simple moral judgment made by the president was his description of Iraq, Iran, and North Korea as "the axis of evil." According to philosopher Peter Singer, in the first two and a half years of his presidency, Bush spoke of evil in 319 speeches, using the word as a noun far more often than as an adjective.[29]

Numerous critics, including former secretary of state Madeleine Albright, have argued that the Bush rhetoric of simple moral judgments is counterproductive to diplomacy. Following the release of the NSS 2006, she observed that Bush's foreign policy reflected a Manichean approach to the world. She wrote, "It is sometimes convenient, for purposes of rhetorical effect, for national leaders to talk of a globe neatly divided into good and bad. It is quite another, however, to base the policies of the most powerful nation upon that fiction."[30] Clearly, Albright cannot really mean that evil is a fiction or that it is impossible to classify regime behavior as good and bad. Hannah Arendt, no disciple of simple moralism, had no trouble in naming Nazism and Communism as "absolute evil." The challenge, then, is not to avoid simple moral verdicts, but rather to avoid using simplistic moral language that obfuscates political conditions.

Excessive Self-Confidence

Niebuhr would have been troubled by the alleged self-confident and self-righteous nature of the Bush foreign policy. Niebuhr greatly admired Abraham Lincoln because he combined a moral resolve with a profound religious perspective about human beings and historical change. According to Niebuhr, Lincoln exhibited the "almost perfect model of the difficult but not impossible task of remaining loyal and responsible toward the moral treasures of a free civilization, on the one hand, while yet having some religious vantage point over the struggle."[31] For Niebuhr, bringing a religious dimension to political conflict was essential in maintaining a balanced moral perspective—one that acknowledged the limitations of human initiatives while providing direction and inspiration for political action. Such a perspective is important because it can nurture both moral confidence necessary to choose among alternatives as well as modesty and humility in carrying out actions.

The perception that the BD is excessively self-confident and self-righteous is no doubt due partly to the dominance of American power and the unilateralism of American foreign policy. It is also no doubt due to the repeated moral claim that people have an inherent right to dignity and freedom—a claim that some have interpreted as an assertion of American political ideology. Finally, the charge of self-confidence has been justified by the universality of the doctrine's moral claims, coupled with a belief in the benevolent role of the United States in the world. The moral legitimacy of the American project is illustrated in the following statements:

> Freedom is the nonnegotiable demand of human dignity; the birthright of every person—in every civilization. . . . Today, humanity holds in its hands the opportunity to further freedom's triumph over all these foes. The United States welcomes our responsibility to lead in this great mission.[32]

> Americans are a free people, who know that freedom is the right of every person and the future of every nation. The liberty we prize is not America's gift to the world, it is God's gift to humanity.[33]

We have a responsibility to promote human freedom. . . . The United States will stand with and support advocates of freedom in every land.[34]

It needs to be stressed that the tensions between Niebuhrian thought and the BD arise in part from the different styles of thought and contexts in which ideas are expressed. Niebuhrian realism is a Christian perspective on public life that is rooted in biblical, theological, and philosophical analysis. As a preacher, teacher, and ethicist, Niebuhr sought to influence the social and political thought of his time by bringing biblical and theological perspectives to bear on the concrete political and social issues of his time. In short, Niebuhr provides a Christian framework in which to assess political thought and action. George W. Bush, by contrast, is a political leader. As president, he is responsible for guiding and inspiring collective action—a task that is best achieved in simple, direct language. Whereas thinkers and analysts have the luxury of presenting different perspectives and interpretations along with multiple policy alternatives, leaders must decide, frequently having to do so by compromising ideals.

Conclusion

Both Niebuhr and Bush affirm a politics based on realism and idealism. Although they express the integration of power and morality in different ways and in different eras, both champion moral ideals with moral courage and a reliance on political power. To a significant degree, their shared perspective of principled realism is rooted in the Christian faith and, more particularly, a Christian anthropology, serving as a source of both hope and caution. Although Niebuhrian ethics and the Bush doctrine represent different ways of conceiving political action, they share a principled moral discourse that is essential in pursuing a more peaceful and just world order. At the same time, the BD challenges Niebuhrian political ethics through its excessive optimism and confidence in progressive social change.

Notes

1. For a discussion of traditions that have historically influenced the conduct of American foreign policy, see Walter Russell Mead, *Special Providence: American Foreign Policy and How It Changed the World* (New York: Routledge, 2002), and Walter A. McDougall, *Promised Land, Crusader State: The American Encounter with the World Since 1776* (New York: Mariner Books, 1997).
2. McGeorge Bundy, "Foreign Policy: From Innocence to Engagement," in *Paths of American Thought*, ed. Arthur M. Schlesinger, Jr., and Morton White (Boston: Houghton Mifflin, 1961).

3. Reinhold Niebuhr, *The Children of Light and the Children of Darkness: A Vindication of Democracy and a Critique of Its Traditional Defense* (New York: Scribner, 1960), xiii.

4. For an overview of Niebuhr's views of sin and human nature, see Reinhold Niebuhr, *The Nature and Destiny of Man*, vol. 1, *Human Nature*, and vol. 2, *Human Destiny* (New York: Scribner, 1964).

5. It should be noted that Niebuhr was a vocal pacifist during his early years, but the evil realities of Nazism made him change his position. For this reference, see Reinhold Niebuhr, "Why the Christian Church Is Not Pacifist," in *The Essential Reinhold Niebuhr: Selected Essays and Addresses*, ed. Robert McAfee Brown (New Haven, CT: Yale University Press, 1986), 111.

6. Reinhold Niebuhr, *The Irony of American History* (New York: Scribner, 1952), 72.

7. Reinhold Niebuhr, *The Structure of Nations and Empires* (New York: Scribner, 1959), 298.

8. In his short study of American history, Niebuhr develops this perspective, arguing that American history is ironic precisely because the hopes and ideals are unconsciously betrayed by the collective behavior of its people and government. See Niebuhr, *Irony*.

9. Niebuhr, *Nature and Destiny*, vol. 1, 220.

10. Niebuhr, "Why the Christian Church Is Not Pacifist," 114.

11. Kenneth Thompson, "The Political Philosophy of Reinhold Niebuhr," in *Reinhold Niebuhr: His Religious, Social, and Political Thought*, ed. Charles W. Kegley (New York: Pilgrim, 1984), 249.

12. Robin Lovin, *Reinhold Niebuhr and Christian Realism* (Cambridge: Cambridge University Press, 1995), 176.

13. Reinhold Niebuhr, "Repeal the Neutrality Act!" in *Love and Justice: Selections from the Shorter Writings of Reinhold Niebuhr*, ed. D. B. Robertson (Philadelphia: Westminster, 1957), 177–78.

14. Robert Jervis, for example, argues that the doctrine involves four elements: a belief that the nature of government determines foreign policy; a belief that threats from nonstate actors necessitate new strategies, including preventive war; the possible need for unilateral action; and the need for American primacy to maintain international order. See Robert Jervis, "Understanding the Bush Doctrine," *Political Science Quarterly* 118, no. 3 (Fall 2003), 365–88. In a subsequent article, Jervis eliminates the demand for U.S. primacy and instead highlights the danger posed by terrorism, especially when linked to tyrannical regimes and WMD. Although one of the distinctive features of the Bush doctrine is its integration of power and morality, Jervis offers a conceptualization of the doctrine that focuses completely on power and security, neglecting altogether the role of political morality in promoting human dignity and fostering political democracy. See Robert Jervis, "Why the Bush Doctrine Cannot Be Sustained," *Political Science Quarterly* 120, no. 3 (Fall 2005), 351–77. Ethicist Peter Singer also has a limited view of the BD. He conceives of the doctrine as involving two elements: the belief that no distinction will be made between terrorists and those

who support and harbor them, and the commitment to preemptive force. See Peter Singer, *The President of Good & Evil: The Ethics of George W. Bush* (New York: Dutton, 2004), 144–45.

15. Norman Podhoretz, "In Praise of the Bush Doctrine," *Commentary*, September 2002, 28.
16. Jervis, "Why the Bush Doctrine Cannot Be Sustained," 351.
17. Ironically, the Bush administration has conflated preemptive force with preventive force. Preemption involves the use of force when clear evidence exists of an immanent attack; preventive force, by contrast, is the use of coercive power to eliminate danger before a threat can emerge. The war with Iraq was an example of preventive military action.
18. Podhoretz, "In Praise of the Bush Doctrine," 22.
19. John Gaddis, "The Past and Future of American Grand Strategy" (Charles S. Grant Memorial Lecture, Middlebury College, Middlebury, Vermont, April 21, 2005).
20. For a stinging critique of Bush's ethics, see Singer, *President of Good & Evil*.
21. Podhoretz, "In Praise of the Bush Doctrine," 20.
22. Philip Zelikow, "The Transformation of National Security: Five Redefinitions," *National Interest*, Spring 2003, 17–28.
23. Jonathan Monten, "The Roots of the Bush Doctrine: Power, Nationalism, and Democracy Promotion in U.S. Strategy," *International Security* 29 (Spring 2005), 140. Monten also attributes the emergence of the BD to the rise of progressive thought. But rather than locating the inspiration in fundamental moral ideals like freedom and human dignity, Monten finds the doctrine's secondary source in the ideology of neoconservativism.
24. Quoted in Larry Rasmussen, ed., *Reinhold Niebuhr: Theologian of Public Life* (London: Collins, 1989), 256.
25. Niebuhr, *Children*, 118.
26. The central aim of Niebuhr's book on democracy—*The Children of Light and the Children of Darkness*—was to provide a better defense of such government. He argued that a Christian anthropology was an appropriate basis for a democratic government because such a perspective provided both hope and caution.
27. Niebuhr, *Irony*, 72.
28. President George W. Bush, Graduation Speech, United States Military Academy, West Point, NY, June 1, 2002.
29. Singer, *President of Good & Evil*, 2.
30. Madeleine Albright, "Good vs. Evil Does Not Work as Foreign Policy," *Financial Times*, March 24, 2006.
31. Niebuhr, *Irony*, 172.
32. National Security Council, *The National Security Strategy of the United States of America*, September 2002, Introduction.
33. President George W. Bush, "State of the Union Address," January 28, 2003.
34. National Security Council, *The National Security Strategy of the United States of America*, March 2006, chap. II, sec. 3.

CHAPTER 8

Christian American Political Realism

Peter Augustine Lawler

What do we learn from the Christian view of being human that we might not know otherwise about the truth or the reality of our situation under God? How does Christianity contribute to genuine realism? To begin with the most obvious and maybe the most fundamental observation, our understanding of the dignity of the individual or the person originates with Christianity, particularly with Saint Augustine.

It originates with Augustine's realistic criticism of the civil and natural theologies—the respectable theologies—of the Greeks and the Romans. Both civil and natural theology are based on a reductionistic misunderstanding of what a human being is.[1]

The Dignity of the Person versus Civil and Natural Theology

Civil theology—the gods of the city or political community—is based on the claim that human beings are essentially citizens or part of a city. But that's not true. Human longings point beyond one's own country and can't be satisfied by any kind of political devotion or success. It finally was undignified or untruthful for a Roman to identify himself or his fate wholly with Rome. The realistic Augustine didn't deny that there is a certain nobility or distorted dignity in citizens who subordinate their selfish interests for their country's common good. But even or especially the best Romans were looking in the wrong place for genuine personal security and significance or immortality. They were looking in the wrong place for the most fundamental form of personal meaning or transcendence or perfection.

The polytheism of civil theology was also undignified insofar as it was an offense against the human mind. It required that educated men who knew better to degrade themselves by feigning belief in anthropomorphic gods to fend off moral deterioration as their country became more sophisticated or incredulous. Such moral efforts were also degrading to others; they aimed to stifle the efforts of particular human beings to free themselves from what are ultimately selfish communal illusions. Civil theology, by defining us as citizens and nothing more, hides from us the dignity that all human beings share in common.

Some sophisticated Greeks and Romans, Augustine adds, rejected the gods of their country for nature's God, the God of the philosophers. But that growth in theological sophistication in the direction of impersonal monotheism was only ambiguously progress. All reasonable theology is monotheistic: The orderly universe and essentially equal human beings must be governed by a single God. But Augustine still saw two problems with nature's God. First, he is too distant or too impersonal to provide any real support for the moral duties of particular human beings. Dignified personal action or personal existence can't be based on a God that is finally not a "who" but a "what." Second, natural theology is based on the untrue premise that the human being is a part of nature and nothing more. So it can't account for the realities of human freedom and dignity.

The God of the philosophers is meant to be a replacement for civil theology and, where it is found, biblical theology. The philosopher orients himself toward the truth about God by liberating his mind from all the moral, political, and religious illusions that allow human beings confidently to experience themselves as at home in the world as whole persons. The philosopher frees himself from the illusions that give most people some sense of dignity or significance. The philosopher discovers that only the human mind is at home in the world, and that God must be the perfection of our intellectual capacity to comprehend all that exists.[2] God is the principle of intelligible necessity that allows the human mind—but not whole human persons—to be at home in the world.

We grasp our true dignity—the dignity of our minds—only by seeing that the mind necessarily depends on a body that exists for a moment nowhere in particular and is gone. So, my being at home as a mind depends on my radical homelessness or insignificance as a whole, embodied being. Any being that genuinely appears to us to be eternal—such as a star—couldn't possibly know anything at all. Only a being who is absolutely mortal—or, better, almost absolutely contingent and utterly finite as a living being—could know the truth about the stars and the truth about the insignificance of himself.

Natural theology can establish the dignity of human minds, but only at the expense of denying the dignity of all human lives to the extent they aren't genuinely governed only by thought. The perspective of the philosophers is achieved through its abstraction from the personal dignity of even quite ordinary persons moved by their love of responsibilities to other, particular persons. The very idea of the dignified, personal "I" points in the direction of a God who is a "Who," and not merely a "what," as is, say, Aristotle's God. Socrates asked the questions, What is man? and What is God? Saint Augustine's questions were, Who is man? and Who is God?

So understanding ourselves as wholly natural beings means surrendering any sense of real personal dignity to impersonal natural necessity, to a God that is a principle, not a person. But, according to Augustine, human beings know they are more than merely natural beings. They long to be seen—in their particular, distinctive, infinitely significant freedom—by a personal God *who* knows them as they truly are. Natural theology can't account for the reality of equally free, unique, indispensable, and irreplaceable beings under God, or human persons who can distinguish themselves not only from the other animals and God, but from each other. So the phenomenon of human pride both reveals and hides the truth from us: We can't help but think in terms of our irreplaceable personal significance, but pride deceives us that we can secure our personal existences without the gracious help of a personal God. Proud human beings also can't help but rebel against the reality of the equality of all human beings under God, but a truthful understanding of the personal cause of that rebellion points us in the direction of God.

Natural theology can't account for—much less point to the satisfaction of—the undeniable longing of each particular human being *really to be*. Each particular person longs to be and *is* an exception to the general, necessitarian laws that account for the rest of creation. Each of us has the freedom and dignity that comes with personal transcendence. The law of nature can't account for our free will, for either our sinfulness or our virtue, for our love of particular persons (including the personal God), for the misery of our personal contingency and mortality without a personal, loving God, for our capacity to sense, even without revelation, that we were made for eternal life, through our ineradicable alienation in this world, and for our literal transcendence of our biological existence as whole persons through God's grace.

Actually, that last proposition concerning God grace isn't realistic. There's no uncontroversial empirical evidence that it's true, and Christians hold it to be true only through faith, which, they freely admit, is foolish from the philosopher's realistic view. The philosophers, Saint Augustine says, are blinded by their pride, but it's that intellectual pride that causes them to prefer what they can see with their own eyes and not with the eyes of faith. According to Augustine, reason and empirical observation alone can establish that beings who love particular persons and long to be irreplaceably, personally significant long for a personal God. But that's no proof that such a God exists.[3] "Man is unique," as Chantal Delsol writes, "in that he does not find life sufficient,"[4] but that doesn't mean that he gets to have anything more. (Or, as Patsy Cline allegedly said, everyone knows that people in hell want ice water, but that doesn't mean that they get it.)

The Modern Individual

One way we can view modern thought is as some combination of acceptance of the Christian "personal" or individual criticism of civil and natural theology with disbelief in the personal God of the Bible. The Christian criticism of natural and civil theology, if anything, becomes more pronounced in the thought of the modern philosophers—such as John Locke—who most influenced our founding. Neither civil nor natural theology can account for the freedom of the particular individual to transcend by negating his natural limitations. The human individual, the modern view is, can't help but regard himself as a free, equal, unique, and irreplaceable being. So he has every right to oppose every effort of other human beings—even or especially priests and kings—to risk or even deploy his very *being* for purposes other than his individual ones. That's why he has individual *rights*. Those are the rights he has in "the state of nature," where he is, paradoxically, more than a natural or impersonal or unfree and unselfconscious being. The only animal who possesses natural rights is the one who can freely transform nature with his individual longings in mind.[5] No other animal invents money, government, property, the family, and so forth to improve upon his natural condition. No other animal develops a technology so advanced and extensive that we can say one species now has the future of all the other species in its hands.

The modern, liberal view is that people who understand themselves as citizens or as serving some "natural excellence" of others degrade themselves by denying what they really know about their individual freedom and dignity. But they add that the same goes for foolish suckers who understand themselves as creatures. Given the mystery of human freedom, Locke holds that we can reasonably believe in a Creator. But it's unrealistic to think that a living God really provides for us now, and belief in a Creator is compatible with the uncreaturely thought that God and nature are indifferent to *my* particular existence. The good and the bad of modern news is that I'm perfectly free to provide for myself.[6]

The price for seeing the untruth of natural and civil theology is the heightening of our alienation from our political and natural homes. And surely Saint Augustine exaggerated that alienation for our own good, to show us that our true home is the City of God. But if there's no City of God, uprooted or displaced or free, apolitical individuals are pretty much on their own. They are free to make themselves more secure through their own work, and their lives become longer, freer, and more comfortable as a result. But this success is at the expense of heightening their individual experiences of isolation, loneliness, and contingency, and so the real dignity that comes through the social experience of personal significance fades. They can't help but face rather starkly the Christian truth that it's impossible to secure one's personal significance—one's *being*—without help one can't provide for oneself. It's no wonder that there have been unrealistic efforts to recover civil and natural theology in the modern world. Those efforts have been responses to the understandable longing of modern individuals to discover that they're not individuals—or not really *that* much on their own—at all.

The modern "Enlightenment" was accompanied in some of its forms (Locke, Spinoza, the Declaration of Independence) with attempts at the recovery of "natural theology." Modern natural theology, more clearly even than the ancient version, was an attempt to identify "God" with the laws that govern impersonal natural necessity—the laws of nature and nature's God. An obvious problem with such a natural theology is that it can't really account for what's undeniably real about the experiences of the free individual negating nature to secure better his particular existence. Individuals working to free themselves from the bondage to a nature indifferent to their particular existence could hardly be guided by nature's God. Because nature's God is neither personal nor providential, he gives the free individual nothing of value except his liberty. Free individuals have no choice but to improve upon what they've been given with no particular purpose in mind beyond avoiding personal extinction.

Thomas Pangle, among others, seems genuinely alarmed that some kind of Christian revival in America—or just genuine belief in revelation's truth—might threaten the understanding of nature and nature's God that is the foundation of both "natural rights" and "liberal democracy."[7] The reply of the Christian realist is that the opinion that we are completely and eternally governed by fixed principles of impersonal natural necessity actually can't comprehend the real existence of the individual who possesses and exercises rights. Surely, our modern or enlightened individualism includes our faith in the uniqueness or genuine individuality or true dignity of every particular human being, and it's hard to see how "belief" in "the God of the philosophers" does anything but undermine that self-conception. The truth about or even the pretensions of free individuals or persons, as well as the truth about the invincibility of some of their flaws and limitations, point in the direction of a personal God.

As Tocqueville explains, making the modern idea of nature's God coherent requires denying the real existence of the human individual. So natural theology tends to morph into pantheism, into a doctrine that proclaims the divinity of all that exists.[8] By calling all that exists God, pantheism becomes a lullaby that means to free us from our efforts to make ourselves other than natural beings. The post-Christian religions of the West—such as Western (or not incredibly self-disciplined) Buddhism, New Agey therapism, and a Gnosticism that's actually an elitist form of therapism—tend toward such self-negation. The promise of such pantheistic religion is that human beings could reintegrate themselves into a natural whole through an imaginative surrender of what allegedly only imaginatively distinguished them.

Tocqueville regarded pantheism as such a seductive, radically egalitarian lie that he attempted to rally all the true defenders of the true dignity of human individuality against it. Today, the brilliant French critic Chantal Delsol adds that the pervasiveness of pantheistic speculation is evidence that our idea of human dignity "is now hanging by a thread."[9] But the truth is that, for us, pantheism is just too unrealistic to be all that successful a means of anti-individualistic self-help. I receive no solace from the fact that the matter that makes up my body continues to exist after my death as part of a tree—even a sacred tree. And it's really very, very little consolation for me to know that the genes I spread will live on. I know that I'm not my genes, and I also know that, even if I were, nature would soon disperse me into insignificance. Much of the Christian polemic against Darwinism is against the pantheistic implication of its denial of the significance of particular members of our species. But Christians shouldn't worry that either pantheistic or sociobiological lullabies will really prove to be cures for the alienation or singular greatness and misery of members of our species alone. Pantheism can't extinguish—because it can't really address—the genuine experiences of the modern individual.

Modern Civil Theology

Most of the modern efforts to recover civil theology get their inspiration from the philosopher Rousseau. According to Rousseau, we naturally enjoy the unalienated contentment—the sweet sentiment of existence—given to every animal. But we, alone among the species, have accidentally or mysteriously become free or progressively less natural beings. The record of our freedom, our movement away from nature in no particular direction, Rousseau called "history." The truth is that we accidentally or unwittingly make ourselves ever more restless and miserable in pursuit of happiness. The only way we now can really find unalienated happiness—given that we can't return to nature—is freely to will ourselves to be part of an artificial, political whole that's roughly equivalent to the natural one. We're unalienated insofar as we can make ourselves citizens, and our theology should be reconfigured to connect our political devotion to God.[10]

One problem among many with modern civil theology is that it's too conscious and labored an attempt to negate what we know about our personal freedom. It has morphed into all sorts of monstrous projects—such as Marx's—to make ourselves fully at home, to bring history to an end. Those "totalitarian" projects were all based on the premise that our alienation isn't natural but historical, and that what has a historical cause must have a historical solution. But in truth, our individuality—our alienation from any natural or political whole—triumphed over every cruel and murderous effort to eradicate it. The horribly tyrannical failure of modern civil theology is, in truth, at the core of Europe's current effort to depoliticize itself, to radicalize the modern premise that the individual should never be sacrificed to any cause or principle, political or theological.[11]

Pierre Manent explains that Europeans today view themselves as individuals freed from both natural and civil theology—from any of the limits that come from any form of embodiment.[12] The modern form of the political community, of course, has been the nation-state, which has been shaped by its location on a particular piece of territory and some common conception of purpose. It is necessarily somewhat particular or parochial, based as it is on distinction between one's fellow citizens and all human beings. The political community—from the Greek polis to the modern nation—has been based on the premise that there are limits flowing from our embodiment to our powers of knowing and loving.

Every individual, of course, is also literally located in a natural body that shapes and limits his or her possibilities. A man is not free to be a woman, and an individual can't choose whether to be born or die. But *to be an individual* is to refuse to accept either the goodness or the permanence of any limits to choose or consent, of any barriers to defining one's own identity. The pure liberty the individual seeks—from nature, God, family, and country—is plausible and desirable only if he sees nothing good or necessary in anything connected to his embodiment.

Manent's criticism of European depoliticization or disembodiment is that it makes human liberty impotent. Democracy, radical individualists believe, is good only insofar as it protects individual rights or autonomy, and one of those rights is freedom from the constraints or duties of political life. The purification of our conception of human rights depends on their liberation from civic or natural obligation. So the idea of compulsory military service has become an affront to human dignity. But not only has that irksome and hazardous duty become optional. The same logic of autonomous individualism in Europe has eroded beyond recognition the individual's ties to family and church. The overcoming of the idea of national sovereignty, from this view, is Europe's victory over the final obstacle to the free flourishing of an apolitical democracy composed of equally sovereign and dignified—equally and completely detached from living for anyone or anything but themselves— individuals. They claim to enjoy, in a way, the "otherworldly" freedom promised by the Christian God, but their perception of their transcendence, of course, is, for the Christian realist, simply fantastic. Their liberation from political, natural, and civil theology—not to mention from the reproductive imperatives of sociobiology—is largely imaginary and surely very temporary. Christian realism, in large part, is coming to terms with everything implied in our existence as embodied persons in this world.

Democracy, as a political idea, makes no sense outside the context of the self-government of a particular people. It requires, of course, the effective participation of active citizens in a common political life. Anyone with eyes to see knows that the movement from the nation to the European Union is from fairly democratic political life to an oligarchic, bureaucratic machine imposing meddlesome schoolmarmish policies on the lives of the particular people and persons that compose the union. So the real promise of postpolitical Europe is to deprive the individual, for his own good, of the power that comes from democratic citizenship and the sense of common purpose that comes from the binding ties of religious and familial life. In Europe, Tocqueville's prediction that modern individualism culminates in soft despotism might be becoming true. Or it may be that the self-understanding of the modern individual is just self-destructive. The attempt to abstract one's free existence entirely from the constraints and responsibilities of embodiment makes realistic and effective action impossible. Part of that indispensable human activity—in fact, our basic natural inclination and duty—is having babies, a pleasure and duty shared by most living beings with bodies. Certainly we have to agree that the perverse behavior of the European individual is powerful evidence, if we really needed it, that civil and natural theology—not to mention sociobiology and pantheism—are untrue or, better, not completely true. What other healthy species flourishing in a very favorable environment—an environment it, in fact, has largely created for itself for its comfort and convenience—would suddenly and rather consciously just decide to stop reproducing?

America's Christian Realism

God, citizenship, and parenthood are all far more alive in America than in Europe. We too are increasingly influenced by corrosive individualistic or libertarian fantasies, but, as Tocqueville predicted, we can also take pride in the various ways we combat individualism.[13] One reason among many for the American difference is that our country has always been Christian and realistic enough to find impersonal natural theology and civil theology incredible. Our Declaration of Independence, crafted mainly with Lockean premises by Jefferson, does speak of "nature's God." But thanks to a legislative compromise with more Christian members of Congress, there God is also providential and judgmental, the God of the Bible, if not the Christian God in particular. (From the beginning, our political leaders have talked about a personal God, but never in public about either Jesus or the Trinity.) Our assumption is that political life is limited by each American's transcendent duties to the transpolitical Creator of all free and equal human beings. We understand that those duties liberate us in some measure from the chauvinism or conventionalism of our political life. And contrary to those who believe in the civil theological "cave" described by the classical philosophers as the ineradicable truth about common human blindness to the truth about all things, we assume that some such liberation is possible for us all. Every good American, that means, lives with some alienation or political homelessness, but perhaps not too much, because we're freed from the burden of expecting too much from our political home.

Because our founders assumed, despite the most theoretical among them, that we are more than merely individuals, we're also free from the burden of securing or "saving" ourselves wholly through individual efforts. We do consent, in our freedom, to be governed, but we also understand citizenship to be more than a social or political construction for individual convenience. Citizenship expresses, to us, part of the truth about our being. But only part, and not the highest or lowest part: For us, citizenship is not some clever artifice that ministers either to our basically material needs or our purely spiritual or otherworldly being. We also know, of course, that government should be limited. We are perfectly free to also experience ourselves as parents, children, friends, and creatures, and our founders assumed we would do so. Our freedom of religion, in particular, is clearly freedom *for* transpolitical religion, for our free discovery of our personal duties to our Creator.[14]

We very incompletely Lockean Americans really do believe that both modern individualists and Augustinians exaggerate our political homelessness. America, the Christian author G. K. Chesterton wisely wrote, is all about "the romance of the citizen," about making the politically homeless throughout the world politically at home here as citizens equal to all the others.[15] The truth that grounds our understanding of citizenship is not that we're citizens and nothing more. We believe that our egalitarian political life—based on the thought that, politically speaking, nobody is more or less than an equal citizen—is based on theological premises about human nature that aren't our civic or political construction but are true for human beings everywhere. Our egalitarianism is not our political religion because we're clear that political religion is an oxymoron for equal beings who know the truth about themselves under God.

As Chesterton explains, America's singular and awe-inspiring capability to be a political "home for the homeless depends" on understanding all human beings as not fully at home in any particular place in the world. America is, in more than one sense, a home for the homeless, and those religious Americans who are most at home with their homelessness are those most fully at home in the worldly or political sense in our country. But, in a still deeper sense, we believe that nobody is radically homeless or displaced or a meaningless accident. Our political life, finally, depends on our free and rational conviction that there's a personal center of significance that is the foundation of the irreducible personal significance of every human life. So it depends on our conviction that human liberty is not that of the liberated or isolated individual completely on his own in a universe indifferent or hostile to his particular existence.

Our common acceptance of the truth about the distinctively human existence under God, and not anything else, is what Americanizes us in the political sense. For us, political education is about the articulation of the truth about and the relationships among the material, political, and religious or transcendent dimensions of being—the truth that is presupposed by our egalitarian political life. That means our civic education has to teach us to be citizens in a way that has nothing to do with civic theology. We're all equal citizens because we're all equally more than citizens. Being citizens reflects a real part, but not the deepest part, of what we really know about our personal dignity.

In a way best explained by the Christian realist, our pious and patriotic evangelicals are not wrong to identify Christian America ("under God") with the real America. Our country really does depend upon our common acceptance of the Christian "anthropological" view of our freedom and dignity, although our Constitution is, of course, neutral on whether citizens actually believe in the real existence of the God of the Bible. That's why so few American Christians agree with Stanley Hauerwas and his disparagement of patriotism as un-Christian, and why so few observant Christians think of themselves, as Hauerwas says they should, as merely "resident aliens" in our country. Our evangelicals aren't all that Augustinian because they usually don't really believe that they live in a pagan or alien place.[16]

Our Christians tend to dissent from the view of sophisticated or "Europeanized" secularists that patriotism is both old-fashioned and unjust, and they don't regard cosmopolitan individualism as the more or less inevitable wave of the future. That's surely, in part, because creatures are more grateful for everything they've been given. As Pierre Manent explains, "Christian humility . . . consists in recognizing the essential human dependence: every man needs to know clearly and to feel intensely that he has received and continues to receive his life and being from someone other than himself."[17] Humility is, most deeply, our recognition of our dependence on God for our very being, but it also includes our grateful acknowledgment of the truth about our various forms of this-worldly dependencies, including what we owe to our political community. And for the Christian, the oxymoron political cosmopolitanism—especially when mixed with any form of historical eschatology—is an heretical distortion of our true unity under God. So it's natural but out-of-touch for good citizens to blame Christianity for weaning us away from our political attachments. The City of God—which includes all human beings—does alienate some from the cities of men—but only some. This partial alienation allows us, Christian realists say, to appreciate political life as not more nor less than it really is.

A Christian Appreciation of Political Life

The most thoughtful or philosophic human beings, according to the Christian American political thinker Carey McWilliams, can, quite realistically, experience on their own what Saint Augustine meant when he observed that sinful human beings hate their equality under God. We really know that we're not God.[18] Just by knowing that, we are more than the other animals, if animals still. Our truthful affirmation of what we really know is both a point of pride and a reason for the humble quelling of pride. There is no biblical reason why we shouldn't take pride in what distinguishes us and doing faithfully and well what is required of us, even as we become humbly aware of the great distance between who we are and what we know we should be or become. We can easily take Augustine's polemic against pride as the final

word on that virtue. But according to Saint Thomas Aquinas, genuine magnanimity is perfectly compatible with genuine humility. True greatness of
soul is a truthful or realistic refusal to succumb to the temptation to think of
ourselves as either more or less than we really are.

Modern—or incompletely post-Christian—thought reflects our natural
temptation to unrealistically think of ourselves as both more and less than we
really are. We moderns think of ourselves as both masters of and slaves to nature.
We think that we are simultaneously both completely free or autonomous or
naturally determined like the other animals, only more clever. But we really are
distinguished by being both political and religious animals. The truth is that our
transcendent openness to the personal God doesn't negate the political responsibility that flows from our love of other, particular persons. We are both like the
other animals in some respects, and like God in others. It's because of our singular in-betweenness that we're given the duty and opportunity to display our
dignity, our excellence, as human animals.

Dutiful, egalitarian political life is incompatible with our proud desire to
distinguish ourselves and declare our independence from other human beings
in every fundamental respect. But the elevation we experience through the
self-discipline we acquire through acting on the basis of our truthful moral
affirmation of equality is surely a source of properly human pride. According
to some sociobiological thinkers, our social devotion to equality comes from
some "moral sense." But the truth is that the source of our social or political
duty doesn't come from an instinct we share with some of the other animals.
It is a form of spiritual knowledge that flows from the Christian insight into
the irreplaceable significance of every flawed human person. And that spiritual insight is at the foundation of the proud sense of self that accompanies
the stern virtue practiced by active citizens. We can agree that both classical
or political and distinctively Christian thought reflect the truth about our
natures even while doubting that a coherent synthesis of Aristotle and
Augustine really is possible, while being too skeptical of syntheses to be
Thomists.

Consider more carefully how egalitarian political life corrects the characteristic excesses of the ambiguous virtue of greatness of soul that Aristotle so
skillfully and subtly describes: "The magnanimous man depicted in Book IV
of the NE [*Nicomachean Ethics*]," Mary Keys observes, "has trouble accepting
his humanity precisely where it implies limitation and independence, the
roots of natural sociability." He is unable "to acknowledge frankly and with
pleasure his need of and indebtedness to those others who have contributed
to his flourishing."[19] So he falls short of the truth about human excellence,
and the result is deficient when it comes to both justice and his capacity for

genuine friendship. The right kind of political experience, in effect, corrects his pretensions in the direction of Christian realism; it causes him to surrender or at least moderate his misguided confusion of himself with divine self-sufficiency. No human being, according to Saint Thomas, should even want to be free from debts that come from our dependence and our love.

Christians also rightly oppose natural and civil theology as ways of negating the truth about human finitude and alienation. It's because of the Christian expression of this truth that every attempt to restore natural and civil theology in the modern world has failed. But genuine political life is quite possible without civil theology or with transpolitical religion. Properly understood, it's not meant to be some radical overcoming of our alienation as flawed individuals or persons. Real political friendship doesn't abstract from the eros and the privacy that come with embodiment through the construction of some political fantasy. It presupposes and thrives on the shared personal experiences of beings who are mysteriously alienated from nature, estranged from God through sin, and never completely at home with each other. We're all in the same boat—unable to live without, or in complete possession of, self-knowledge or personal knowledge of each other.

Political equality, as McWilliams explains, is based on a wisdom shared by many philosophers and theologians. Not only are we ennobled by the humbling practical discipline that accompanies "living" political equality, we are elevated by the humbling, Socratic awareness that all human self-knowledge is "radically incomplete and defective."[20] We are distinguished from all else that exists through our awareness of the ineradicable mystery at the core of our being. That is, in large measure, the mystery of being the animal that transcends the rest of nature through its awareness of time and the temporality or finitude of its own being. It is also the mystery of the being that can't help but think of him- or herself as a free and unique and irreplaceable person. Everything else that more obviously distinguishes us—brains, strength, beauty, virtue, talents, skillfulness, and cleverness—is secondary to the mortality that all rational animals with some self-knowledge share. Anyone who really thinks realistically can see that even philosophers, kings, and priests are not fundamentally different from the rest of us.

Much of our dignity comes through living well with what we can't help but know about our dependence on nature, God, and each other. Political life is particularly dignified because the more we depend on each other—on particular someones—the less dependent we are on forces beyond our control—the market, technology, bureaucratic expertise, and no one in particular. It is also in political life that we are held accountable to a common standard, encouraged in our virtue and punished for our vice. It is in political life, at least on a relatively small or personal scale, that our dignity is connected with purposes citizens actually share.

As Harvey Mansfield writes, our "manly" desire to display our nobility as indispensably important, transcendent beings is fundamentally a political characteristic.[21] That desire must be shaped and limited by a realistic standard of perfection that is more than a whimsical personal preference, one that is shared by others whom one really knows and loves. Political life is, in large part, our earthly pursuit of recognition for whom we really are by those we know well enough to love, respect, and admire. The "political" desire to be recognized in our indispensable, irreplaceable personal significance points beyond itself in the direction of a personal God who sees us all as we truly are. Political distinctions are always relatively superficial, and human judgments about justice and the other virtues are often distorted and just wrong. But a realistic perception of the inadequacy or imperfection of all personal judgments doesn't obliterate the distinction between good and bad human judgments. A complete denial of the reality of the human phenomena of citizenship and statesmanship doesn't square with what we can see with our own eyes; it's a strange form of self-denial to be too skeptical about the reality of wonderful and admirable displays of human excellence.

That political life is real and points beyond itself to a more personally satisfying reality is the perception of the citizen who is also a creature. The individual, by contrast, experiences his isolated liberty as "nothing left to lose," and, as Tocqueville explains, his detached and impersonal judgments seem to stifle his personal longings. The resulting apathetic passivity—the "heart disease" portrayed, for example, on *Seinfeld*—is what Tocqueville called, with great precision, individualism.[22] According to the Christian, this apparent "flatness of soul" barely masks the despair of the soul alienated from God and the good. Those, in truth, pathetic souls have been deprived of the personal experiences that would allow them to dismiss, in gratitude under God, the individualistic or libertarian thought that they would be better off as beings who did not know love, virtue, deep longing, truth, and even death. That means of course that freedom, understood as freedom from the demanding and ennobling—if often quite ordinary—experiences of parents, children, citizens, and creatures, is really, as McWilliams says, "a cosmetic form of indignity."[23] People become small and insignificant as they withdraw into themselves. But they never, in truth, escape the miserable despair that accompanies their experience of emptiness.

A genuinely apolitical or completely "liberal" society, McWilliams observes, would be full of people who, in effect, wear the famous Ring of Gyges. They are invisible enough from others to do as they please. They are freed from human responsibility because nobody cares enough about them to hold them accountable. So they are free to indulge in their increasingly petty self-obsessions. Manly nobility—or significant displays of their indispensable and unique personal importance—seem not to be an option for them. The truth is that the pleasures of irresponsibility are fleeting, and they turn us into anxious emotional transients who can't help but exaggerate, far beyond anything actually said in the Bible, the transience of all things human. They come to believe, falsely, that nothing human endures. The progress of individualism in our country—although much more limited and ambiguous than that found in Europe—stands in criticism of our founders for neither understanding clearly nor articulating publicly the full human anthropology that animated their confidence in the goodness of human and political liberty. We're grateful for and challenged by the fact that they built with more Christian realism than they knew.[24]

Notes

1. Augustine, *The City of God*, bks. 5–8.
2. Thomas L. Pangle, *Political Philosophy and the God of Abraham* (Baltimore: Johns Hopkins University Press, 2003), is the source of my account of the case for the God of the philosophers and the philosophic way of life. Pangle's purpose, apparently, is to revive "philosophic civic religion" (62).
3. Augustine, *City of God*, bk. 19.
4. Chantal Delsol, *Icarus Fallen* (Wilmington, DE: ISI Books, 2003).
5. This is the view of the human being presented in both Hobbes' *Leviathan* and Locke's *Second Treatise*.
6. Consider the way Locke relegates the present-tense living God of the Bible to a past-tense God who gives nothing of value in Chapter V, the chapter on property, in *The Second Treatise*.
7. Pangle, *Political Philosophy*, 30–31. According to Pangle, "our liberal democratic politics" is based on "the peculiarly modern dedication to the project of the rational enlightenment of all mankind by means of the intelligent lawfulness of all things as discovered by mathematical natural science." For Pangle and his students, genuine realism means "[m]eeting the challenge of the pious view of the world in a philosophically adequate manner" (Robert C. Bartlett, *The Idea of Enlightenment* [Toronto: University of Toronto Press, 2001], 191).
8. Alexis de Tocqueville, *Democracy in America*, vol. 2, pt. 1, ch. 7.
9. Chantal Delsol, *The Unlearned Lessons of the Twentieth Century* (Wilmington, DE: ISI Books, 2006), 194.
10. Read Rousseau's account of the accidental history of our unique species in his *Discourse on Inequality*, with his account of civil religion at the end of his *Social Contract*. Maybe the most important difference between the American

and the French revolutionary traditions is the status of religion and so the status of citizenship.

11. Delsol, *The Unlearned Lessons*, ch. 12.

12. Pierre Manent, *A World Beyond Politics?* (Princeton, NJ: Princeton University Press, 2006).

13. Tocqueville, *Democracy in America*, vol. 2, pt. 2.

14. As James Madison says in his "Memorial and Remonstrance."

15. The whole account of America's distinctive understanding of citizenship is indebted to Gilbert Keith Chesterton's *What I Saw in America* (New York: Dodd, Mead, 1925).

16. Stanley Hauerwas, *Resident Aliens* (Nashville, TN: Abington, 1989).

17. Pierre Manent, *The City of Man* (Princeton, NJ: Princeton University Press, 1998), 200.

18. See, for example, Wilson Carey McWilliams, "Equality as the Moral Foundation of Community," *The Moral Foundations of the American Republic*, ed. R. Horowitz (Charlottesville: University of Virginia Press, 1986), 195–96. This appreciation of politics is indebted to themes found throughout McWilliams' work.

19. Mary Keys, *Aquinas, Aristotle, and the Promise of the Common Good* (Cambridge: Cambridge University Press, 2006), 184. See also Manent, *City of Man*, 200, where the Christian critique of magnanimity is presented as partly true and the tension between magnanimity and humility basically rooted in the human situation.

20. McWilliams, "Equality," 195.

21. Harvey C. Mansfield, *Manliness* (New Haven, CT: Yale University Press, 2006).

22. Tocqueville, *Democracy in America*, vol. 2, pt. 2, ch. 2.

23. Wilson Carey McWilliams, "Politics," *American Quarterly* 35 (Spring/Summer 1983), 22.

24. This essay is an overview of some themes I explore more deeply in my book (*Homeless and At Home in America* [South Bend, IN: St. Augustine's Press, 2007]) and in a somewhat different way in a study on dignity I'm preparing for the President's Council on Bioethics.

CHAPTER 9

International Institutions and the Problem of Judgment

Daniel Edward Young

In this essay I wish to explore the idea that there is a role for international institutions in international life consistent with a strand of Christian realist discourse. Drawing on the recent work of Oliver O'Donovan, I contend that international institutions can play a role in moral discrimination in international life. This analysis of the role of international institutions is consistent with a Christian realist analysis of politics (the balance of power, interest-seeking, checking the consolidation of power, etc.), for it does not depend on international institutions being able to enforce their judgments. However, O'Donovan's perspective on institutions is not consistent with the contractarian political theory and positivist legal theory that seem to be lurking in the mainstream of Christian realism. Christian realism's analysis of politics is reliant on its rearticulation of the doctrine of original sin and its suspicion of natural law theories. I argue that while retaining the former, Christian realism ought to reconsider the latter, for the latter assumes richer theories of human nature than those typically assumed by Christian realism. However, there are Christian realists who may not be convinced by the natural law tradition. For them, I suggest that constructivism and the English School of international relations theory may be amenable to a Christian realist reading of politics. In fact, the thought of the Christian realist Martin Wight is ancestral to these schools and coheres with an understanding of the evolution of international life that includes a greater role for international institutions.

I begin this essay by discussing the realism-idealism debate in the context of O'Donovan's concept of judgment. I then move on to the question of international institutions, which O'Donovan views as being called forth by the necessity of judgment. In the course of this discussion, the inevitable question of natural law is raised, leading to the traditional impasse of Christian realism versus neo-Thomism. Finally, I conclude that Wight's intellectual children, the English School and constructivism, may help us escape this impasse.

Realism, Idealism, and the Concept of Judgment

For Oliver O'Donovan, probably the most important contemporary political theorist working in the Christian tradition, the central political concept is judgment.[1] He distinguishes the biblical concept of politics as justice-as-judgment from the Roman concept of justice-as-right and the Greek concept of justice-as-virtue. Although he sees all three as relevant and acknowledges their role in the history of Christian political thought, it is justice-as-judgment that is foundational for O'Donovan.[2] For him, the authority of secular government resides in the practice of judgment; his recent book *The Ways of Judgment* explores its implications for domestic and international politics. O'Donovan defines *judgment* as "*an act of moral discrimination that pronounces upon a preceding act or existing state of affairs to establish a new public context.*"[3] Thus, it involves discerning right from wrong, regarding particular past actions, in such a way as to create a more just public moral context.

Furthermore, judgments must be both true and effective. This raises the question of whether judgment is effective without punishment. Does enforcement equal effectiveness? What does nonenforcement look like? To explore this question, O'Donovan devotes an entire chapter of *The Ways of Judgment* to the realism-idealism divide that has divided political theory, including Christian political thought, for centuries.

> It is, perhaps, the most fundamental of all political questions whether and to what extent judgment is possible. How are we so to pronounce as to establish? How are we to make the truth appear effectively? Of God it is said that "He spoke and it was done." "God said, 'Let there be light,' and there was light." The word of God carries the power of God within itself; to echo the old phrase from sacramental theology, it effects what it signifies. But can the human word effect what it signifies? Are we given to renew the life of human communities by a word of truth, or is this an unattainable ideal, from which we have to fall back upon the "messiness" and "compromise" of politics?[4]

The answer to this question divides the idealists from the realists. O'Donovan traces the origins of the realist strand to Marsilius of Padua, who notes that voiceless coercion makes good the impotent word. According to this view, judgment is impossible without coercion. (It is interesting that he does not trace it to Augustine.) The idealist tradition he traces to John Wyclif, who sees judgment as noncoercive. The bishop and priest represent this judgment in contrast to the coercive power of the king. In an imperfect world, the latter may be needed to enforce judgment, but it is not *part* of judgment. "The realist critique of idealism is that it fails to acknowledge the brutal rupture implied in the transition from speech to action. The idealist critique of realism is that it allows too little distinction between rational force and irrational violence,"[5] O'Donovan wrote. Thus, we see that realism links force and judgment, while idealism separates them. It is difficult to pigeonhole O'Donovan into either of these categories. At times he sounds a realist note; at times, an idealist one.

A key idea for O'Donovan is that judgment is primarily addressed to the community, not just two individuals in dispute. As such, the question of punishment is secondary. Rather, judgment's primary purpose is to articulate the moral convictions of a society. This is the idealist O'Donovan. On the other hand, force is not absent from judgment, and indeed force may be necessary to create the new public context. Thus, the realist O'Donovan: "There could be no clearer illustration of this than the circumstances leading up to the Dayton Agreement of 1995, which ended the Bosnian civil war. Until serious external military force was thrown into the scales, every deal that was signed was broken before the ink was dry."[6] Overall, O'Donovan's argument is that punishment is a subset of judgment; it is judgment enacted. However, not all judgment is punishment; legislative acts, for example, single no one out for punishment.[7]

Political theorists in other traditions may think that O'Donovan is too ambitious about the purpose of politics. His notion of the authority of government is, of course, different from other proposals such as the assorted social contract theories that derive the authority of government from the people, those theories which see the state simply as an arena in which diverse pressure groups in society compete for influence over policy, or those theories that simply see the notion of justice as a power move by elites. Is politics really about judgment at all, one might ask, or, more along the liberal conception, is politics about keeping the ship afloat and allowing, or enabling, each of us to pursue our particular way of life? It is beyond the scope of this essay to answer these questions; O'Donovan develops his argument in detail in *The Desire of the Nations*, and readers can peruse that volume and judge for themselves. For the sake of argument, I will simply assume that O'Donovan's account is generally on target and use it to probe some Christian realist assumptions about international politics.

Institutions and Judgment

I have examined the realist-idealist divide and their view on the relationship of judgment and punishment. Does institutional context matter? That is, is the rule of law necessary for effective judgment to occur? Many thinkers draw a distinction between the possibility of justice in the domestic realm, where there is a state apparatus that can enforce law, and the international arena, which is a realm of anarchy. However, for O'Donovan, this is not so; international judgment can be done. In fact, for him it is one of the three strands of the just constitution of a state, along with legitimacy and the appropriate conception of the powers of government (executive, legislative, and judiciary).

The question here is whether there is an analogy between rendering judgment in the circumstances of balance of power politics in the international arena and rendering judgment in the circumstances of the interest group politics of pluralist theory in the domestic arena. While the international arena is one of anarchy and the domestic arena one of the rule of law, the realist sees both as characterized by the struggle for power.[8] While the outcome of legislation by Congress, in O'Donovan's terms, is presumably a rendering of judgment, it is arrived at largely by means of bargaining, cajoling, logrolling, negotiating, and strong-arm tactics, rather than rational deliberation as to the good.[9] Christian realism's enduring contribution to political discourse was to note that this continual struggle for power should be unsurprising given the theological doctrine of original sin. But, even if it is the case that politics is a struggle for power, does it mean that judgment *cannot* be rendered? If judgment is *possible* (however unlikely) in the struggle for power in the domestic arena, then presumably it should be *possible* (however unlikely) in the international arena. A realist reading might likely say that true judgment seems unlikely in either arena, whereas an idealist might be more optimistic. Yet even such a realist reading goes against our intimations that politics *should* be about justice. Is this simple wishful thinking, or does it point us toward a more adequate conception of politics? Realists have defined politics as the struggle for power. Is this the best definition? Is "rendering judgment in a public context" a better one?

An essential idea to keep in mind as we discuss this issue is that for O'Donovan, judgment is an act, and furthermore, an act not necessarily dependent on an institution. Institutions *facilitate* judgment, but they are not *necessary* for it to occur, as judgments are made by human beings. Thus, if institutions are absent, it does not follow that judgment cannot be done. Instead, judgment can be "improvised," in O'Donovan's words.[10] Take a domestic example: If the police, an authorized instrument of judgment, are not present during commission of a crime, does it follow that judgment cannot be done? According to O'Donovan, no. If the criminal is threatening the life of an innocent bystander, then citizens may use force, perhaps even lethal force, to stop the criminal. Of course, this requires discrimination as to the likelihood of whether actual harm would come to the bystander. But if there is a reasonable judgment that actual harm will occur before the police arrive, one need not wait for them. (My use of the word *criminal* is not accidental: The assailant has not been found guilty of a crime by a court of law, yet the citizens judge that he has broken the law and must be stopped.)

Likewise, in the international arena, justice must be done and judgment must be rendered. Let us assume for the moment that no international institutions exist. Does it follow that judgment cannot be done? No, for if it is true in the domestic arena that judgment can be improvised, it would also seem to be true in the international arena. This is the purpose of the so-called just war theory, which O'Donovan describes as a proposal for doing justice in the theater of war.[11]

Improvisation of judgment may be necessary, but presumably is not desirable, as it would likely lead to a less rigorous or perhaps biased formulation of judgment. Therefore, judgment calls forth institutions. Judgment in the domestic arena calls forth the necessity for domestic institutions, and judgment in the international arena calls forth the necessity for international institutions. This is the act of "political foundation."[12] O'Donovan's act of political foundation is different from the act of political foundation in social contract theories. Whereas in the latter, the state is a conscious creation of the will of the people, in the former, it simply emerges through the enactment of judgment.[13]

The difficulty here is, of course, the lack of enforcement capabilities in the absence of institutions that lack a means of enforcement. There is no world army or world police force. No international thinker of any enduring significance has seriously advocated a world police force or world state, seeing such a thing as an almost certainly tyrannical entity. O'Donovan is no different. He considers the European Union project to be suspect as it attempts to construct a multistate entity in the absence of a true European identity.[14] So, if an attempted regional state like the European Union is of dubious value, it seems pretty clear a world state is of no value, even if possible. How then, absent enforcement, is judgment possible? Again, we must recall that judgment for O'Donovan is an act. Any person or group may render judgment; punishment does not necessarily occur.[15] And furthermore, failure to render judgment in specific circumstances does not mean that judgment itself is impossible. Thus, a refusal to judge by a particular international institution is a shirking of its duty, not a demonstration of judgment's impossibility.

Laws and institutions differ in different cultures and historical periods, and new circumstances give rise to new possibilities of judgment. "The existence of international institutions makes some things practicable now that were impracticable before," such as, for example, war crimes trials.[16] O'Donovan thus argues that we need to construct international institutions that remove the locus of judgment from individual states. It does not follow that those institutions ought to have the coercive power needed to force recalcitrant states to obey their will.

According to O'Donovan, "the United Nations is important precisely as an agent of earthly politics, introducing an *international point of reference that is to frame the decisions of national governments*. As such it commands action, and its judgments are as much human compromises, sometimes good ones, sometimes bad ones, as all other judgments that command action."[17]

This, in my view, is the crux of the issue. Domestic politics is every bit the struggle for power that international politics is. But the frame of reference in both arenas is justice, even when it is acknowledged through hypocrisy. Everyone claims that their policies further justice. This must be because people believe the purpose of politics is to further justice. It seems, then, that for O'Donovan, the importance of international institutions of judgment in international politics, even if there is no enforcement, is to act as a point of reference. A judgment rendered by an institution is an address to the community, as we saw above; in this case, there is an address to international society. Absent this, we wind up privileging a state's particular morality as beyond questioning.

It is important to note that O'Donovan does not claim that all enforcement of international justice needs to be done by an international institution. In fact, he contends that it is generally preferable for national courts to administer international law, with exceptions for matters such as war crimes, in which the appearance of neutrality in the administration of justice is barely present, if at all. Note again, from the quote above, O'Donovan's conception of the United Nations as an international point of reference for *national* policies.

It is at this point that Christian realists will be hesitant, but perhaps not for the usual reason. Realists have repeatedly cautioned us that international institutions do not work, or at least they are highly flawed. That is true enough, and the charge can be leveled at domestic institutions as well. But Christian realists may have a problematic theoretical issue lurking in their thought here as well: Are Christian realists working with an overly Hobbesian conception of the state? Realists generally see the sovereign state as the only legitimate representative of citizens and as the only real purveyor of force, and they believe that states have few or no moral obligations to other states.[18] Furthermore, realists see international institutions as simply being the creatures of their member states and having no real *authority* over them. Where do they get that authority if not from the sovereign state?

That seems to be true in today's world. But is not this view dependent on a contractarian view? That is, for an international institution to have authority (if only moral authority), does it have to receive it from particular states in an act of will? Does an international institution have to be explicitly authorized, in the Hobbesian sense? What if an institution's moral authority simply emerges from the necessity of doing judgment, as O'Donovan suggests? The realist perspective also seems to be dependent on a post-Westphalian conception of sovereignty, in which the sovereign state is responsible solely for its own national interest. What if these ideas about the nature of state obligations are reshaped?

If, as the realist says, the purpose of politics is to create some sort of balance of power in order to facilitate some approximation of justice, then it would seem that political institutions are not themselves truly instruments of justice, merely instruments of collective selfishness serving the purpose of order.[19] On the other hand, O'Donovan sees politics itself as judgment, not an amoral precondition for judgment. Underlying this dispute is this difference: Christian realism and O'Donovan define the purposes of politics differently. Is the purpose of politics simply to create a mere balance of power? Or does an adequate conception of the purpose of politics draw on a richer account of human nature and human sociability?

International Judgment and Natural Law

Inescapably, the question of international institutions raises the basic questions of the philosophy of law. To oversimplify, is law a product of law-making entities or does law exist antecedent to the institutions? Furthermore, is it a necessary property of law to be enforceable? That is, if there is no entity that can enforce the law, is it truly law?

O'Donovan notes that the idea of international judgment is only coherent with the idea of natural right, and this is where he most clearly diverges from the most representative Christian realists: "It is the authority of the law that is prior to any international institution and prior to any international convention, the 'law of nations,' an aspect of the natural right of God within creation, confirmed as such by the time-honored customs and usages of states in their dealings with one another. The whole realm of international authority is unintelligible without the supposition of such a law."[20]

In a book on the justice of war, O'Donovan puts it this way: "By definition war arises in the absence of an adequate formal authority to resolve a dispute. But public order abhors a vacuum. The just belligerent is supposed to venture, informally and with extraordinary means, the judgment that *would* be made by a formal court, *if* there were a competent one. The move clearly identifies the proposal [the just war tradition] with a natural law rather than a positive law orientation. Institutions of right are called forth by the relations of right themselves; they are not foundational for the relations of right."[21]

The role of international institutions, O'Donovan contends, is to help shape these common customs into an agreed international practice that *can be applied by individual states within their jurisdictions.*[22] Clearly, O'Donovan comes down on the naturalist side of this debate. Notice again that the primary agent of international politics is still the state.

Christian realism has typically been quite skeptical of the idea of natural law; thus by default it is on the positivist side. This suspicion derives from its emphasis on human imperfection and sin, which affects a person's ability to discern right from wrong. If natural law is problematic, then so is the concept of the just war or, for that matter, any other form of political judgment.[23] The controversy over the existence and efficacy of natural law is the primary gap between Protestant and Catholic political theories. Of the various Protestant traditions, the Anglicans have typically been the least skeptical of natural law theory. An Anglican himself, it is not surprising that O'Donovan would be open to natural law. However, there are some indications that non-Anglican Protestants are beginning to rethink this position, for it is fairly clear that the magisterial Reformers had little problem with the concept of natural law.[24] Since Christian realism has generally drawn on Protestant theology, and if contemporary Protestantism is beginning to reconsider the validity of natural law, then what implications does this have for Christian realism? That is, if the natural law perspective is the mainstream of the Christian tradition, both Protestant and Catholic, and realism rejects (or is at least skeptical of) natural law, does that render "Christian realism" a contradiction in terms? What does Christian realism need to rethink? Some Christian realists may seek to create a revised account of politics that includes natural law, while others may retain their skepticism of natural law. However, even for the latter, there are ways of thinking about international politics that may make space for international institutions.

Reframing the Question

For those Christian realists still skeptical of natural law, I would like to suggest that perhaps we can make an end run around this realist versus idealist (or Christian realist versus neo-Thomist) debate by exploring schools of thought on international relations that take into account the social interactions among states, but are not reliant on a theory of natural law. Among these schools are constructivism and the English School. Both of these perspectives have great internal diversity that I will not elaborate on here; rather, I will focus on the core concerns of these schools, and so will be painting with a very broad brush.[25] In addition, I suggest that these perspectives are not alien to Christian realism, but can actually be found as a major strand of thought in one of its major figures: Martin Wight. One of Wight's great challenges to realism is that he questions the reduction of political analysis to simple formulations such as "interest defined by power." Instead, using his famous three traditions of international theory, he focused on the multiple motivations of political actors. My intent in this essay is simply to suggest that those sympathetic to the Christian realist position ought to engage more thoroughly these strands of contemporary international relations theory.

Why do the cultures of advanced modernity not accept theories of natural law?[26] If people do not conceive of themselves as being social creatures, as being part of a community, they cannot have a conception of the common good. Rather, they hurl incommensurable and subjective rights-claims at one another, sorted out by power and experts. Likewise, we can extend this analysis by contending that if states do not conceive of themselves as part of an international society, then there are states hurling incommensurable and subjective rights-claims at one another on behalf of their states, sorted out by sheer power and perhaps exacerbated by cultural differences. This distinguishes an international society from an international system.[27]

Wight begins *Power Politics*, his most realist text, by highlighting a shift from "right" to "power" as the basis for international politics.[28] He contended that medieval European polities had a self-conception of being part of an international society with rights and duties, while the self-conception of the modern states-system was that of egoistic states accountable only to their own national interest. In medieval times, there was of course no shortage of war, but such wars were fought under the pretext of securing legal rights that were understood commonly; that is, all the European polities saw themselves as part of Christendom. After the breakup of Christendom, relations among states came to be governed by sheer force, by Leviathans knowing no law but their own power. Wight goes on to comment that this sense of unity was thoroughly weakened by the rise of the independent state so that "international society" has become merely the sum of its parts. Thus, from Wight's perspective, the modern state was an organization of power emancipated from right.

Because in his writings Wight highlighted so much the role of ideas of law and justice, one could argue that he hoped (although likely did not expect) that international society would reclaim its self-conception as being an international society—that is, as having a membership with rights and duties—as opposed to two other possible self-conceptions that correspond to his three traditions of thought about international relations: realism, rationalism, and revolutionism.[29] The first, realist self-conception was that of egoistic states motivated solely by self-aggrandizement. The second possible self-conception was of revolutionary movements that saw no quarter possible with the "infidel." Doctrinally based wars were very difficult to compromise on, and Wight speculated that "just wars" (wars following certain rules and conventions) took place in international societies while "holy wars" (crusades to crush the "infidels" or "heretics") were between doctrinally ruptured factions in international society or between international society and the "barbarians." If either of these newer self-conceptions—that is, a self-conception of egoism (corresponding to Wight's account of the realist tradition) or self-conception of revolution (the revolutionist tradition)—could be displaced by the older conception (the rationalist tradition), perhaps the ferocity of wars could be diminished. This has given rise to the "solidarist-pluralist" debate in the English School, which explores cultural solidarity in the international system (or the lack of it) and how that affects the interactions of states.

Realism focuses on material interests and downplays ideas and instead looks at the national interest as the source for state behavior; ideology is often seen as arising after the fact to justify preserving (or overthrowing) the existing states of affairs. Idealism focuses on the "oughtness" of ideas; that is, we should try to reshape the world according to more noble ideas than that of the national interest. Constructivism and the English School help us get around the realist-idealist impasse because it contends that ideas play a crucial role in how interests are conceived and pursued. They study the rules of the international system and how those rules affect the behavior of states. Hence, if the dominant ideas of a social system change, then the perceptions of interests, and the appropriate way to pursue those interests, can change as well. The Christian realist, while rightly retaining a focus on power, and in particular the ideological uses to which ideas can be put in the service of power, ought to be careful in ruling out the independent validity of ideas. Perhaps significantly, early realist thinkers like E. H. Carr and the early Reinhold Niebuhr of *Moral Man and Immoral Society* were highly influenced by Marx, who of course is suspicious of the independent validity of ideas. Wight, as we saw above, noted the importance of the role of ideas in how the international system was constituted. Furthermore, Wight in his three traditions seems to be attempting to get beyond the monolithic realist approach of focusing on power. Power of course is important, and perhaps even overwhelmingly dominant, but there are other motivating factors as well.

Along with Wight, more recent scholars have noted that there have been changes in the rules of the international system.[30] For example, new Protestant ideas reshaped notions of legitimacy leading to the creation of the Westphalian system. This shift took place when the idea of natural law was commonplace, but the shattering of the European theological consensus led to the modern period's skepticism about natural law. If a shift in rules has happened in the past, there is no reason why it could not occur again in the future. How do states conceive of themselves? Are they power maximizers, concerned only with security conceived in a narrow sense, or are they citizens of an international society with rights and duties that come with membership in a society? According to both constructivism and the English School, it does not follow that anarchy makes states behave *solely* as self-regarding power maximizers: As Nicholas Onuf has written, "Anarchy is a condition of rule in which rules are not directly responsible for the ways agents conduct their relations. To be sure, there are rules in the background. They make sure that the unintended consequences of agents' many choices, and not rulers, do the job of ruling. If unintended consequences *seem* to rule, it is because some agents intend for them to do so."[31] Or as Alexander Wendt puts it, "Self-help is an institution, one of various structures of identity and interest that may exist under anarchy."[32]

In the constructivist paradigm, the identities and interests of states shift through interaction and could move from a situation in which self-help is the rule (a realist world) to one in which other-regarding is the case (an idealist world). It is possible then for agents to alter the rules of the system so that it is no longer the case that non-other-regarding behavior is permissible. That is, although states might conceive of themselves as sovereign entities unaccountable to other states, in actuality the practice of the society of states is that of disciplining states that break the rules. Gradually states become aware of this and recognize that one condition of rule (self-help) has been replaced by another rule (law-based). Of course, powerful states dominate the system and set the rules for the weaker states. However, no state is so powerful that it can ignore the other powerful states in the system. The disciplining of a recalcitrant state may have the effect of changing the recalcitrant state's attitude toward its obligations to the international society. It is also possible, of course, that the continued breaking of the rules and ineffective disciplining would lead to the breakdown of that particular situation of rule and to a genuinely anarchic situation of rule. Furthermore, it need not be the case that it is only the disciplinary actions of other states that shape the system's rules. There is no reason why the ideas and beliefs of the agents themselves would not cause them to conceive of the international system as an international society and hence act accordingly.

Conclusion

This essay has been somewhat theoretical in nature, but it does have practical implications, for constructivism and the English School are indeed about practice: How do agents conceive their interests and act to achieve them? Do agents conceive of themselves as in an anarchical society, with commensurate rights and duties? Nothing in these schools of thought compel Christian realism to reject its core beliefs about human sinfulness and power politics. They make no promise that a shift in the self-understandings of states is inevitable. If the constructivists and the English School are correct, however, O'Donovan's proposal, and other proposals that see international institutions as instruments of justice, should be taken with added seriousness. If these schools are right, the venues for power politics and the content of the national interest are changeable. If so, it is possible to create international institutions able to render a judgment that would be acknowledged by the states of the world.

Notes

1. Oliver O'Donovan was recently appointed Professor of Christian Ethics and Practical Theology at the University of Edinburgh and was for many years Regius Professor of Moral and Pastoral Theology at Oxford University. Along with his wife, Joan Lockwood O'Donovan, he has been a pioneer in attempting to articulate a political theory that is both evangelical and traditional; that is, a theory that is rooted in the gospel as illuminated by the whole of the scriptural witness and yet is thoroughly grounded in the two-thousand-year-old tradition of Christian political thought. This exploration has resulted in several difficult and challenging books by O'Donovan, in particular, *The Desire of the Nations: Rediscovering the Roots of Political Theology* (Cambridge: Cambridge University Press, 1996) and its sequel, *The Ways of Judgment* (Grand Rapids, MI: Eerdmans, 2005).
2. O'Donovan, *Ways*, 7.
3. Ibid. This section draws on ch. 1.
4. Ibid., 13.
5. Ibid., 15.
6. Ibid., 29n2.
7. Ibid., 108–9.

8. See, for example, Hans J. Morgenthau, *Politics Among Nations: The Struggle for Power and Peace*, 6th ed., rev. Kenneth W. Thompson (New York: Knopf, 1985), ch. 3.
9. However, rational deliberation is not entirely absent. See, for example, Joseph M. Bessette, *The Mild Voice of Reason: Deliberative Democracy and American National Government* (Chicago: University of Chicago Press, 1994); Martha Derthick and Paul J. Quirk, *The Politics of Deregulation* (Washington, DC: Brookings Institution, 1985).
10. O'Donovan, *Ways*, 234.
11. Oliver O'Donovan, *The Just War Revisited* (Cambridge: Cambridge University Press, 2003), vii.
12. O'Donovan, *Ways*, 135.
13. Ibid., 128.
14. Ibid., 176.
15. Ibid., 109.
16. Ibid., 21.
17. Ibid., 218 (italics mine).
18. In this essay, I speak of states as having moral obligations. This is, of course, a useful fiction. A state is not an actual person but a collective of persons. Those who make policy for states do have moral obligations, some of which may be regarding the people of other states.
19. See, for example, Reinhold Niebuhr, "Why the Christian Church Is Not Pacifist," in *The Essential Reinhold Niebuhr: Selected Essays and Addresses*, ed. Robert McAfee Brown (New Haven, CT: Yale University Press, 1986), 116; Reinhold Niebuhr, *Moral Man and Immoral Society* (New York: Scribner, 1960).
20. O'Donovan, *Ways*, 218–19.
21. O'Donovan, *Just War*, 23.
22. O'Donovan, *Ways*, 219.
23. Not surprisingly, Reinhold Niebuhr argues for the extremely limited usefulness of just war theory in *The Nature and Destiny of Man: A Christian Interpretation*, vol.1, *Human Nature* (New York: Scribner, 1941), 283.
24. See, for example, David L. Weeks, "The Uneasy Politics of Modern Evangelicalism," *Christian Scholar's Review* 30 (2001), 403–18; Stephen J. Grabill, *Rediscovering the Natural Law in Reformed Theological Ethics* (Grand Rapids, MI: Eerdmans, 2006).
25. For an accessible summary of constructivism, see Nicholas Onuf, "Constructivism: A User's Manual," in *International Relations in a Constructed World*, ed. Vendulka Kubalkova, Nicholas Onuf, and Paul Kowert (Armonk, NY: M. E. Sharpe, 1998). The seminal article is Alexander Wendt, "Anarchy Is What States Make of It," *International Organization* 46 (1992), 391–425. The classic English School scholars are Martin Wight, Hedley Bull, and R. J. Vincent. Contemporary scholars working in this tradition include, among others, Tim Dunne, Barry Buzan, Richard Little, and Robert Jackson. For a useful discussion of the diversities within these two schools and how they could fruitfully interact, see Christian Reus-Smit, "Imagining Society: Constructivism and the English School," *British Journal of Politics and International Relations* 4 (2002), 487–509.

26. For what follows, I am indebted to Alasdair MacIntyre, "Theories of Natural Law in the Culture of Advanced Modernity," in *Common Truths: New Perspectives on Natural Law*, ed. Edward B. McLean (Wilmington, DE: ISI Books, 2000).
27. Hedley Bull, *The Anarchical Society: A Study of Order in World Politics*, 2nd ed. (New York: Columbia University Press, 1995), 8–19.
28. Martin Wight, *Power Politics*, ed. Hedley Bull and Carsten Holbraad, intro. Jack Spence (Leicester, UK: Leicester University Press, 1995), 26. The following paragraph is adapted from a paragraph in my essay "Martin Wight: Politics in the Era of Leviathan," in *The Christian Realists: Reassessing the Contributions of Niebuhr and His Contemporaries*, ed. Eric Patterson (Lanham, MD: University Press of America, 2003), 120–21.
29. For a brief overview of the three traditions, see "An Anatomy of International Thought," in Martin Wight, *Four Seminal Thinkers in International Theory*, ed. Gabriele Wight and Brian Porter (Oxford: Oxford University Press, 2005). For the complete discussion, see Wight, *International Theory: The Three Traditions*, ed. Gabriele Wight and Brian Porter (New York: Holmes and Meier, 1992).
30. Daniel Philpott, "The Religious Roots of Modern International Relations," *World Politics* 52 (January 2000), 206–45, is a good example.
31. Onuf, "Constructivism," 63.
32. Wendt, "Anarchy," 399.

CHAPTER 10

Christian Realism and Utopian Multilateralism[1]

Eric Patterson

Two generations ago, voices on either side of the Atlantic called isolationist America and pacifist mainline Anglo-American churches to accept responsibility for resisting evil by fighting against Nazi and later Communist tyranny. At the root of this clarion was the debunking of the utopian claims made by idealists that the West could rely on diplomacy and moral suasion manifested as international treaties, organizations, and law to keep the peace. Unfortunately, it took *blitzkrieg* and Pearl Harbor to shatter the idealists' illusions that the Axis powers were interested in consensus and accommodation.

The dissenting voices were the Christian realists such as Reinhold Niebuhr, John Foster Dulles, Herbert Butterfield, and their contemporaries. Their worldview was grounded in orthodox Christian faith and sought to apply that ethos to the real-world political dilemmas of their day. Classical Christian realism was Christian and realistic in its evaluation of human sin and human potential, both in the individual and corporate realms. This school of thought never had a doctrinaire set of positions, but was associated with principles of political responsibility, international security, and justice.[2] This chapter suggests that there is a renewed utopianism in international affairs, and that one important element of this worldview is an ideology of multilateralism: the faith that trans- and supranational institutions and international law are morally superior to state-centric international "power politics." This chapter disagrees with the idealism of contemporary multilateralism, arguing that political realism should be the foundation for efforts at international cooperation.

The Original Debate: Classical Christian Realism versus Idealism

Liberal Idealism in the Interwar Period

Classical Christian realism—that associated with Niebuhr and his contemporaries in the 1930s to 1950s—was a reaction to the liberal idealism of the interwar era that included a strong faith in multilateralism. This idealism informed many academic and political elites in the interwar era because many in the West blamed the First World War on the *realpolitik* of national and imperial governments in the years preceding August 1914. In international politics, the aversion to such Machiavellian realism resulted in "liberalism," or political idealism, and this school of thought is most identified with Woodrow Wilson's legacy and the faith in international law (Washington Conference System, Kellogg-Briand Pact) and organizations (League of Nations, Geneva Disarmament Conference, World Court) to banish war from international life. Perhaps the most notorious example of this faith in negotiation and accommodation was Neville Chamberlain's short-lived diplomatic "success" at Munich.

The gist of Wilsonian idealism is that conflict in international life is not caused by human sin manifesting itself through individuals and groups as competitiveness, egoism, and greed. Instead, idealists felt that war was caused by a poorly managed international system that allowed imperialist exploitation, exacerbated misunderstanding through secret diplomacy and poor information flows, aggravated competition through trade barriers and arms races, flouted international law, and was unresponsive to domestic public opinion.

The failure of domestic and international mechanisms to check World War I led to a variety of liberal policy prescriptions. Wilson, modeling Kant, Locke, and Bentham, argued for transparent multilateralism based on international law and organizations to manage the peace.[3] Wilson's famous "fourteen points" called for "open covenants . . . openly arrived at" (no secret diplomacy), freedom of the seas and free trade, massive disarmament, national sovereignty and "the freest opportunity to autonomous development" (self-determination), and "a general association of nations . . . affording mutual guarantees of political independence and territorial integrity" for all states.[4] In short, Wilsonian liberals put a great deal of trust in multilateral arrangements to commit states to peace and hoped that commerce and democratic institutions would make war unlikely. Unfortunately, this utopian multilateralism did little to thwart the threats of the 1930s.

The Christian Realist Riposte

The Christian realists attacked the idealism of the 1920s and 1930s, disparaging it as utopian, sentimental, hypermoralistic, and even mawkish. They rejected the liberal optimism in societal evolution to restrain the use of force in favor of law, negotiation, and arbitration. The Christian realists called this vision utopian because it failed to take into account the sinful nature of individuals and their communities.

Niebuhr recognized that there were multiple variants of liberalism, such as Joseph Schumpeter's free trade liberalism, Woodrow Wilson's vision of self-determination and transparent diplomacy, John Dewey's rationalism and focus on education, the Social Gospel, mainline Protestant pacifism, and the like. Niebuhr argued that the variants of liberalism shared a creed:

- That injustice is caused by ignorance and will yield to education and greater intelligence.
- That civilization is becoming gradually more moral and that it is a sin to challenge either the inevitability or the efficacy of gradualness.
- That appeals to love, justice, goodwill, and brotherhood are bound to be efficacious in the end. If they have not been so to date, we must have more appeals to love, justice, goodwill, and brotherhood.
- That wars are stupid and can therefore only be caused by people who are more stupid than those who recognize the stupidity of war.[5]

Niebuhr concluded that "liberalism is, in short, a kind of blindness." He and other realists charged that this blindness resulted in a fallacious view of international politics, proceeding from the illusion that human nature was essentially rational and good. Thus, liberals believed that "enlightened" mass publics and their elected officials would realize that it was morally wrong to go to war and that multilateral commitment would keep the peace. Realists countered that not only were individuals egoistic, but that their collectives were even more so—motivated by nationalism, prejudice, and competition, operating primarily on the basis of self-interest. Furthermore, because Christian realists did not agree with liberal optimists that enlightened self-interest would lead nations to eschew war, they were certain that the liberal international order of law and organizations was powerless to stand against the determined behavior of a predatory state unless states believed that it was in their interest to act. With the rise of fascism in the 1930s and Communism in the late 1940s, Christian realists argued that liberal idealism made the West unprepared to fight against tyranny. Christian realists did not disparage the existence of international organizations such as the League of

Nations, but were disappointed that states neglected their moral responsibility and long-term interests by not fulfilling their obligations to collective security.[6]

Contemporary Utopian Multilateralism

In the past two generations, the world that Wilson and Niebuhr knew has changed in many ways. However, both the idealists and the realists would quickly recognize the essence of contemporary debates regarding international law, the authority of the United Nations (UN), and multilateralism. Christian realism contributes to the debate by critiquing the weak philosophical underpinnings of utopian multilateralism and articulating a more realistic view of international politics, including a defense of the appropriate role of multilateralism in international affairs.

The Ideology of Utopian Multilateralism

Multilateralism is a term bandied about much of late, but few scholars have attempted to demarcate it with any precision. John Gerard Ruggie considers multilateralism to be an idea of "an architectural form" organizing international life.[7] In a famous article a decade ago, political scientist James Caporaso asked, "Why is multilateralism neglected in international relations theory?" Caporaso suggests a "distinction between multilateral institutions and the institution of multilateralism." The former refers to formal organizations with addresses and secretariats; the latter "appeals to the less formal, less codified habits, practices, ideas, and norms of international society."[8] Caporaso goes on to say that "multilateral" can refer to an organization or activity, but "multilateralism" "is a belief that activities ought to be organized on a universal basis. . . . As such, multilateralism is an ideology 'designed' to promote multilateral activity. It combines normative principles with advocacy and existential beliefs."[9] Caporaso concludes that multilateralism is not merely a means to a political end, but for many actors and activists it is an end unto itself.[10]

Multilateralism is an ideology. "Utopian multilateralism" is the perspective that a twenty-first century world epitomized by international law, multilateral organizations, and transnational movements is practically and morally superior to the power politics of past millennia. Such postmodern politics are said to be practically superior because they are better equipped to deal with the global nature of contemporary issues.[11] Utopian multilateralism is morally superior in that it recognizes some harmony of human interests across borders and employs dialogue and consensus, as opposed to coercion, to achieve its aims. Often this multilateralism has shades of economic neoliberalism, which believes that economic interests dominate all political questions, but it nonetheless remains utopian in its faith in overcoming individual interests and creating situations of mutual gain. As one author writes, European multilateralism in the form of Kyoto, Ottawa, and the International Criminal Court "shows the ability of the Europeans not only to reach consensus but to reflect the aspirations more widely shared at the global level for a more egalitarian international society with greater respect for the law."[12]

In contrast, unilateralist state action is morally suspect because it is selfish and self-interested, resulting in, at the least, diplomatic competition, and at the worst, outright confrontation, including the use of military force. Furthermore, utopian multilateralists hold that authentic multilateralism takes place in formal settings governed by rules, procedures, and memberships. Thus, only structured institutional arrangements really meet the conditions of multilateralism, and ad hoc alliances, such as the recent "coalition of the willing" that toppled Saddam Hussein, are illegitimate. As Kofi Annan recently opined, "'[T]he legitimate interests of all countries' must be accommodated for multilateralism to work."[13] Utopian multilateralism calls for structured multilateralism on nearly all issues, from trade to international security, regardless of efficiencies or domestic political factors. In practice, the assumption of equal states with harmonious interests in pursuit of universal goods, such as collective security, cooperating and compromising via diplomacy is the essential foundation of utopian multilateralism.

Rethinking the State and Collective Security

Much of the inspiration for multilateralism comes from the perceived flaws inherent in the state system. Indeed, many utopian multilateralists tend to be critical of the nation-state itself as a historical artifact outdated due to contemporary global dilemmas or as the epicenter of national problems rather than a font of national solutions. From a historical perspective, the purpose of the nation-state since Westphalia was to be the fundamental unit of security for a group of people living in a defined territory. However, states were often characterized by a handful of thuggish elites or, at best, the parochial interests of the citizenry, which in either case tended to be exclusivist, self-absorbed, and competitive in international affairs. Local and regional identity politics based on creed or race were often the cause of local repression and international aggression, justifying discriminatory strife and even ethnic cleansing.

Moreover, utopian multilateralists argue, national governments continue to be barriers to people achieving their aspirations or engaging in transnational organizations and culture. Kofi Annan denigrated state sovereignty in favor of what he calls "individual sovereignty . . . the human rights and fundamental freedoms enshrined in our Charter," which the UN has an obligation to defend "from the peoples, not the governments, of the United Nations."[14] In sum, if the state itself causes human insecurity, utopian multilateralism argues, then we should do something to mitigate its power.

A second charge leveled against the contemporary nation-state in favor of robust multilateralism is that globalization has incapacitated states in dealing with "postmodern" threats to security that are said to "transcend" national borders: environmental degradation, diseases from AIDS to avian influenza, international terrorism, and the like.[15] Utopian multilateralists rightly point out that such phenomena cross borders and therefore require flexibility and creative action to deal with. Václav Havel writes, "[I]n the next century I believe that most states will begin to change from cult-like entities charged with emotion into far simpler, less powerful . . . administrative units," while power will be abdicated "upward to regional, transnational, and global organizations."[16] However, utopian multilateralists often assert that such transnational issues divine a deeper truth—the emancipation of humanity from the old limitations of parochial power politics and the advance of a new pacific millennium characterized by a cosmopolitan citizenry. Utopian multilateralists are most derisive in their characterization of modern and premodern relations among states as "power politics." Utopian multilateralists deplore Vegetius' admonition, "*Si vis pacem, para bellum.*"[17] The old model associated with Paleolithic warriors from Julius Caesar to Ronald Reagan of unilateral "peace through strength" is simply dangerous, rooted in a Hobbesian (or Waltzian) view of international affairs characterized by security- or power-seeking states in conditions of anarchy. That go-it-alone, Wild West, competitive world of unilateral states motivated by nationalism and militarism is precisely what utopian multilateralism wants to do away with. In short, power politics are evil because they are competitive and self-interested.

In contrast, utopian multilateralism assumes that systems of rules, exhaustive diplomacy, overlapping institutions, and moralistic political declarations demonstrate the moral resoluteness of effective multilateralism and can result in collective security to throttle threats. Potential wars can be averted by diplomacy because increased dialogue will ultimately achieve some form of compromise short of violence. Former French President Jacques Chirac asserted, "There is no alternative to the United Nations,"[18] and he went on to argue that "no one can act alone in the name of all, and no one can accept the anarchy of a society without rules."[19] Most important, utopian multilateralism suggests that when states stand shoulder to shoulder in support of collective security, the world is safer because aggressor states will back down in the face of the overwhelming moral, political, economic, and military superiority of the collective (e.g., apartheid South Africa).[20]

Hence, utopian multilateralism is optimistic that we can reform power politics by diluting the sovereignty of individual states through embedding them in international institutions within a new world order.[21] Multilateral approaches may take many forms, be it interagency cooperation across borders (e.g., INTERPOL), treaties to address cross-border initiatives (e.g., the Kyoto Protocol), international bodies like the Organization for Security and Cooperation in Europe (OSCE) and the African Union (AU),[22] or inviting nongovernmental organizations "to the table" as political players in international fora such as the UN.[23] Perhaps the most evolved of such international entities is the European Union, which has taken decisive steps to implement integrative regulations and procedures that are distinctive and beyond the ken of national parliaments or public referenda. Furthermore, there are those who long for an entirely new world order—a global parliament or world government or terrestrial federation—that would abolish great power politics and usher in a chiasm of peace. As one former U.S. official stated, "Within the next hundred years, nationhood as we know it will be obsolete; all states will recognize a single global authority."[24]

Christian Realism and Utopian Multilateralism: Power, Responsibility, and Morality

Power Politics and the State

Christian realism does not dispute that cooperation is often a good means of international politics, but as noted below, Christian realism does call into question the philosophical assumptions of utopian multilateralism. Christian realism also need not take a strong position on whether the state should give way to a new form of authority and governance, but many are skeptical that nation-states are a relic that will quickly be superseded by some new form of government that is morally and practically superior. In addition, Christian realism is certainly concerned about issues that cross borders and is critical of those national elites who oppress their citizens and neighbors.

A Christian realist analysis of international affairs recognizes that power is central to international politics—it is still power politics out there. Power is the fundamental currency of security. Domestic and international structures may evolve from tribes to empires to democracies, but the fundamental need for order and security has not changed. Furthermore, the nature of the specific threat as well as the unique means employed to defend oneself or one's collective from that threat may change, but the reality of human history is that power—understood fungibly—is the critical element for security.[25]

Thus, it is a fallacy to believe that states are subordinating their national interests in favor of global interests, or that postmodern states have given up on power politics.[26] In contemporary international affairs, states continue to be self-interested and seek to promote their interests within the international playing field available to them.[27] For a variety of reasons, many states have decided to pursue their national agendas—economic, security, political— through multilateral institutions rather than unilaterally. One obvious reason for such behavior is the desire by smaller states to utilize the mechanisms of multilateral organizations to promote their individual interests, such as by free-riding on the coattails of larger states. As Chris Patten, external relations commissioner for the European Commission, observed in 2004: "Militarily weaker by choice and by taxpayer demand, we Europeans recoil from using arms to solve problems except as a last resort. Our appetite for negotiation, for soft not hard power, and our contention that this approach is morally superior to the Americans, is a flight from responsibility, only available as a political option because we can always count on Uncle Sam to keep us safe and to bear the civilized world's burden."[28]

A second reason that states self-interestedly promote multilateralism is as a tool for weaker states to constrain the strong. Although it is often said that the European Union (EU) transcends power politics, the simple truth is that it aspires to be an international economic and political counterweight to the United States, and certainly there remain internal disputes over power. More important, one of the foundations of the EU is the attempt by weaker states, like France and the Benelux countries, to tie down colossal Germany within a framework that will limit Germany and strengthen them. Christian realism recognizes these facts and demands that we deal with the world as it is, rather than lying to ourselves that contemporary international affairs is morally superior to the politics of the last century.

Power Politics and Responsibility

At the heart of utopian multilateralism is the idealistic faith that dialogue can always achieve compromise or consensus. Hence, success in the operation of international organizations, such as the UN, is the achievement of consensus, not necessarily action on some initiative. Consensus means that every party's equities were taken into account and that the outcome document, statement, or initiative has the approval of all involved. Consensus need not result in action, for the achievement of even a modest consensus is a diplomatic triumph in and of itself, regardless of whether concrete action is taken.

Christian realism realizes that consensus is a morally problematic form of decision making. If it is necessary to get all or most actors to agree on a given document, be it in the area of arms control, human rights, or environmental policy, it is likely that a consensus decision or treaty will be at the lowest common denominator, not the highest. As Australia's foreign minister once quipped, "[Multilateralism] is a synonym for an ineffective and unfocused policy involving internationalism of the lowest common denominator."[29] Christian realism does not descry political consensus; rather, it expects it as the reality of real-world politics. Indeed, we should be hopeful that modest, least common denominator steps in the right direction can lead to real solutions for concrete political and social problems. However, if action is taken, it is taken because states see it in their interest to act.

The fundamental problem with the "multilateralism is moral" school of thought is that consensus can dissolve the notion of responsibility. States may be abdicating their responsibility for individual moral action by excusing themselves under the guise of "no international consensus." As one writer says, "[M]ultilateral action is clearly preferable. There is only one problem with this conclusion: Experience has shown that multilateral action is frequently impossible . . . even with causes on which there is broad international agreement."[30] The genocides of the 1990s are cases in point. No European state was willing to intervene individually in the Bosnian bloodbath, and Europeans absolved themselves by pointing at both the EU's and the UN's lack of consensus and political will to stop the genocide.[31] Similarly, African governments, both individually and collectively via the Organization of African Unity, refused to intervene to stop the bloodbath in Rwanda (and elsewhere).[32] Again, states obfuscated their real reasons for choosing inactivity by hiding behind the cover of "no international consensus in our organization" to keep from taking moral action.

Christian realism recognizes that responsibility is a key feature of political decision making for individuals and for collectives. A political ethic of state responsibility recognizes that a certain level of self-interest, such as self-defense, is a moral response to threats. The Golden Rule also informs an ethic of responsibility in political affairs in the protection of the weak as well as the punishment of wrongdoing.[33] Unfortunately, consensus-based utopian multilateralism does not necessarily have the moral resources to justify political action or intervention on moral grounds—it must wait and abide by the consensus. If the vote is "no, there is no genocide in Darfur," or "something is happening in Darfur, but we are not going to act," then for the multilateralist, "that is that." [34] For the Christian realist, such inaction may be imprudent, or it may be sin.

Of course, responsibility does not mean that one can or must do everything. It is ludicrous to think that the United States or the United Nations has the capacity to solve every humanitarian, political, and social crisis around the globe. Responsibility is about the freedom to take some action, when possible, to ameliorate the tragic conditions of insecurity in human affairs.[35] Nonetheless, in contemporary international life, states still have the legitimate monopoly on the use of force and are the repository of collective morality for the citizens they represent. Action, or inaction, has moral content in international affairs, but the alleged demise of the nation-state suggests increasing lack of ethical accountability and an unwillingness to respond to specific crises beyond passing resolutions. Moreover, the utopian multilateralists' optimism about international law and organizations changing international life fails to consider, or is cleverly disingenuous about, individual states having a moral responsibility to utilize the various types of power at their disposal as appropriate.

Neutrality and Moral Equivalence

Perhaps the fundamental moral crisis for utopian multilateralism is that all of its hopes for a world of amity require shared values. The present crisis in international affairs suggests the opposite—that there is no such cosmopolitanism. For multilateralists, perhaps the only alternative is the relativism of postmodernity. Such relativism sees the intractable conflicts of political life as problems to be solved mechanistically, rather than imbued with the moral significance of good and evil.

This relativism makes the political equality of states at international organizations possible—regardless of size, regime type, or human rights record. Of course, it is not called relativism at international fora; rather, it is trumpeted as the principles of "collective equality" and "political neutrality." Such neutrality is very different from the ethic of political responsibility discussed above.

If the United Nations or other international instrument can only approach the aggressor and the victim as equal parties, such as the "equal" application of an arms embargo on both the sophisticated Serbian military and barely armed Bosnian Muslims, there is a lack of moral insight. Jean Bethke Elshtain calls this "moral equivalency." Her example is the choice by many Western religious and academic elites to not distinguish between Al Qaeda's barbarism directed at unsuspecting civilians and America's conventional military response in Afghanistan as categorically different uses of violence.[36] The classical Christian realists also railed against this moral equivalency. In Niebuhr's day, many in the church and academy argued that the United Kingdom was an empire, as was the Third Reich, and as both were sinful, there could be no justice on the British side. Niebuhr countered that all political systems have an element of sinfulness in them, but that the British

Empire was a far lesser evil than the satanic Nazis and therefore should be supported.

Christian realists recognize that the claim to "neutrality" by international institutions often masks something else. For example, it is routinely in the interest of the African Union to turn a blind eye to genocide in its bailiwick because identifying the killing fields of Rwanda, Congo, or Sudan as "genocide" would prompt action by state parties. Or, perhaps international organizations like the UN claim neutrality because they realize their own real impotence in most cases of conflict. Again, the argument of moral neutrality is a thin veneer trying to hide the much larger questions of power politics and responsibility in international life.

Christian Realism and International/Multilateralism

The fact that utopianism underlies contemporary internationalist and multilateralist programs does not mean that such political means should be condemned out of hand. Christian realism disagrees with the idealistic presuppositions that are based in liberal philosophy, but affirms many aspects of international law and organizations.

For instance, Christian realism rejects the assertions of neorealists and neoliberals (institutionalists) that international relations can only be understood at the "third level of analysis."[37] Christian realists, along with classical scholars of politics, refuse to rule out the centrality of individual human beings and human nature, both individually and collectively, in influencing international affairs.

Of course, Christian realists accept the existence of universal values, such as the value of individual human life, but reject the international legal paradigm that asserts that such values arise out of the consensus of nations, or the constructivist account that we are experiencing a "norms cascade" based on the heavy lifting of norm entrepreneurs who promoted a change in societal values that is belatedly taking root in current history. Instead, Christian realists affirm the dignity of individual human beings as children of God and refer to divine or natural law as the origin of all moral systems. This further judges the exclusive claims of some national and state groups as idolatrous.

Therefore, the universalization of some norms that have achieved prominence in international life, such as discriminating between combatants and noncombatants, the genocide convention, and human rights, is positive. But, such gains in the international political realm were the consequence, in part, of a curious mixture of state interests, backroom dealing, good intentions, face-saving, moral suasion, power politics, and a measure of deceit. Furthermore, statements of such values, such as in the Universal Declaration of Human Rights, are substantively more than the consensus of legal scholars or governments; they are rooted in universal morals valuing individual human beings as children of God. However, Christian realism is pragmatic and willing to work with others from a plurality of traditions to promote these goods, as well as introspective in recognizing the failings in our own civilization. In the end, we must be practical—for such values to have force, they must be vitiated by political power.

There is a spiritual dimension to politics disdained by the positivists and post-positivists alike—the existence of evil in the world. Much of the social scientific world has dispensed with the idea of evil, unless one means "structural" forms of evil or violence, such as ignorance and poverty. Christian realism returns to the classical notion of evil in human affairs—that individuals are moral agents capable of good and evil and that the actions of citizens and their leaders, whether locally or internationally, have immediate and long-term moral consequences. *Ergo*, multilateral cooperation that provides security to the insecure, such as through a peacekeeping mission in the wake of civil war, has positive moral content. Similarly, the choice by national leaders to sign onto, but not abide by, an international covenant, such as the Convention on Torture, is an immoral act of hypocrisy.

A related point is that Christian realists respect the manifold creativity of individuals and collectives to seek solutions to many of humankind's historical dilemmas. International institutions that manifest this positive creativity toward ameliorating the conditions of a fallen world, be it the International Committee of the Red Cross, the World Health Organization, or UNICEF, demonstrate the universal Law of Love as well as God's unique gift to humankind—free will to choose to do good.

As often as not, interests are involved in philanthropic or humanitarian action. Christian realists are not naïve in thinking that moral principles alone will goad states into right action. Instead, Christian realism recognizes the nexus of values and interests in every collective endeavor and realizes that this is the natural order of politics.[38] For instance, the Geneva Conventions do not only limit the actions of our state, they also theoretically protect our soldiers captured by the enemy. This *quid pro quo* does not rob the Geneva Conventions of their moral worth; rather, it roots them in the *terra firma* of human experience.

Therefore, we should be wary of the claims of utopian multilateralists that international and supranational organizations are more moral than self-interested states. The same claim has been made regarding the alleged moral superiority of governments over individuals and interest groups. It is true that there is great potential for organizations and international law to do some work in promoting goodwill and seeking solutions to the thorny knots of international security, but we should also recognize that collectives tend to be less morally sensitive than individuals. This is because groups, from mobs to labor unions to governments, may face less immediate moral restraint on their activities than do individuals, because groups tend to compromise among their members to achieve consensus—regardless of the fact that this often results in a lowest common denominator morality. Furthermore, collectives tend to enhance group egoisms at the subnational, national, and regional levels, manifested as ideology (e.g., Communism) or nationalism: "Society merely cumulates the egoism of individuals and transmutes their individual altruism into collective egoism so that the egoism of the group has double force. For this reason, no group acts from purely unselfish or even mutual interest, and politics is therefore bound to be a contest of power."[39]

This does not mean that Christian realists reject international law, treaties, or organizations. Instead, Christian realism reminds us that the pitfalls attendant to all human collectives likewise exist at the international level. Moreover, Christian realists traditionally have pointed to the concepts of power and interests as critical to understanding domestic and international politics. In the discourse of utopian multilateralism, power and interests are often forgotten. However, in truth, multilateralism and international institutions are often designed to promote the interests of some members. Certainly, the UN Security Council is a case in point. France's constant calls for multilateralism are grounded less in a philosophy of consensus than in France's interests in remaining a player, albeit an increasingly weak one, in international life.

In short, the case for multilateralism in all of its forms must rest on a realistic appraisal of the continuing centrality of power in international life. State and nonstate actors seek power and influence in international life. The value of international institutions is to bind states together in ways that they can pursue their own interests and accommodate others' without the resort to war. A goal of multilateral efforts is the division of labor and costs in international life. Most important, the value of collective security arrangements, such as Chapter VII of the UN Charter, as well as regional alliances like NATO and international instruments such as the Geneva Conventions, is to create checks and balances on power in international life.

Finally, this discussion reminds us that Christian realism differs from some other Christian perspectives, such as pacifism or monasticism, in articulating a collective notion of responsibility. Monks and some pacifists withdraw from society because they understand their individual devotion to trump obligations associated with society at large. However, individuals—be they day laborers or presidents—are moral agents both as individuals and as part of their community. Similarly, governments and international organizations are complex moral agents constituted of individual and group interests. Such institutions do have some moral responsibility based on their identity or charter, and therefore their action (e.g., to save Kosovar civilians from genocide) or inaction (e.g., to neglect Bosnian civilians facing genocide) does have moral content. This notion of morality and responsibility should commission international organizations that have clearly defined moral imperatives to go beyond reflection to action.

Conclusion

Christian realism was not really a new phenomenon in the 1930s—it is heir to a historic tradition spanning the author of the epistle to the Romans, Augustine, Aquinas, Calvin, the Puritans, and others, and it continues to be the thoughtful, practical, hopeful, and sometimes anxious attempt to engage real-world political dilemmas, with feet rooted in the soil of a fallen world but hearts seeking the City of God. Christian realists have typically been frustrated by the utopian claims of those who prescribe solutions rooted in idealistic worldviews to the tragedies of politics. In contrast, Christian realism articulates a conception of political responsibility for action to engage evil, recognizes the ubiquity of power politics in world affairs, and suggests pragmatic solutions for matching power with power in order to find proximate solutions to the issues of competition and struggle in social relations.

This chapter suggests that the worldview underlying much of the contemporary rhetoric regarding multilateralism is utopian, for it lacks a realistic consideration of the inherency of power to politics and often fails to consider responsibility in cases of moral tragedy. Christian realism provides an alternative conception of international politics that reminds us of the centrality of power to any notion of international law and organizations and the necessity of backing up the rhetoric of security and human rights with the political force necessary to protect them.

Notes

1. A draft of this chapter was presented at the annual meeting of the American Political Science Association in Philadelphia on September 2, 2006. I am grateful to the panel discussant Jean Bethke Elshtain, as well as members of the audience, for their comments on the original draft.
2. There is no contemporary school of Christian realism led by a charismatic individual like Reinhold Niebuhr; indeed, Roger Epp (1993) has suggested that with

the passing of Niebuhr and the fragmentation of the movement over the Vietnam War, Christian realism lost its coherency. Some of the novel and strange applications or comparisons of Christian realism bear out this loss of coherency: feminism and Christian realism (Hinze, 2004), communitarianism and Christian realism (Dorrien, 1997), liberation theology and Christian realism (McCann, 1981), process theology and Christian realism (Bennett, 1982). Niebuhr himself has been contrasted with everyone from John Dewey (Rice, 1993) to Emmanuel Levinas (Flescher, 2000).

3. For an overview of the liberal tradition that includes Immanuel Kant's *Perpetual Peace* and Jeremy Bentham's work by the same name, see Michael W. Doyle's *Ways of War and Peace* (New York: W. W. Norton, 1997): ch. 6–8.

4. For a comprehensive discussion of Wilson's Fourteen Points speech, see Thomas J. Knock, *To End All Wars: Woodrow Wilson and the Quest for a New International Order* (Princeton, NJ: Princeton University Press, 1995).

5. Reinhold Niebuhr, "The Blindness of Liberalism," *Radical Religion* 1 (Autumn 1936), 4. Niebuhr's list was even longer than the four points enumerated here.

6. Reinhold Niebuhr, *The Irony of American History* (New York: Scribner, 1952), 116.

7. John Gerard Ruggie, "Multilateralism: The Anatomy of an Institution," *International Organization* 46, no. 3 (Summer 1992), 568.

8. James A. Caporaso, "International Relations Theory and Multilateralism: The Search for Foundations," *International Organization* 46, no. 3 (Summer 1992), 602.

9. Caporaso, "International Relations Theory," 603.

10. Ibid., 603–4.

11. The mammoth opus that suggests the nature and ramifications of these changes is David Held et al., *Global Transformations* (Cambridge: Polity, 1999). A more accessible version by Held et al. is *Globalization* (London: Foreign Policy Centre, 1999).

12. Pascal Boniface, "Reflections on America as a World Power," *Journal of Palestinian Studies* 29, no. 3 (Spring 2000), 15.

13. "Annan Plays to Harvard Crowd with Bush Jab," *Boston Herald*, June 11, 2004, 22.

14. Quoted in Marc A. Thiessen, "Out with the New," *Foreign Policy*, March/April 2001, 64.

15. Victor D. Cha, "Globalization and the Study of International Security," *Journal of Peace Research* 37, no. 3 (2000), 391.

16. Thiessen, "Out with the New," 64.

17. "If you want peace, prepare for war."

18. "It's Time to Choose the UN's Future Path, Says Secretary-General," *Financial Times*, September 24, 2003, 8.

19. "The Future of World Politics," *Irish Times*, September 24, 2003, 15.

20. Although it is true that international pressure played a major role in bringing down apartheid, it is nonetheless remarkable that South Africa so frequently shows up as the exemplar of collective action in international life when there was

no war being fought there. Better recent examples, of failure or success, would seem to be Gulf War I, Bosnia, Rwanda, Zaire/Congo, Chechnya, Kosovo, Sudan, Macedonia, Nagorno-Karabakh, and Gulf War II. In successful cases, diplomacy was backed by military power.

21. See Robert Cooper, *The Postmodern State and the New World Order* (London: Foreign Policy Centre/Demos, 2000).

22. Mark Leonard, "Soybeans and Security," *Foreign Policy*, March/April 2001, 67–68.

23. Michael Edwards, *NGO Rights and Responsibilities: A New Deal for Global Governance* (London: Foreign Policy Centre/NCVO, 2000).

24. Strobe Talbott, quoted in Thiessen, "Out with the New," 64.

25. There has been vociferous debate in recent years on the nature of security and security studies. For more, see David Baldwin, "Security Studies and the End of the Cold War," *World Politics* 48, no. 1 (1996), 105–121; David Baldwin, "The Concept of Security," *Review of International Studies* 23, no. 1 (1997), 44–59; Barry Buzan et al., *Security: A New Framework for Analysis* (Boulder, CO: Lynne Rienner, 1998); Peter Glieck, "Water and Conflict," *International Security* 18, no. 1 (1993), 15–37; Keith Krause and Michael Williams, "Broadening the Agenda of Security Studies," *Mershon International Studies Review* 40., no. 2 (1996), 135–60; Roland Paris, "Human Security: Paradigm Shift or Hot Air?" *International Security* 26, no. 2 (2001), 154–72.

26. In the rational choice and collective action areas, there is lengthy and profound literature that discusses how actors will cooperate because they see it to be in their interests. See Russell Hardin, *Collective Action* (Baltimore: Johns Hopkins University Press, 1982); Robert Axelrod, "The Emergence of Cooperation Among Egoists," *American Political Science Review* 75 (June 1981), 272–91; Michael Taylor, *The Possibility of Cooperation* (Cambridge: Cambridge University Press, 1987).

27. On the debate regarding the competition between global governance and state sovereignty in the United States, see "Trends in Global Governance: Do They Threaten American Sovereignty?" *Chicago Journal of International Law* (Fall 2000), 9–21.

28. Right Honorable Chris Patten, "Europe and American: Has the Transatlantic Relationship Run Out of Road?" (speech, Lady Margaret Hall, Oxford, United Kingdom, February 13, 2004), http://ec.europa.eu/comm/external_relations/news/patten/sp04_77.htm.

29. Quoted in Michelle Gratton, "The World According to Howard," *Age* (Melbourne), July 2, 2003, A2.

30. Evelyn Gordon, "The Pitfalls of Multilateralism," *Jerusalem Post*, October 26, 2004, 15.

31. One scholar observes that governments are relinquishing their involvement in such affairs by hiring private security firms. For instance, U.S.-based MPRI trained the Croatian military in the early 1990s, and Bahamas-based Sandline, Inc., provided security in Sierra Leone. The same is true with the outsourcing of

humanitarian and quasi-military services such as landmine abatement, security, and refugee services to NGOs and private companies. See Elke Krahmann, "The Privatization of Security Governance: Developments, Problems, Solutions," *Arbeitspapiere zur Internationalen Politik* (working paper, January 2003).

32. Eric Patterson, "Rewinding Rwanda: What If? (A Counterfactual Approach)" *Journal of Political Science* 33 (2005), 61–79.

33. This point is part of the classical just war tradition associated with Augustine and Aquinas. See James Turner Johnson, "Just War, As It Was, and Is," *First Things*, February 2005, 14–24.

34. An oft-quoted story originating from the Rwanda debacle is that the UN Secretary-General felt that he simply could not "use the G-word" in trying to motivate action. The text of the "Convention on the Prevention and Punishment of Crime of Genocide" deals primarily with punishing genocide after the fact. Only Article 8 deals with prevention: "Any Contracting Party may call upon the competent organs of the United Nations to take such action under the Charter of the United Nations as they consider appropriate for the prevention and suppression of acts of genocide."

35. Robin Lovin's excellent article on freedom and responsibility deals with this dilemma; see "The Limits of Freedom and the Possibilities of Politics: A Christian Realist Account of Political Responsibility," *Journal of Religion* 73, no. 4 (1999), 304–35.

36. Jean Bethke Elshtain, *Just War Against Terror* (New York: Basic Books, 2002), ch. 2 and 7.

37. Kenneth Waltz, *Man, the State, and War* (New York: Columbia University Press, 1954).

38. One liberal institutionalist account of this view is Lisa L. Martin, "Interests, Power, and Multilateralism," *International Organization* 46, no. 4 (Autumn 1992), 245–71.

39. Niebuhr quoted in Kenneth Thompson, "Moral Reasoning in American Thought in War and Peace," *Review of Politics* 43 (July 1981), 189–205.

Index

accountability, political. *See* responsibility, political
Afghanistan, 4, 176
Al Qaeda, 4, 28, 176
Anscombe, Elizabeth, 61–63
Aquinas, Thomas, 28, 60, 84–85, 87–88, 148
Augustine, 3–6, 29, 74, 87–89, 119, 122, 137–41

Battle of Algiers, 90, 91, 94
Blair, Tony, 2, 24, 32
Bosnia, 14, 155, 176, 180
Buchan, John, 91
Bush Doctrine, chap. 7
Bush, George W., 24, 26, 32, 26, 39, 117, 122–24, 128, 131, 133
Butterfield, Herbert, 2, 4, 23, 25, 29

caritas (charity), 5, 86
civil theology, 137, 138, 140, 144, 145, 149
civilians. *See* discrimination
Clausewitz, Carl von, 26, 30, 92, 94
Cole, Darrell, 59, 63–64, 66, 68
combatants, categories of, 29–31, 61–65
competition, economic, chap. 5, 168
crusade(r), 27, 29, 75

democracy, 6, 11–13, 34–37, 77, 85, 123–24, 128–29, 141, 143–44
deterrence, 6, 31–33, 76, 85, 124
discrimination and noncombatant immunity, 29, 61–65

Elshtain, Jean Bethke, 4, 177
English School, 153, 154, 162, 163
equivalence, moral, 177
European Union (EU), 22, 26, 157, 173–74

freedom, 16, 35, 74, 46–78, 104, 119, 122–26, 143–45, 148, 151, 176

genocide, 2, 14, 175, 177, 180
Germany, 5, 40, 62, 76
global war on terrorism. *See* war on terrorism
globalization, 100, 109–13, 172

Hannay, Richard. *See* Buchan, John
humility, 7, 27, 32, 35, 74, 119, 121, 132, 147–48
Hussein, Saddam, 25, 33, 85, 171

idealism, 6–8, 11–12, 37, 54, 73–76, 89, 100, 117, 118, 123, 153–55, 162, 168–69
intention. *See* right intention principle
international community, 129, chap. 9